Alfred Hope Patten
and the Shrine of Our Lady of Walsingham

Michael Yelton is the author of *Anglican Papalism: An Illustrated History 1900–1960* (Canterbury Press, 2005) and, with Rodney Warrener, of a biography of Martin Travers, the leading twentieth-century ecclesiastical artist.

He is a County Court Judge and he lives in Cambridge.

Also by the same author and available from Canterbury Press:

Anglican Papalism: An Illustrated History 1900–1960

'Here is a wealth of material which deserves further detailed exploration.'
New Directions

ALFRED HOPE PATTEN

and the Shrine of Our Lady of Walsingham

MICHAEL YELTON

CANTERBURY
PRESS
Norwich

First published in 2006 by the Canterbury Press Norwich
(a publishing imprint of Hymns Ancient & Modern
Limited, a registered charity)
9–17 St Alban's Place, London N1 0NX

www.scm-canterburypress.co.uk

British Library Cataloguing in Publication data

A catalogue record for this book is available
from the British Library

ISBN 1-85311-753-6/978-1-85311-753-4

Typeset by Regent Typesetting
Printed and bound in Great Britain by
William Clowes Ltd, Beccles, Suffolk

CONTENTS

INTRODUCTION AND ACKNOWLEDGEMENTS

When I wrote my last book, *Anglican Papalism: An Illustrated History 1900–1960*, which the Canterbury Press published in 2005, I commented that 'Hope Patten was an interesting and complicated man of whom there is as yet no full life'. At that time I had no thought of following the apparently logical course of writing such a biography myself, but in due course the idea grew and work began.

I am acutely aware that in some ways such a life is bound not to find favour with all its readers. There remain those who consider that Hope Patten was a saint who could do no wrong. There remain others who consider that he was a humourless autocrat whose vision has nothing to offer to the Church of England or the wider world. I am equally well aware that any biographer of Hope Patten walks in the shadow left by his successor as administrator of the shrine, Canon Colin Stephenson, who wrote *Walsingham Way*, published by Darton, Longman & Todd in 1970. The anecdotes in that book are told with Father Stephenson's characteristic humour and style, but it did become clear as I trawled through the archives that, although he did not reference the documents he had used, he was sometimes selective in the quotations from them which he incorporated into the text. Also, a great deal of further information has become available since 1970, especially on Hope Patten's family background, as the census returns for 1841 to 1901 are now readily accessible. The picture which is now apparent of Hope Patten's family background and early life is far fuller than has been portrayed before.

While no successor can hope to emulate the wit and aplomb of Colin Stephenson (and this author did not attempt to do so), it is hoped that this book paints a fair and rounded picture of a man with many facets, who was neither without fault nor without many great gifts.

Any writer on Walsingham owes a great debt to Father F. T. W. Smith, then parish priest of St Salvador, Edinburgh, who in 1961 advertised for material about Father Patten with a view to writing a biography which he never in fact completed (any may indeed never have started). However, the letters which he received, together with other letters which were subsequently written to Father Stephenson and to Father Charles Smith when the latter was administrator, provide an invaluable source of information in relation to Hope Patten's early years and his time as a curate. Most of the writers are of course now dead and their testimony would otherwise have been lost.

This is not in any way an 'official' biography, but it could not have been written without the very ready assistance and encouragement of the Guardians of the Shrine and in particular of the present administrator, Father Philip North, who has been unfailingly helpful and hospitable. It will also be apparent to anyone reading it that the documents in the shrine archive have formed the basis of much of what I have written (they are referenced throughout as 'WA'). No one could have been of greater assistance than the honorary archivist of the shrine, Isabel Syed, who with her husband Keith have encouraged and aided me at every step. I am also very grateful for the support shown by Canon Peter Cobb, who was the Master of the College of Guardians during the period when the book was being written and who very generously agreed to contribute the Foreword.

I am also very sensible of the assistance given by John Shepherd and by Stanley Smith, both of whom were very ready to talk to me about their close involvement with Hope Patten and the shrine in later years, and by Michael Farrer, who was a schoolboy at Walsingham during the war and later a teacher there. Other members of the Anglo-Catholic History Society, of which he is the Secretary, have as always encouraged me and provided further information.

The publishers have again been enthusiastic and helpful, particularly in the light of the short time available before the seventy-fifth anniversary of the translation of the image, at which it is hoped the book will be available.

Last but by no means least my long-suffering wife Judith has again had to put up with my absences from home and incessant two-finger typing in the house as the manuscript was completed. I thank her as always.

The views expressed in this book are mine alone: so are any mistakes which have escaped my own vigilance and that of those who have so kindly assisted me.

Michael Yelton
Feast of St Augustine of Canterbury, 2006

FOREWORD

It is very appropriate that a new biography of Father Hope Patten and his work should be published now, in this year which marks the 75th anniversary of the translation of the image of Our Lady of Walsingham from the parish church to the restored Holy House and shrine church in 1931. As the author says, the translation was 'an event of enormous significance in the life of Hope Patten and of the revival of the Walsingham shrine'.

To date we have had to rely on Colin Stephenson's *Walsingham Way*, published in 1970. He had the advantage of knowing Hope Patten from 1935, and had been a Guardian since the early 1950s. His book was on the whole well received, but some who knew Hope Patten well, and felt indebted to him and his ministry, thought he had been too flippant in places and were offended.

Michael Yelton's research for *Anglican Papalism*, published only last year, enables him to provide in greater depth the ecclesiastical context for Hope Patten's life and achievements. He too has made use of the census returns, which have enabled him to throw light on Hope Patten's background on both sides of the family, and to correct the version that Hope Patten liked to put out.

He tells us more about what Stephenson called his 'monastic dreams and frustrations', the unhappy story of the Community of Our Lady of Walsingham, and the chequered history of the College of St Augustine, and more importantly he gives us a sympathetic and perceptive appreciation of Hope Patten himself.

Peter G. Cobb
Master of the College of the Guardians of the
Holy House of Our Lady of Walsingham 1996–2006

Family tree

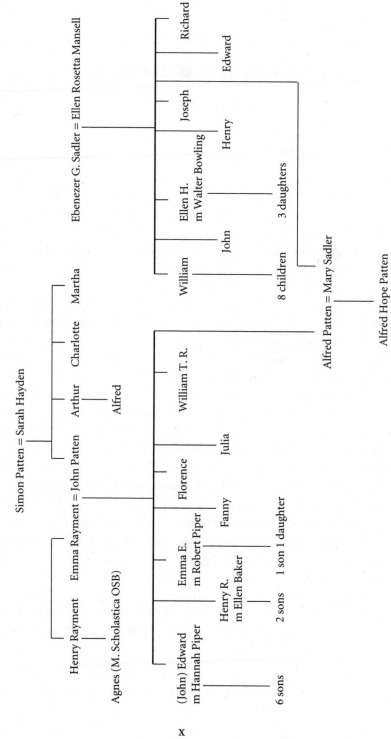

Simon Patten = Sarah Hayden

Henry Rayment Emma Rayment = John Patten Arthur Charlotte Martha

Agnes (M. Scholastica OSB) Alfred

(John) Edward Emma E. Florence William T. R.
m Hannah Piper m Robert Piper

Henry R. Fanny Julia
m Ellen Baker

6 sons 2 sons 1 son 1 daughter

Ebenezer G. Sadler = Ellen Rosetta Mansell

William Ellen H. Joseph Edward Richard
m Walter Bowling Henry

John 3 daughters

8 children

Alfred Patten = Mary Sadler

Alfred Hope Patten

1

BACKGROUND AND EARLY LIFE, 1885–1901

Alfred Hope Patten, priest, was born on 17 November 1885 in Sidmouth in Devon; he died on 11 August 1958 in the place with which his name was then and has since been most closely identified, Little Walsingham in Norfolk. So far as is known, his birth was uneventful; his death, however, was to be as dramatic and public as could be imagined.

Alfred Hope Patten was the only child of Alfred Patten (1862–1917) and Mary Patten, née Sadler (1854–1943). He was given his first Christian name after that of his father; it was a name which certainly in maturity he disliked and rarely if ever used.

There are many mysteries surrounding Hope Patten, often of his own making, and one on which ink has been expended in the past is the origin of his second Christian name, which he later almost always used rather as if he had a double-barrelled surname, invariably signing himself 'A. Hope Patten'. However, as with many of the facets of his life, the truth appears now on further investigation to be quite straightforward. Although Hope was by the late twentieth and early twenty-first centuries used exclusively as a forename for girls, in the mid-Victorian era it was found with reasonable frequency as a Christian name, usually a second such, for boys. It was becoming somewhat outdated by the time the young Patten was born, but it would not have excited much comment among those who were told at the time. It equates perhaps with the fashion in the inter war period for calling men Evelyn, which has now all but disappeared. It is perhaps a curious parallel that Hope Patten's long time collaborator and promoter, Revd H. J. Fynes-Clinton, should have been given the second Christian name Joy, usually found only among women, after the more conventional Henry.

The life of the young Hope Patten, as he will generally be referred to hereafter, in accordance with his own preference, is not entirely easy to trace, not least because he himself, to quote the words of a man who knew him better than anyone, Derrick Lingwood, never spoke about his early days.[1] Another long-standing priest friend also said that he 'never spoke to me about his life before ordination'.[2]

There are therefore few landmarks for a biographer to follow in this subject's own recorded recollections of his background, and in any event he was inclined sometimes to rewrite events retrospectively. However, the recent availability of partial census returns for 1841, and full returns for 1851 and every ten years thereafter to 1901, does enable certain facts to emerge with clarity from what would otherwise be an almost entirely foggy background. There must still be an element of speculation as to some of the matters, especially the whereabouts of the dramatis personae between census returns.

It may be helpful to look first at the wider family into which Hope Patten was born. In later years, perhaps under the influence of his friend Father Fynes-Clinton, who was genuinely and closely connected to the landed aristocracy, Hope Patten became very interested in genealogy and armorial bearings. In 1943 and again shortly before his death he attempted to carry out enquiries into his Patten forebears, writing in particular during the Second World War to the then vicar of Clavering in Essex in terms which suggested that he knew very little even about his immediate family on his father's side. There is, however, by contrast, in his personal papers a professionally researched and printed family tree of the Sadler family, with some members of whom he was certainly in close and friendly communication throughout his life.

The Patten family is undoubtedly an old one, with roots many centuries back in Lancashire. Hope Patten's researches late in life resulted in an elementary family tree, in which he included a distant relative, the politician John Wilson-Patten (1802–92), who was raised to the peerage as Baron Winmarleigh, and after whom Wilson Patten Street, in the centre of Warrington, then in Lancashire but now in Cheshire, is named. More characteristically, Hope Patten endeavoured to establish a kinship with Richard Patten of Waynfleet or Waynflete (Lincolnshire), whose son, William Patten alias Waynflete, was the founder of Magdalen College, Oxford, in 1458. He asserted to the priest in Clavering that 'the arms of

---

1 Letter of 20 May 1961 from Derrick Lingwood (WA).
2 Letter of 23 May 1961 from Revd Frank Harwood (WA).

John Patten and so of my family are the same as Waynfleet but without the Eton lilies'. He then drew out in his notebooks some suggestions for his own coat of arms.[3]

Whatever the distant connections, the particular branch of the Patten family from which Hope Patten came had long since left the northwest and had been established for some centuries prior to his birth in what remains even to this day a very agricultural and sparsely populated area of the southeast of England, on the borders of Essex and Hertfordshire and to the north of Bishop's Stortford, and its members were largely involved in farming and associated activities.

Derrick Lingwood refers to Father Patten as thinking that 'trade' was somehow unbecoming.[4] In fact, the Patten side of his family was almost entirely involved in farming and associated businesses, all of which would undoubtedly be classed as 'trade': his mother's side of the family, the Sadlers, by contrast were more academic by inclination.

Hope Patten's great-grandparents, Simon Patten and his wife Sarah (née Hayden), married at Meldreth, Cambridgeshire, in 1812 and farmed at Langley, just on the Essex side of the border with Hertfordshire, in the early nineteenth century. Simon's brother, Isaac Patten, married Sarah's sister, Susan Hayden, but in his case only after eloping with her.

Simon Patten predeceased his wife and in 1851 she was farming on her own account at Brent Pelham, Hertfordshire, with her son Arthur and daughters Charlotte and Martha. Although all those children were unmarried, the household included a five-year-old granddaughter, who must therefore have been born out of wedlock, a fact of which Hope Patten would have been deeply ashamed had he known of it.

Simon and Sarah Patten's oldest son John, Hope Patten's grandfather, was born in Langley in 1821. In 1847 he married Emma Rayment, born about 1825, the daughter of a Hertfordshire brewing and farming family, and initially farmed himself at Langley Bower, Upper Green, Langley. In 1851 he had 93 acres there, employed six men and is described in addition as a 'dealer'. The first six children of the family were born at Langley, and a further two followed after they moved to Great Hormead in Hertfordshire in about 1860. By 1861 John Patten's brother Arthur had returned to Langley Bower to work as a farm bailiff; he later married and

---

3 WA.
4 Letter of 20 May 1961 (WA).

raised a family at Wormley, Hertfordshire, where he was a grocer. He too had a son named Alfred.

By the time of the 1861 census John and Emma Patten were living at Hare Street House in the hamlet of Hare Street, near to the small town of Buntingford. Part of the hamlet was then in the parish of Great Hormead, including their house, part in the parish of Layston, which is a village now disappeared and over the site of which Buntingford has grown. At the time of the 1851 census the house was occupied by Thomas Titchmarsh, who described himself as a 'landed proprietor'; he had no apparent connection with the Patten family and it appears that the move there by John and Emma Patten was a result of upward social mobility and increasing prosperity.

Hare Street House is a substantial and very pleasant property, which, by one of those ironies which occur from time to time, was sold by the Patten family in due course to Monsignor R. H. Benson, the son of Archbishop E. W. Benson of Canterbury. Robert Hugh Benson had been ordained in the Church of England before converting to Rome. After his conversion, he wanted a base for writing and for his preaching tours, and bought Hare Street House for that purpose. He had a chapel inserted into the property, which on his early death he left to the Archdiocese of Westminster, which still owns it. Hope Patten never seems to have alluded to the fact that a house he knew well as a small child had been given this unexpected addition, which seems to conform to his general practice of almost neglecting the Roman Catholic Church in this country, however much he admired and imitated what he saw of it in Europe.

A. C. Benson, in his memoir of his brother Hugh, left a description of the house in the pre-First World War period, as well as including a picture of it at that time in his book.[5] Although Hugh Benson had altered it, he did not change the fundamental nature of the building, which remains visible today. It has a red brick façade with cornice and parapet above and a substantial door in the centre with two windows on each side and five above, placed at regular intervals. A. C. Benson remarked that it looked 'just the sort of house that you would find in a cathedral close'. That appearance is deceptive, however, as the front, built in the eighteenth century, conceals the fact that the main part of the house is considerably older.[6] The back wall has plaster with characteristic pargetting, or patterns, as are often

5 See A. C. Benson: *Hugh* (Smith Elder & Co., 1915).
6 See N. Pevsner: *Buildings of England: Hertfordshire* (Penguin, 1977), p.156.

found locally. The dining room has a Tudor fireplace and the substantial kitchen has stone flags on the floor. The main bedroom, which Hugh Benson used, was panelled in wood. The chapel was adapted from an old brew house at the back of the house, and there were substantial gardens, including a vegetable garden and an orchard, together with stables. The house also had an adjoining cottage, which Benson bought at a later date, and a paddock.

It is also significant that Hugh Benson believed that the house was haunted. He, like Hope Patten, was very sensitive to and interested in the occult throughout his life and it is interesting that he recounted the story of haunting independently of anything that came from the Pattens. In the somewhat lyrical style of the time, A. C. Benson said of Hare Street House: 'There is no sign of wealth about it, but every sign of ease and comfort and simple dignity.'

The nature of the property shows, however, that John Patten was a prosperous farmer. He lived in the house until his death at the age of 71 on 19 September 1891. His widow Emma died only a few months after him at the age of 66.

It is not without significance that one of Hope Patten's cousins on the Sadler side told one of his prospective biographers that there were no Patten cousins, and that Alfred Patten had only one brother, who was childless. This information was repeated by Colin Stephenson in *Walsingham Way*, but was wholly inaccurate. In fact Alfred was the youngest of eight, many of whom had children of their own. The importance of the story may rather be to illustrate how far Hope Patten and his mother had cut themselves off from his father's family and had either deliberately or by neglect suggested to the other side of the family that there were no relations who actually had to rely on commerce for their living.

Some indication of the scale of John Patten's enterprise can be seen from the detail contained in the 1881 census. That shows that he was then farming 574 acres and employing 30 men as well as women and boys. He also had one or two live-in servants at the house during the High Victorian years.

John and Emma Patten had four sons and four daughters, born between 1849 and 1862. The oldest son, named John after his father but always known by his second Christian name of Edward, was born in 1849. Henry Rayment Patten followed two years later, taking his second Christian name from his mother's maiden name, then after another two years came the eldest daughter, named Emma after her mother but referred to here as Emma Elizabeth to distinguish her. Fanny came next, a year younger, then a gap of three years to Florence, and another gap of one year to Julia. These were the six born at Langley, and after the move to Great Hormead two further sons appeared, William Thomas Rayment in 1860 and finally Alfred in 1862.

It may be helpful to look at the situation of the various Patten aunts and uncles as at 1885 when Hope Patten was born. His paternal grandparents, John and Emma, were of course still living at Hare Street House at that time. (John) Edward had initially assisted his father on the farm and is listed as his assistant in 1871. However, in 1874 he married Hannah Louise Piper, who was about seven years his senior, and was the daughter of Francis Catori Piper, also of Hare Street, but in the parish of Layston. In 1881 Edward was farming some 250 acres at Thorley Wash, Hertfordshire, and employing six men and a boy. It may possibly be that he had a personality clash with his father and therefore left to set up on his own account. He and his wife had six sons, one of whom died young; their youngest, William, was born the same year as Hope Patten, at which time (Edward) George was 9, John 6, Drury 4 and Frederick 2. When Hope Patten started his own research in 1943, the local vicar referred him to his cousins George, then farming at Whitebarns Farm, Furneux Pelham, also nearby, and John, who farmed even nearer to Hare Street, at Little Hormead Hall. This reference suggests strongly that he was not then in close touch with them himself.

Henry, the second son of John and Emma, was not initially a farmer but was very definitely in trade. In 1871, although still living at home, he was described as a grocer. In 1876 he married Ellen Mary Baker, born at East Dereham, Norfolk, who was two years his senior. Certainly by 1891 he was living at 82, Fore Street, Hertford with her and their sons Henry (born about 1881) and Cyril (born about 1884 and thus very near in age to Hope Patten). Since they had three live-in servants it appears that they were reasonably prosperous.

Emma Elizabeth, the oldest daughter, also married in 1876, in her case to Robert Dean Piper, four years her senior, who was the younger brother of her sister-in-law Hannah. They moved away for a time, and in 1879 had a daughter, the third generation to be named Emma, followed by a son four years later. In 1881 they are recorded as living at 68, Church Road, Richmond, Surrey, where their household included not only two servants but also Hope Patten's father Alfred, who is described in his relationship to the head of the house as 'pupil'. Since Robert Piper was then entered as a brewer, and Alfred was then 19, this suggests strongly that he was learning that trade from his uncle by marriage.

The three youngest daughters were all unmarried and living at Hare Street House in 1881, so it is likely that they still formed part of Hope Patten's grandparents' household when he was born.

William Patten, the brother nearest to Alfred in age, seems to have been the most enterprising. As early as 1881, when he was scarcely 20, he was farming on his own account at Little Hormead Bury, very near Hare Street, and employing ten men. He had not married at that time.

Very little has been recorded of Hope Patten's father Alfred by his contemporaries. We know nothing of his early life save that he was born at Great Hormead and by 1881 was in Richmond, probably as an apprentice brewer as already suggested. Although, as again already noted, there had been a brew house at the rear of Hare Street House, there is nothing to suggest it operated commercially at that time.

The real brewing enterprise within the family was carried on by the Rayment branch. They had had a brewery in Furneux Pelham since the eighteenth century, and in 1860 Emma Patten's brother Henry Rayment, Alfred Patten's uncle, built a new facility there. Rayments continued to produce beer there until 1987 and the brewery has now been converted to housing, although the Brewery Tap public house survives. There appears to be no evidence, however, that the Patten/Piper side of the family were concerned in this enterprise.

The other particular interest in relation to the Rayment branch of the family is that Henry's daughter Agnes (born 1857) became in due course a sister at the enclosed Roman Catholic Benedictine Abbey of St Scholastica at Teignmouth, Devon. It appears that she broke with family tradition by her secession and Hope Patten never seems to have mentioned her presence there to outsiders, although she played a cameo role in his life very much later. She was professed about 1882, shortly before his birth.

The next document which throws some light on Alfred is that evidencing his marriage on 17 January 1885 to Mary Sadler at Horley Parish Church, near Reigate in Surrey. He was then 22, and she was 30; the considerable age difference was coyly disguised on the certificate by describing both of them as of 'full age'. The residence of the groom is given as Sidmouth, indicating that he had been living there prior to the wedding.

Before turning to Hope Patten himself, it is interesting to look at his mother's family, with whom in later years he was to be much closer. The printed family tree indicates that they came originally from Wroughton, near Swindon. Mary Sadler was the sixth of the eight children of Ebenezer Gosling Sadler (1823–97), who had been born in Clerkenwell, and his wife Ellen Rosetta, née Mansell (1823–62), who had been born at Richmond, Surrey. They married in 1844. Gosling was a family name from some generations back.

Ebenezer Sadler was a schoolmaster who eventually ran his own establishment. In earlier years, however, he was somewhat itinerant, as can be seen from the places of birth of his children. William (1845–1930) was born in Paddington, John (1847–1925) and Ellen Hephzibah (1849–1931) in Great Yarmouth, Norfolk, Henry (1851–71) in York, Joseph (1852–1901) in Islington, Mary herself (1854–1943) and Edward Paul (1857–91) in Canterbury, and Richard Woodall (1859–1925) in Tottenham.

In 1851 Ebenezer Sadler was at the Yeoman School, York. By 1861 the family was established in Tottenham High Road; after Ebenezer Sadler was widowed the following year the family continued to live in the area, and in 1871 they were all at 7, Percy Villas, Tottenham, save William, who had left home, and Henry, who was drowned in Australia in that year. By 1881 Ebenezer Sadler had moved to become headmaster of Albert Road Grammar School, Horley, where a number of boys boarded; the census returns of that time revealed whoever had stayed at the address on the day the count was taken, regardless of whether they actually lived there permanently and the pupils were thus included. Ellen, Mary and Richard were then still at home.

William Sadler was ordained deacon in 1868 and priest in 1870 in the Diocese of Calcutta. He remained in India for a time, returning in 1875 to a curacy in Norfolk, but in 1876 was appointed as rector of the tiny Lincolnshire village of Dembleby, near Sleaford, where he lived with his wife Charlotte, by whom he had eight children of his own. Dembleby had a population of about 50, so it is unlikely to have involved the rector in too much parochial work, but in 1897 he added to his cure the equally small adjoining village of Aunsby. William Sadler's daughter Mary Ethel Grace Sadler, born about 1878, was particularly friendly with Hope Patten. William Sadler was described by one who knew him[7] as rather 'High

---

7 Wilfred Leeds.

Church' in rather an old-fashioned sense; he was certainly not an advanced Anglo-Catholic. William Sadler's daughter Anne married Canon William Oldfield, of Lincoln and there was another clerical connection in the family, in that his brother Edward married the daughter of the vicar of Horley.

Little has come to light of John or Joseph Sadler save that each married and had two children. Richard became a member of the Stock Exchange, lived in Tottenham, and married a widow from Jersey who had two children of her own; they also had their own child. Ellen Hephzibah Sadler and her children were to play a more significant part in Hope Patten's life, as will be described.

The marriage of Alfred Patten and Mary Sadler was solemnised in the presence of the bride's brother William, and a number of members of each family signed the certificate as witnesses.

Thus it was that ten months after his parents' marriage Hope Patten was born in the Town Brewery, Old Fore Street, just behind the seafront in the somewhat exclusive South Coast resort of Sidmouth. Some conclude that those southwestern seaside places such as Sidmouth which were served by the Southern, as opposed to the Great Western, Railway developed less and remained more genteel, and certainly that is true of Hope Patten's birthplace, which had at one time been a very fashionable retreat for the aristocracy. It is ironic that he was born in a brewery, since throughout his life he was very abstemious where alcohol was concerned and took little if any interest in wine.

The brewery was then owned by Thomas Ford & Son. It is not clear how long the Pattens remained in Devon, although certainly by 1889 the local trade directories show another man as manager.

Hope Patten was baptised in Devon on 3 February 1886. In later years he was to lament that his parents had not named him Hugh in memory of St Hugh of Lincoln, on whose feast day he was born, and to whom he showed a strong devotion in adult life. His parents appear to have had no particularly strong religious beliefs, and his father is said to have been somewhat Low Church in outlook. His mother's family, as we have seen, were more involved in ecclesiastical affairs and it may be that she was more inclined to the ideas of the Oxford Movement than was her husband even before her son began his own religious development.

The next definite sighting we have of the family is six years later, at the time of the 1891 census. Hope Patten was then five, and he is shown as living with his parents at 2, Queensberry Place, Richmond, Surrey. There were to be no more children, unusually for a Victorian household. Alfred Patten is then described as a 'wine and spirit merchant'. It is not clear whether he was working for the same employers as had he and his brother-in-law in 1881, but the return to Richmond may be significant. There were no live-in servants, which suggests no great prosperity. The house still exists and is one of what would now be described as a bijou Georgian terrace, near Richmond Green.

The 1890s were to be a traumatic decade both for Hope Patten's wider and for his immediate family. At the time of the 1891 census his paternal grandparents were still alive and living at Hare Street House with their unmarried daughter Fanny, but their married daughter Emma Elizabeth with her husband Robert Piper and their two daughters had moved in with them. His maternal grandfather Ebenezer Sadler was then at his school in Horley: the only other member of his family still resident with him was his daughter Ellen Hephzibah, who had married Walter Henry Bowling, the mathematics master at the school, in late 1885. He came from Sheffield, so it is not clear why they married in Fulham, but in any event he continued to work at the school and the couple had three daughters, Ellen Hesse Bowling (born 1887), Jane Mansell Bowling (born 1889; given her second name after her late maternal grandmother) and Winifred W. Bowling (born 1893). Mary Patten was very close indeed to her sister Ellen and the three daughters were the closest cousins to Hope Patten. Neither Ellen Hesse (known as 'Hessie') nor Winifred Bowling married and in later years they lived at Sheringham and remained in touch with him, visiting Walsingham from time to time.[8]

As already set out, John Patten died on 19 September 1891. His death occurred at home and was attributed to chronic bronchitis, asthma and congestion of the lungs, and his wife followed him very shortly thereafter. His will, made as long ago as 8 January 1870, was proved on 22 December 1891 by his brother-in-law Henry Rayment, the brewer, who was also a substantial farmer at Furneux Pelham, and by Augustus Hawks, a solicitor in the town of Hertford. The estate was clearly of importance to the remaining members of the family because of the deceased's prosperity relative to all his children, although it must be born in mind that at that time England was in the grip of a deep agricultural depression, with much

---

8 See letter of 9 May 1961 from Winifred Bowling (WA).

farm land worth next to nothing. The depression affected this area of the country particularly badly.

The will is a long document of some 1,300 words, much of it containing verbiage rendered superfluous by subsequent legislation. However, the effect of it was quite straightforward given the events which had occurred, and particularly that all the testator's children survived him. All the deceased's property save for his personal effects was left on trust for his widow for life and thereafter to his eight children in equal shares. Since his widow survived him for such a very short time, the property therefore had under the terms of the will to be sold and the proceeds divided between the children.

In fact Hare Street House was not sold for a very long time afterwards. It was empty for a number of years and was eventually sold to R. H. Benson, as already mentioned, in 1908, who found that it had 'long been unlet, and that no one would buy it'. His brother continues: 'It was all going to ruin and the owner was glad to get rid of it on any terms.' The owner at the time of the sale was Ellen Mary Patten, the widow of Henry Patten, who presumably had bought it from the executors.[9]

The personal estate of the deceased was valued for probate at £6,712 4s 8d, a very considerable sum for the time.

It is clear that after the death of John Patten and before the sale of the property the house was occupied on occasion by members of the family; it was, however, empty by the time of the 1901 census and appears to have remained so until Hugh Benson purchased it. Edward Patten did not return there, but remained in Thorley with his family; he died at an early age in 1898 and it is conceivable that it was that event which precipitated the vacation and putting on the market of Hare Street House, because his own family would have needed funds.

Henry Patten continued living with his family in Hertford but died aged only 53 in 1903. Robert and Emma Piper moved from Hare Street House at some time after John Patten's death and by 1901 were at Newport, Essex, another nearby village. Robert Piper died in 1910 aged 61.

William Patten remained at Little Hormead Bury; in 1891 his sisters Florence and Julia were there with him and Julia remained so throughout that decade. Certainly by the early years of the twentieth century he was

---

9 The Westminster Cathedral Archivist kindly confirmed the identity of the vendor.

farming the land which was attached to Hare Street House. He then became lord of the manor of Little Hormead and later married, dying in the late 1920s or early 1930s. His nephew John (Edward's son) assisted him on the farm, and, as Hope Patten was to be told later, continued to live in Little Hormead thereafter.

Kelly's directory lists 'the Misses Patten' (who would be Fanny and Florence) as living at Hare Street House in 1895, after which they are listed at other addresses elsewhere in the immediate neighbourhood.

More relevantly, it appears that for a period of time Alfred Patten and his family returned to Great Hormead. There are two important pieces of evidence which point that way, one being a letter written by Alfred to Christ's Hospital in late 1896 from Hare Street House, the other being that when he signed his will on 31 March 1897 he recited that he was then living in the property. Derrick Lingwood also recalled Hope Patten telling him later that he remembered staying in the house and hearing outside the tramp of pilgrims passing by: the road had been on a pilgrim way to Walsingham in the Middle Ages.

Nothing has come to light in relation to Hope Patten's schooling prior to 1896, when he was almost 11. On 14 November 1896, however, he was admitted to Christ's Hospital, then still in London, on the petition of his father.[10] There is photographic evidence of his presence there, but he stayed only until 14 September 1898, in other words for almost two years, when he was discharged to his mother (rather oddly) who was then said to be living at Crosby House, Redhill. It may be that she was staying there with her sister Ellen Bowling, whose husband had died at a young age in 1895, leaving her with three young daughters to bring up. Hope Patten was released on the grounds that he was 'not strong enough for school life', although the only specific note that the school had was that he was 'subject to colds which generally go to the chest'.

Winifred Bowling, who was then of course very young, recounted later[11] that while in Redhill Hope Patten was taught locally. He in fact attended Reigate Grammar School for that short time, and is said to have boarded there along with six or seven others. Reigate Grammar School had been founded in 1675 and for many years the headmasters were also vicars of St Mary, the local parish church. In 1862, however, it was

10 See letter of 24 May 1961 from Christ's Hospital (WA).
11 See her letter of 9 May 1961 (WA).

reformed as a proper grammar school, with a small group of boarders. Although the connection with the parish church ended with the reconstitution, clerical influence remained and the headmaster of the school when Hope Patten attended it was Revd H. A. Hall, who had been ordained priest in 1887 and had thereafter pursued a career in teaching before being appointed to Reigate in 1895.

A more obvious place to send Hope Patten would have been his grandfather's school in nearby Horley, but Ebenezer Sadler had died in 1897 while Hope Patten was at Christ's Hospital.[12] Reigate Grammar School is now once again independent, but it is not and never has been a public school.

The other very interesting aspect of the records held by Christ's Hospital relate to Alfred Patten's health and work record. There is no mention of him having any paid employment after that which can be gleaned from the 1891 census. It is clear that in later years he was regarded as something of an invalid and Winifred Bowling said that he 'rarely left the house'.[13] Other relatives thought that he had had a railway accident at some undefined point, about which there was some mystery. In his petition to allow his son to enter Christ's Hospital, however, Alfred Patten said that he was dependent on relatives, as he had been injured while at his work as a brewer, and at time of writing to the school he had been unemployed for five years. This is of course a contemporary document and therefore worthy of special attention. It would have been an unusual lie for Alfred Patten to have told if his injury had not occurred as he said, namely in connection with his work, and the dates tally with the other known facts set out above.

It is possible, however, that the petition concealed as much as it revealed. The late Theodore Williams, who was to be under Hope Patten's guardianship in the post-Second World War period, thought that Alfred Patten had a problem with alcohol, which would not have been discussed openly, but might account not only for the lack of knowledge of his exact condition in the family but also perhaps for his son's abstinence.[14] It might

---

12 There is no record of probate being granted in relation to his estate, which suggests that he left very little.

13 See her letter of 9 May 1961 (WA).

14 Information from Michael Farrer, who interviewed Theodore Williams before his death.

of course have been that a problem with alcohol, very common in the liquor trade, led to an injury at work.

What is clear is that by 1901 Alfred and Mary Patten had moved to the Brighton area, where they were to stay for some years, in contrast to their earlier peripatetic lifestyle. Although Hope Patten is usually referred to as having grown up in that area, with its strong Anglo-Catholic influences, in fact he does not appear to have gone there until about the turn of the century at the earliest, at which time he was around 15. In the 1901 census his parents are shown at 19, Russell Square, Brighton, and Ellen Bowling was also there, although she may of course only have been staying the night; her daughters were not with her and certainly the younger two were boarding at the Drapers' School in Tottenham. Alfred and Mary Patten had not been at Russell Square at the time of the 1899 Kelly's directory and it may be that it was temporary accommodation: a later Directory lists that address as 'apartments'.[15]

At the date of the census Hope Patten was boarding at a further educational establishment, this time at 5, St Anne's Road, in nearby Eastbourne, which was run by one Arthur E. Heinhardt and his wife. It appears to have been yet another attempt by his parents to complete what had clearly been a fractured education, but it was far from the conventional public school which most of his clerical contemporaries would have attended. It consisted of a small number of boys, some of whose parents were abroad with the Empire, being tutored together. Hope Patten and another boy were at 15 the two oldest. His stay there does not appear to have been very lengthy. He was soon to return home, his external education complete for the time being.

Hope Patten's bookplate.

15 It is now a hotel; it is very near the new Churchill Square shopping centre.

2

THE BRIGHTON YEARS, 1902–11

The way in which Hope Patten saw his life in the years between 1902, by which time he had finished such schooling as he had had, and 1911, when he went to Lichfield Theological College with a view to ordination, is not easy to ascertain, although we do have evidence from a witness who knew him well over that period, Wilfred Leeds, who was to be ordained himself and indeed later to work as Hope Patten's curate at Walsingham.

Arthur Wilfred Leeds was much younger than Hope Patten; he was born about 1891 and in 1901 was living at 45, Montpellier Road, Brighton, with his elderly father, rather younger mother, brother and sister. He recalled[1] coming back from holiday in 1902 or 1903 and then meeting Hope Patten at St Michael, one of the bastions of Anglo-Catholicism in Brighton, which was very near his own home. Wilfred Leeds was already a server there and Hope Patten had begun to assist while the younger boy was away.

At that time Alfred and Mary Patten were living at an address in the rather sophisticated Brunswick Road, Hove, again on a temporary basis, but they moved by 1905 at the latest to 'Ravensworth', 31, Wilbury Villas, Hove, where they lived for about ten years. This was a pleasant but not particularly substantial semi-detached villa in a good area which must then have been on the edge of the built-up zone. It seems unlikely that they were in a financial position to afford to purchase that property, bearing in mind their dependence on money derived from the family. Alfred Patten, however, thereafter always insisted on referring to himself as 'of independent means', and even Mary Patten's death certificate many years later referred to her as being the widow of 'Alfred Patten of independent means'. This may have concealed some genteel poverty.

There is no doubt that Hope Patten's education had been less than full,

---

1 Letter from Wilfred Leeds, 28 November 1961, on which much of the next section is based (WA).

and that it was hampered by his illnesses, which were to continue in various forms throughout his life. Wilfred Leeds recalled that at about the age of 17, when he first knew Hope Patten, the latter had all his teeth removed, a most unusual step for one so young and also one which may explain the rather tight-lipped expression on photographs of him over the years. He further described Hope Patten as from time to time passing into a form of delirium and imagining the presence of various historical figures, another trait which was to manifest itself in later years. Another witness to his state at this time was Revd John Markham, whose father, Revd R. H. Markham, had been a curate at St Michael from 1906 to 1912. He recalled his mother referring to Hope Patten as that 'ailing invalid boy' and thinking that he was too handicapped by his ill-health to achieve anything much in life.[2]

While these observations are no doubt accurate, there are other important facets of the picture of the late teenage boy. He was very keen on cycling, not only on the hilly streets of Brighton and Hove, but also for long distances, which at first sight appears inconsistent with a tendency to bodily weakness, although his frequent physical collapses were often caused by mental strain of one sort or the other, usually from examinations or the thought of them. Mary Sadler recalled him riding ahead of her at great speed on his bicycle, singing 'I fear no foe with thee beside me'.[3]

What is clear is that at no time between 1902, when he was 17, and 1911, when he was 25 and went on to train for the priesthood, did Hope Patten ever work gainfully. His parents appear to have kept him in some comfort, probably to their own detriment, and Father Leeds never thought him short of money. However, another priest who knew him in 1913, when he was 28, said that even at that age he was unaware of how to draw a cheque.[4]

It also appears that Hope Patten's parents themselves appreciated that his education had not been satisfactory. After meeting Wilfred Leeds, Hope Patten and he rapidly became very close friends despite their considerable age difference. They shared a tutor in about 1902–3, Mr F. W. A. Docker of Sackville Gardens, Hove, although it is not clear why Wilfred Leeds required assistance of that nature. Hope Patten was by then a voracious reader, largely of religious books, and took extensive notes on them. However, his spelling was, and remained throughout his life, erratic; his

2 Letter from Revd John Markham, 6 December 1961 (WA).
3 Letter from Mary Sadler, undated (WA).
4 Letter from Revd E. F. Bailey, 27 April 1961 (WA).

command of Latin, then regarded as a sine qua non of education among the middle and upper classes, was rudimentary at the very best.

It is possible that Hope Patten was mildly dyslexic: that condition was not of course recognised at that time, but the fact that his spelling was so consistently below the level expected of a man who read so much, coupled with his visionary artistic talents, suggest that as a plausible diagnosis. That would also explain why such an obviously intelligent boy had so much difficulty with formal schooling and fell into a state of terror at the thought of examinations.

Wilfred Leeds thought that the Patten household was not unhappy, but somewhat subdued and with the atmosphere of a sickbay. Alfred Patten was regarded by all as an invalid. The house at Wilbury Villas only really came alive at Christmas when Ellen Bowling and her three daughters nearly always came to stay. Revd William Sadler, who had been widowed in 1896, also stayed at the house about twice a year. Father Leeds did not mention the Patten side of the family at all, although he had been told that Alfred Patten had been in brewing.

It is of course possible, although it must be speculation, that there had been some family row over the will trusts of John Patten; certainly by moving to the South Coast, perhaps for health reasons, Alfred had cut himself off geographically from the other members of the Patten family and after the move it appears that he had little to do with his own relations.

Apart from his religious interests and his cycling, Hope Patten was at this time very keen indeed on amateur theatricals, in which he performed frequently and at which he was thought to be accomplished. His theatrical instincts were to stay with him throughout his life although they found expression in other ways. He was keen on and adept at sketching, and he could sing, although he had no great musical talents. He was undoubtedly, even at that stage, possessive of friends and prone to lead and even to dominate those to whom he was attached. It was easy of course for him to do that with Wilfred Leeds because the latter was so much younger than him. Although very fond of his cousin Mary Sadler and of the three Bowling girls, and an attractive presence to other young women, he tended to shy away from any close involvement with the opposite sex.

There is absolutely no doubt, however, that even by the time Wilfred Leeds first encountered Hope Patten, the latter had absorbed the ethos and beliefs of Anglo-Catholicism as a choate whole, and thereafter he only once appears to have wavered from that position, although he himself strongly disapproved of the expression 'Anglo-Catholicism'; he always referred to Anglo-Catholics simply as 'Catholics'.

It is important to remember that by the beginning of the twentieth century the Catholic Revival in the Church of England had already been in existence for almost 70 years. The first generation of Tractarian priests, who were often very restrained indeed in their liturgical practices, had passed on and a new cadre of more forceful exponents of what had come increasingly to be known as Anglo-Catholicism had taken their place. Although these developments were unpopular in many circles, the attempt in 1874 and the following years to use the clumsy instrument of a criminal prosecution to regulate the worship of the Church of England, resulting in the imprisonment of a number of devoted clergymen, had neither restricted the spread of Ritualism nor given much satisfaction to its opponents. The best known of those so imprisoned, Revd Arthur Tooth, became something of a hero to Hope Patten.

Ceremonial use among Anglo-Catholics had increasingly begun to follow Roman examples, and the increased devotion to the Blessed Sacrament was manifested at that date particularly in some religious communities; public reservation was virtually unknown in parish churches as at 1900, as was overt appreciation of the role of Mary in the life of the Anglican Church. The condemnation of Anglican orders by the Papacy in 1896 had, contrary to the expectation at the time, especially in the Roman Church, not led to a mass exodus of priests or people. Further, the early years of the twentieth century saw the beginnings of a definite Papalist Movement in the Established Church, with the goal of corporate reunion between Canterbury and Rome expressed as an attainable object of policy to be achieved as soon as possible.[5] The commencement of an organised tendency in that direction can be dated to the feast of St Peter, 1900, when a sermon was delivered at St Matthew, Westminster, by Revd Spencer Jones. Among the congregation was H. J. Fynes-Clinton, then still a layman, but subsequently to play an important part in Hope Patten's life.

Henry Joy Fynes-Clinton (1876–1959) came from a very different background to Hope Patten; he was a product of a strongly clerical family with connections to the aristocracy, and had been educated at King's School, Canterbury, Trinity College, Oxford, and then Ely Theological College. He was ordained deacon in 1901, and priest in 1902.

---

5 See Michael Yelton: *Anglican Papalism: An Illustrated History 1900–1960* (Canterbury Press, 2005), Chapters 1 and 2.

During the Edwardian period, which coincided almost exactly with the period when Hope Patten was in and around Brighton, Anglo-Catholicism began to move forward and nowhere was that tendency more apparent than in the area where he lived. The snide comment that Ritualism, as it was still sometimes called, was a London, Brighton and South Coast religion (a play on the railway of that name) had more than a little truth behind it. The enormous expenditure on churches in Brighton by the Wagner family had contributed to its standing as one of the leading centres of the Movement. By the time that Hope Patten and his family moved to the locale, there was a variety of churches available to the devotee of bells and smells which was probably unequalled anywhere else in the country outside London. Within a small compass were to be found the very large St Martin, Lewes Road, the twin-naved St Michael, Victoria Road, the pioneering St Paul, West Street, the towering St Bartholomew, Ann Street, and the rather more hidden Church of the Annunciation, Washington Street, as well as other less well-known missions and also some churches in Hove itself.

It is not clear exactly when Hope Patten's absorption into this world of birettas and intrigue, underlain by solid and committed devotion, had begun; it may indeed have been even before he moved to Brighton, but it was certainly in the incense-sodden churches of that town that it was completed. Father Leeds recalled that when he first met Hope Patten, which was after the latter had been attending St Michael for a very short time, the walls of his room were covered with brass rubbings from Downland churches, and he could already be described as a 'spike'. The term 'spike', attributed to the eccentric Revd L. S. Wason, is often used derogatively to indicate one whose interest in the minutiae of religious practice is greater than in the discipline demanded by traditional teaching, but that criticism could not even at that stage be used of Hope Patten. There is no doubt that even by that early period he not only took his religious obligations very seriously, but also that his almost obsessional interest in devotional practice came from his faith, rather than the other way about.

Not only did Hope Patten collect brass rubbings from his cycling tours to Sussex churches, but he also collected religious books from the many second-hand bookshops which even then could be found in the centre of Brighton. Hope Patten exemplified the Romantic, somewhat Gothic, tendency often found in Anglo-Catholics of the nineteenth and early twentieth centuries. He was fascinated by hagiography and by accounts

19

of the religious life in community. He was particularly influenced by Montalambert's *Monks of the West*, and it is tempting to think that even at that time he may have acquired a copy of *Customs of Augustinian Canons* by J. Willis Clark, published in 1897, which related specifically to Barnwell Priory, Cambridge, but which was subsequently to influence his thinking very profoundly.

Father Leeds recalled that in the period in question, Hope Patten went to mass almost daily and to confession most weeks, in addition to observing days of abstinence and of fasting with great severity. Father Markham recollected too that Hope Patten and Wilfred Leeds, when serving at St Michael, used to prostrate themselves at the elevation at high mass, a flamboyant but not atypical gesture, which led other members of the congregation to term them 'the twin soles'. The perfectionism which Hope Patten later applied to his own saying of mass was apparent even when merely serving at the altar and even then he was very ready to lose his temper with those who were not as meticulous as was he.

Although he generally attended St Michael, Hope Patten used Revd F. F. Smallpiece, curate of St Bartholomew, and later Revd C. E. Roe, curate of St Paul, as confessors and also attended the backstreet Church of the Annunciation, particularly for benediction on Thursday evenings. In 1904 Father Fynes-Clinton arrived in the town to take up his second curacy, at St Martin, and stayed for about two years before moving back to London where the whole of the rest of his very long ministry was based. That period would appear to have included the first meeting between the two men, who were to become firm friends and collaborators in due course.

It would also seem that it was during the early years of the twentieth century that Hope Patten first visited Europe and saw for himself the devotional practices of Roman Catholics in those countries where the Reformation had had little effect. The exact timing of his first trip abroad is not clear, although it appears to have been early on in his time in Brighton, and possibly when he was still 16, but it seems to have been to Belgium, a country for which he retained thereafter a very deep affection. He was not alone among the new generation of Anglicans who saw in that country a model which they hoped to reproduce in the Church of England: Belgium was near and easily accessible and had been largely free of the anti-clericalism which had affected France and some other countries. Hope Patten was particularly captivated by Bruges and by the piety he saw there, as were many others, and he returned there time after time thereafter. It was in 1910, some years after his first visit, that three men – Samuel Gurney, a wealthy layman, Ronald Knox, a brilliant scholar who was to be ordained deacon the next year, and Revd Maurice Child, the *enfant terrible* of Anglo-Catholicism, already a priest – met each other in Bruges; and from that meeting resulted the Society of SS Peter and Paul, which specifically aimed to replace the externals of Anglican worship with those of contemporary European Roman Catholicism, adopting the premises not only that the Reformation was an entirely tragic episode for England but also that the pretence should be adopted that it had not in fact ever occurred. That Society encapsulated many of Hope Patten's own ideas.

Hope Patten coupled his general enthusiasm for the piety of the Continent with a specific enthusiasm for relics of all types, fuelled by his deep but narrow reading on the lives of the saints and allied subjects. He was enthralled by the holy bones he saw and, it is fair to say, was not over-sceptical over their provenance. At this stage he had retained his own particular strong devotion to St Hugh of Lincoln, and also to all those saints whose shrines had been set up in English cathedrals and parish churches. Father Leeds thought that Hope Patten's specific interest in shrines of Our Lady followed from this general cast of mind, rather than the other way about. There can be little doubt, however, from the capacity which he displayed for self-learning on such matters that he was fully acquainted with the existence and history of the Shrine of Our Lady of Walsingham, and of its later suppression under Henry VIII.

The enthusiasm for the religious life which Hope Patten exhibited did not, as might have been expected, draw him towards one of the established communities for men within the Church of England, such as the Community of the Resurrection or the Society of St John the Evangelist. He may have thought them insufficiently forward (or in other words too Anglican) in ethos for him. He did, however, draw up for himself and Wilfred Leeds a rule for a form of Third Order of St Benedict; in doing so his imagination and vision rather ran ahead of reality, not for the first time in his life. The two of them found that they could not recite all the day offices and in addition rise at 2 a.m. for the night office, apart from the fasting which was strictly insisted upon. The experiment was therefore short-lived.

It may be wondered what his parents thought of this almost all-

consuming enthusiasm, which was coupled with an apparent unwilling-
ness either to enter remunerated employment or to train for any profession. There is no doubt that he was spoiled by his parents, and in
particular by his mother, and it appears that no great pressure was placed
on him to move on. Father Leeds recorded that there was no hostility to
his religion at home, although his parents did not overtly encourage him
either.

By the summer of 1906 Hope Patten and Wilfred Leeds had already
been on a number of cycling holidays together, including a visit to
Canterbury. That year, however, saw a very extensive tour planned, which
included a number of cathedrals, with a finale at the Benedictine Community which was then at Painsthorpe, Yorkshire. The itinerary, a considerable undertaking bearing in mind Hope Patten's health problems,
appears to have been accomplished without any difficulty. Starting in
Brighton, they visited Rochester, Bury St Edmunds, Ely, Norwich,
Peterborough, Lincoln, Beverley and York before arriving at Painsthorpe
for the feast of the Assumption. En route they stayed with various friends
and relations, including particularly Revd William Sadler at Dembleby
Rectory in South Lincolnshire, with whom they spent a weekend.

A number of myths have developed in relation to this tour, particularly
the suggestion emanating later from Hope Patten himself[6] that he saw the
signpost to Walsingham but did not take the road, saying either that the
time for that had not yet occurred, or that there was insufficient time that
day to divert. This appears to be a retrospective gloss on what actually
happened, which is that they passed not very far from Walsingham while
cycling between Norwich and Peterborough. Father Leeds was asked
specifically about this, and it is worth quoting his reply exactly: 'It has been
said that [Hope Patten] deliberately denied himself a visit to Walsingham,
having a feeling that 'this was not the time'. This may be so, but although
I was his very intimate companion he never hinted anything of the sort to
me nor to my recollection was there ever any suggestion that we should
consider Walsingham.' He went on to say that the whole purpose of the
trip was to visit the various cathedrals and, pertinently, that their journeys
were regulated by the distances they had to travel to reach the hospitality
of their various friends and relations on the way. In other words, a diver-

---

6 In *Our Lady's Mirror*, spring 1946.

sion to Walsingham would have disrupted the carefully planned schedule, but in any event was not ever considered.

In fact, that schedule was indeed then varied as a consequence of the impact made on the two travellers by the Community at Painsthorpe. They were so entranced by what they saw there, and by experiences such as getting up for the night office, that they extended their stay so much that they were forced to return to the South coast by train instead of cycling back.

Hope Patten was not the only young and impressionable Anglo-Catholic to be so affected by what he saw of the Benedictines. The interesting question is why he did not, then or shortly afterwards, join the Community, because in so many ways it represented what at that stage he saw as the way forward for the Church of England.

The attempt to revive the Benedictine life in the Anglican Communion was the brainchild of a young medical student, Benjamin Carlyle (1874–1955), who took the name in religion of Aelred. There are strong parallels between his character and that of Hope Patten, some of which of course were conditioned by the ethos of the age in which they lived. Both thought instinctively that in order to show that the Church of England was a true part of the Catholic Church it should be able to demonstrate outwardly that it could produce religious communities, shrines and the like, equivalent to those which they had seen in Europe. Both had a Romantic view of monasticism, influenced by their reading. Both were fascinated by the occult. They were both forceful characters with an obvious charisma which attracted some but repelled a few. They were each hopelessly impractical in dealing with finance. They both enjoyed the company of young men. Each, although committed to the tenets of the developing Anglican Papalism Movement, was devoted to the very High Anglican (as opposed to Anglo-Catholic) cult of King Charles the Martyr.

However, there were also significant differences between their characters. Hope Patten was in many ways extraordinarily self-disciplined, more so than Aelred Carlyle, who had a much more substantial streak of self-indulgence. Although Hope Patten was financially extraordinarily incompetent, he was not dishonest, whereas Aelred's behaviour in that respect became both irresponsible and reprehensible. Although they both enjoyed leading on young men into religion, Hope Patten's friendships of that nature were conducted with the utmost propriety, whereas with Carlyle there was an underlying unhealthiness in the way in which he favoured some members of his Community, took one at a time up to act as his valet, and so on. The homoerotic atmosphere at Caldey is hinted at by those who have written about it, and was undoubtedly picked up by some of the visitors.

It may be that although he was entranced by the liturgical practices of the Benedictines, Hope Patten was acute enough to see that beneath the surface all was not well. It has also been said that Carlyle revealed something said to him under seal by Hope Patten, which, if true, would provide an entirely plausible explanation for the latter not joining the Benedictines: he was always very scrupulous about observance of the confidentiality of the confessional.

The Community was not very old when Hope Patten and Leeds visited it in Painsthorpe, but had had a peripatetic existence since its foundation, with time being spent in the Isle of Dogs in the East End of London, Guiting Power in Gloucestershire, Milton Abbas in Dorset, and then from 1902 onwards in Yorkshire. Lord Halifax, the grandest and wealthiest supporter of Anglo-Catholicism, allowed them to use his house at Painsthorpe, and although he himself was conservative in his liturgical tastes and perfectly satisfied with the use of the Prayer Book of Edward VI, which was used in his family church at Hickleton by permission of the Archbishop of York, he did not stand out against the very evident adoption of Roman spirituality by Carlyle.

Hope Patten and Leeds were so taken with what they had seen that the following year they visited the brethren again. By this time they had moved to Caldey Island, off Tenby in southwest Wales. Another who arrived on Caldey in the same year was Revd William Prideaux, who subsequently took the name in religion of Denys. Hope Patten met him in 1907 and in later years, as Abbot of the reborn Community, he was to be an important supporter of the revival of the Walsingham devotion.

Hope Patten, together with many other supporters, visited Caldey precisely because it appeared to them that a Church which could produce a flowering such as was found on Caldey was capable of being transformed into a wholesale reproduction of the Roman Catholic Church in Belgium or Italy. There was nowhere else in the Church of England, even in Brighton or London, where the spirituality was as ultramontane. Latin was used for all the services, to which in fact Hope Patten had an aversion throughout his life, possibly to disguise his known lack of knowledge of the language, but equally there were frequent devotions such as exposition and benediction of the Blessed Sacrament which were rare if not unknown elsewhere and by which he was much taken. Ronald Knox and his friend Vernon Johnson, both later to become prominent converts to Rome, also came and were delighted by what they saw. Others arrived who were in a position to offer some of the financial assistance which Carlyle so badly needed, including of course Halifax, but also Samuel Hoare (later a well-known and ultimately disgraced politician), Niall Campbell (later Duke of Argyll), Athelstan Riley and Samuel Gurney. Riley, a rich and enthusiastic layman who promoted Anglo-Catholicism in many ways, famously wrote in the Benedictines' magazine *Pax*: 'Caldey is to me the greatest phenomenon in the Anglican Communion at the present day.'[7] Halifax, after being present at exposition of the Blessed Sacrament and compline in the chapel, was moved to write to his daughter: 'It really was the chief dream of my life realised.'[8]

One of the problems which Carlyle faced at Caldey was one that was to replicate itself many years later when Hope Patten tried to establish his own religious community. It was difficult when pushing forward the boundaries of the Church of England to attract stable and intelligent personalities who would make an order run without drama. Each of them was too anxious to take in any who showed an interest in the religious life, and the chronicler of Caldey, Peter Anson, who did not arrive until 1910, has set out the problems there which were partly attributable to an over-rapid growth sustained by the recruitment of many, such as himself, whose education had been either perfunctory or at best fragmented; Hope Patten would of course have fallen into that category also. There is no evidence that at this time he met Peter Anson (who was then using the forename of Richard, after the martyred last abbot of Glastonbury, whose supposed relics Carlyle had acquired and had brought to the island), although they encountered each other on a number of occasions in later years.

In fact, life on Caldey at that time followed a quasi-Cistercian pattern devised by Carlyle which included abstinence from meat at any time. It may be that another reason for Hope Patten holding back was that he appreciated that his own health problems would have prevented him from following the rule, something that Anson, who had very similar troubles, failed to see until much later.

---

7 Quoted in Peter F. Anson: *Abbot Extraordinary* (Faith Press, 1958), p. 120.
8 Letter of about 1908, quoted in J. G. Lockhart: *Charles Lindley Viscount Halifax, Part Two* (Centenary Press, 1936, p. 208).

Following this contact between Hope Patten and Carlyle, the latter stayed for two or three days at Wilbury Villas while conducting a mission at St Martin, Brighton. It is another indication of the support given by Alfred and Mary Patten that they were prepared to put up in their own home one of the most controversial figures in the Church of England at that time.

Carlyle had grandiose plans for an abbey on Caldey with a chapel larger than most English cathedrals, on which work began in 1910. There is still in existence a short letter from Carlyle to Hope Patten[9] dated 2 June 1912, when the latter was at Lichfield Theological College. Carlyle refers in it to there being 87 men at work on the buildings on the island. In the meantime the Community lived in a group of terraced houses known as the cottage monastery. However, he used the device, later emulated by Hope Patten at Walsingham, of inserting stones from various pre-Reformation abbeys into the reredos of the new high altar, to stress the continuity which he was attempting to demonstrate.

When in 1913 the majority of the Caldey monks made their submission to Rome, Hope Patten was distressed, but not tempted to join them. The episode, however, strongly affected his thinking for the future and he was anxious when he revived the shrine at Walsingham to ensure that it could not be lost to the Church of England by the defection of a subsequent incumbent.

Having resisted the attractions on offer at Caldey, Hope Patten seems to have decided that he did indeed have a vocation. It is not clear exactly when that conviction developed, but after one false start, to be described shortly, he had a characteristically strong, indeed inflexible, commitment to that priestly calling.

In 1910 Hope Patten's health suffered yet another breakdown. A trip to Switzerland was prescribed, and Wilfred Leeds was asked to accompany the patient, who recovered with great rapidity once their destination was attained and there were ecclesiastical sites to be toured. It was while on holiday there that the two travellers encountered by chance Revd E. R. Shebbeare, curate of the Church of the Annunciation, Brighton, who told them of the uncertainty which was then taking place in advanced Anglo-Catholic circles in the town. One of the sporadic attempts by the episcopate to control the use of non-authorised liturgical practices led in due

---

9 Addressed to 'My dear Hope' (WA).

course to a wave of secessions by both clergy and laypeople: this became known as 'the Brighton troubles'. One of the most poignant images of those years is conjured up by the singing by the clergy and congregation of the Annunciation of 'God be with you till we meet again' after a last service of benediction, the devotion which had been banned by the bishop. Thereafter the vicar, Revd H. R. Hinde, and two of his three curates including Father Shebbeare himself, went over, together with Revd A. R. C. Cocks, the vicar of St Bartholomew, and members of both congregations. These final events had not occurred when the travellers met Father Shebbeare in Switzerland, and it may be that the priest was simply considering his position at that stage.

The false start mentioned above was a short-lived attempt to found an entirely new religious community in Aberdeen, which took place in 1910–11, according to notes which Hope Patten made in 1913.[10] The other potential participants were Revds F. P. Williamson and P. F. Gateley.

Father Williamson was a much older man, born in 1865. He was rector of St Margaret, Aberdeen (the church founded by the designer Ninian Comper's father, Revd John Comper) from 1898 to 1901 when he resigned; the parish wanted him back but the Bishop did not, and he went to serve for six years as curate of St James, Plymouth, a city which was a leading light in advanced Anglo-Catholicism at the time. However, in 1907 he returned to the same church in Aberdeen as rector, and stayed until 1913, when he went over to Rome. He does not appear to have been reordained, because in 1916 he is recorded as an assistant master at Carlisle Grammar School. The curate at St Margaret was Revd H. L. Williamson, who was probably Father Williamson's brother; he certainly shared an Irish background with him, and was actually ordained in the Church of Ireland. He arrived at St Margaret in 1906, although he too had had an earlier spell there, between 1897 and 1899. It does not appear that he was involved with the community, as he was married.

Hope Patten had met Father Percy Gateley after he arrived as a young curate at St Martin, Brighton, in 1909, and the contact with Father Williamson was through him. Father Gateley's time in Brighton was short and unrecorded in *Crockford*, but he had earlier served at St Paul, Leicester, and then St Jude, Birmingham, a well-known Anglo-Catholic church which he left in 1908.

---

10 In a notebook in WA.

The little venture was so short-lived that it never even appears to have acquired a name, or, more probably, none has survived. Hope Patten was reticent about the matter, and such information as has been handed down comes largely from Peter Anson, who acquired it from Father Gateley when the latter was at Caldey. The end of the enterprise was somewhat dramatic: Hope Patten had been sent to Edinburgh to meet a potential novice, and while at Waverley Station he received a telegram telling him not to return as the experiment was ending. Certainly, although both the other participants eventually became Roman Catholics, neither conversion was immediate and in Father Gateley's case was preceded by a stay at Caldey as an Anglican, so that cannot have been the reason for the failure of the Community. It appears rather to have been a failure of organisation and indeed of the basis on which the Community should be run. It would have been difficult in any event for Hope Patten to be the junior member, and the only one not ordained, of such a small Community. His monastic vocation was undoubtedly to be a leader rather than a foot soldier. He did, however, note the reasons for the failure in his notebook as: (1) having no definite leader; (2) having no ideal in view; (3) different ideas as to the nature of the house they were involved in; and (4) the difficulty of combining living in an order with parochial work, warnings which he did not heed in later years.

Father Leeds recounts that Hope Patten was 'a bit woe begotten' after the failure of the Aberdeen venture but neither that nor the secessions and the uncertainty to which they led among the milieu in which they moved had, however, any long-term effect on Hope Patten and Leeds and they were by this time both convinced of their vocation to the secular priesthood in the Church of England.

3

ORDINATION AND CURACIES, 1911–21

It may be that Hope Patten had appreciated the practical difficulties which, because of his lack of educational attainment, lay in the way of him being ordained, and that this had delayed his decision to put himself forward. Although the system of selecting ordinands was then very haphazard, it was normally required that a candidate had been to university. There were, however, some colleges which would accept candidates without that academic achievement, provided that they undertook a preliminary course.

Hope Patten was first intending to go to Lincoln Theological College, a predictable choice bearing in mind his devotion to St Hugh, and was promised a place there, but was not able to take the entrance examination which was demanded of him. His reaction to the prospect of sitting the paper was to become physically ill, and Lincoln then would not keep the place open for him.

In 1911, however, Hope Patten was admitted to Lichfield Theological College for their preparatory class, and after several attempts he did finally manage to pass the preliminary examination: he was then put on the ordinary two-year course for non-graduates. Later in the same year, he was joined by Wilfred Leeds, who reported that Hope Patten had entered well into the life of the College and was liked; no doubt he was considered somewhat eccentric and certainly there were some who deliberately effected a spoonerism and termed him Pope Hatten, a rather obvious but telling joke.

The recurrent breakdowns did not, however, cease. Father Leeds says that on one particular occasion after he was taken ill, and despite being perfectly well looked after in Staffordshire, Hope Patten insisted upon being taken back to Hove in a special coach attached to the regular train, with a doctor and nurse to attend him, as he was convinced that he would not recover while at Lichfield.

The College was not particularly Anglo-Catholic in its ethos, but Hope Patten appears to have coped with that. Some years later he clearly remembered his time there with pleasure: on 21 October 1952 he wrote to an ordinand of his acquaintance[1] saying that he hoped he would be as happy at Lichfield as he had been and that there was much to appreciate in the cold and Book of Common Prayer type of worship experienced there. Surviving photographs show convivial groups including Hope Patten standing around the grounds of the College.

The course completed, however, Hope Patten still had to face the final examination which would allow him to proceed to his ordination. He again broke down and took to his bed. There are those who in later years were ready to doubt the veracity of these repeated breakdowns, but it does seem that they were genuine reactions to stresses which most people could have tolerated without any untoward consequences. He was fortunate, however, in that he wished to be ordained for the Diocese of London, which is itself interesting in demonstrating that he did not want to return to Sussex after at last breaking away from home. Bishop A. F. Winnington-Ingram, a straightforward, kindly man who combined a conventional, mildly High Church, attitude to his religion with an extreme administrative incompetence, was in many instances far too ready to ordain men without proper enquiry into their backgrounds. He of all bishops of the time was unlikely to stand in the way of a man whose real talents were no doubt apparent to those who had taught him, and who seemingly had a real vocation. His examining chaplain[2] is said to have interviewed Hope Patten at the latter's bedside, and decided after a few perfunctory questions on theology that he should indeed be approved. The episode almost certainly shows less about the perspicacity of Winnington-Ingram and his chaplain than it does about the casual way in which the system of approving those wishing to be ordained was then operated.

It appears also from the notes which Hope Patten made on the failure of the Aberdeen experiment, which are dated 1913, that even then he was still giving thought to the foundation of a religious community, on explicit Augustinian lines. This was an idea which never deserted him, even if it

---

1 The later Revd John Foster: see letter of that date (WA).
2 Identified by Colin Stephenson as Archdeacon Phillimore, but that name does not fit with any of the listed examining chaplains of the time.

was put to the back of his mind for the time being in favour of the secular priesthood.

Hope Patten was ordained deacon in St Paul's Cathedral on the feast of St Thomas the Apostle, 21 December 1913, to serve his title in the Church of the Holy Cross, Cromer Street, St Pancras. The church was in an area of a type for which little in his rather sheltered upbringing to that date had prepared him. It was a densely populated inner-city parish very near to King's Cross Station, in the streets of which prostitution and drunkenness were rife. Most of the area was tenement blocks. The church had been built in 1888 to designs by Joseph Peacock, and from its foundation had stood for what were regarded as the forward elements within the Anglo-Catholic Movement.[3]

The vicar at the time that Hope Patten arrived was Revd F. E. Baverstock. He was brought up within a family which worshipped at the nearby St Alban, Holborn, and was the younger of two brothers, both of whom became well-known priests. Francis was less in the public eye than his brother Alban, who wrote many pamphlets and from 1899 to 1930 carried on a notable rural ministry at Hinton Martel in Dorset, which paralleled in some ways that which Hope Patten was later to achieve in Walsingham. Francis Baverstock's ministry was entirely within London: he had served his title at St Michael, Bingfield Street, Islington (1899–1905), where his vicar was Revd E. L. Reeves, who in 1904 left the dingy side streets on the other side of King's Cross from Cromer Street to become vicar of Walsingham. Father Francis Baverstock then spent four years at All Saints, Notting Hill before becoming vicar of Holy Cross in 1909. In later years he returned to West London and was parish priest of St Clement, Notting Dale, for many years.

In order to assist him in the parish, Father Baverstock had three curates, of whom Hope Patten was obviously the most junior. The other two were the Revds E. F. Bailey and L. F. Barrett, and all four lived at the clergy house, which at that time was at 62, Cartwright Gardens, some distance away from the church, as did a layman, R. H. Stapley.

It is clear from those who remembered Father Baverstock that he was a stern taskmaster who worked extremely hard himself and drove his staff to emulate him. He liked Hope Patten, who appears to have made a good

---

3 For further information see M. Farrer and W. Young: *Faithful Cross* (Cromer Street Publications, 1999), especially the appendix by Michael Farrer on Hope Patten.

impression during his short time in the parish. However, Hope Patten found life in the clergy house restricting and uncongenial, not least because one facet of Father Baverstock's system of operation was to keep a very close eye on his curates and to check up on their comings and goings. That did not equate well with Hope Patten's independent frame of mind, and the result was that in due course he moved out of the clergy house and into his own flat at Tonbridge House, which was then quite modern, having been constructed in 1904, and was in Tonbridge Street, a road which is just opposite the church. There is a story that he left the clergy house because he thought that it was haunted and was terrified to remain there, but that seems to be another of the many myths which Hope Patten has attracted, and certainly Father Bailey, who was after all there when the move took place, knew nothing of it.[4] It would also seem that the other curates did not take each other as solemnly as Hope Patten did himself and the ordinary banter in a group he found difficult to live with. His lack of experience in money matters may also have led to unkind comments from the others, and certainly he had an air of unworldliness about him at that time. On the one hand, the phrase 'religion de luxe' was used of him, but in fact he was certainly not well off: on the other hand the public school bareness of the clergy house was not his natural environment.

Despite its reputation for being in the forefront of Anglo-Catholicism in London, in fact the clergy at Holy Cross at this time had fallen behind some other churches in their liturgical use. The Prayer Book was used for mass, with the Roman canon said secretly. The Blessed Sacrament was reserved, but not openly within the main body of the church, and at that time benediction was not a devotion practised at Holy Cross.

In December 1914 Hope Patten was ordained priest and on 22 December celebrated his first mass with considerable ceremony, although no details of it appear to have survived save for the card which he had printed, showing mass being celebrated before a theophany (a representation of God). It was printed for him in Paris.

Hope Patten took the priestly status very seriously indeed. He never allowed himself to appear in any parish where he served dressed other than in clerical garb and was scornful of priests who acted otherwise. On one occasion many years later he met a priest at Walsingham who was in mufti. When he was greeted, Hope Patten remarked, 'I am so sorry Father,

---

4 Letter from Revd E. F. Bailey, 27 April 1961 (WA).

I did not recognise you' – a carefully delivered and utterly devastating put-down.[5] On the other hand, he himself did wear lay clothes on holiday abroad, often including plus fours, and his passport photographs show him so dressed. He was quite convinced of the need for clerical celibacy, although unlike some of that frame of mind he was charming to clergy wives whom he knew and liked. For clergy who fell beneath the high standards he set himself, he had little sympathy.

While at Holy Cross, it is said that Hope Patten arrived wearing a frock coat and top hat, but he went around the parish in a soutane, that is a cassock with cape attached. In the clergy house and church he wore a biretta, the party badge of the time, but in the street he wore what Father Bailey described as a 'furry hat with strings' such, no doubt, as he had seen the clergy wear abroad.

Hope Patten's time at Holy Cross was short. He left in January 1915, after barely 14 months in the parish. He did not leave on bad terms and indeed was subsequently asked back to preach. It was said at the time that he was leaving on doctor's orders because his health was insufficiently strong for the work required in that area, to which Father Baverstock characteristically added that he looked fit and strong enough to him, and that his sermons would be missed.

It was while Hope Patten was at Holy Cross that Father Baverstock produced at breakfast one morning a small statue of Our Lady which was to be sent to Father Reeves at Walsingham. Father Baverstock was involved with the League of Our Lady, which had been founded about 1904 and was one of the three streams which led in 1931 to the formation of the Society of Mary and the image was provided by the League. The display of such images was then very unusual in the Church of England, especially in a country parish, and demonstrates the advances which had already taken place in Walsingham. As already mentioned, it is clear that with his profound knowledge of shrines in England, Hope Patten would have been well informed of the history of devotion at that place. His own account later that he had forgotten all about Walsingham until this was mentioned to him, and then forgot it again until the living was offered to him, does seems to contain a certain amount of poetic licence.

---

5 On the same occasion he turned to another priest he did not like, who hailed from the West Midlands and was with the object of his first satirical comment. He enquired, 'How's Birmingham? Collapsing without you?'

On leaving Holy Cross, Hope Patten went to the more salubrious surroundings of Teddington, a very pleasant area on the Thames, then in Middlesex. He was curate to Revd A. M. Cazalet, who had been vicar of the parish of St Alban since 1908. Father Cazalet had been priest in charge of the famous inner-city church of St Michael, Shoreditch, in 1903–4, a difficult situation for him since the vicar and one of his curates had just gone over to Rome. He was then at St Alban, Fulham, until moving to Teddington. He left in 1918 for St Olave and St John, Southwark, which was later demolished and the unusual dedication recreated at St Olave, Mitcham.

Father Cazalet was a sound Anglo-Catholic, who was extraordinarily vague and easily distracted, often forgetting appointments and even services; Father Leeds described him as 'a man of great charm and forgetfulness'. That trait must have been a trial to the punctilious Hope Patten, but despite that the two appear to have worked well together. It may well be that Father Cazalet allowed Hope Patten the freedom to carry on and develop his own ministry rather than over-supervising him.

The church of St Alban, now converted to residential accommodation, was once known as 'the Cathedral of the Thames Valley'; although narrow, it is enormously tall and designed by W. Niven on French Gothic models. In addition to his parochial duties Hope Patten acted as chaplain to an army camp and a Red Cross hospital nearby. It was typical of him that even the cataclysmic events taking place on the Continent appear to have made relatively little impact other than to bring these additional responsibilities. He was completely uninterested in politics or current affairs generally, and several people who knew him well never recalled him ever reading a newspaper.

At Teddington, Hope Patten was instrumental in suggesting changes to the liturgy to move forward. High mass was sung for the first time in 1915, and it is said was enlivened by the extraordinary antics of the subdeacon, who had a background in the music hall. Hope Patten also organised parish clubs and encouraged the sacristans to make items to his design.

At Teddington also Hope Patten developed his style in the pulpit and became a confident, clear preacher whose sermons were not too overlong. Although perhaps rather shy in dealing with all situations, he was particularly good with the young. One particular friend whom he made there was Oliver Richards, who was a server and certainly for a time considered ordination. He was a gifted musician and when Hope Patten moved to Walsingham in 1921 Richards went too and lived in the vicarage for some years. Another who went to Walsingham with him was a young man called Thomas Tapping, although he initially stayed in Norfolk for a very short time. He too appears to have met Hope Patten at Teddington.

Another young member of the Teddington congregation[6] recalled that Hope Patten invited him and his friend round to play billiards and he used to tell them ghost stories, which they found frightening but fascinating. There was perhaps an element of living a youth which Hope Patten himself had missed; the same observer says that there was also what was then called 'ragging' or horseplay, but that when they attempted 'Chinese torture' on Hope Patten he unexpectedly fainted and for a few moments they thought that he was seriously ill.

Phyllis Bishop was another young parishioner who got to know Hope Patten, in her case because she was a friend of Oliver Richards' sister. She makes the interesting comment that Hope Patten was quite at ease with her as she was youthful and friendly and posed no threat to him, but he was terrified of another woman from the church who was 'not so young' and who had 'followed him'.[7] He was always extremely wary of women who were attracted by his evident good looks and by the aura which he carried with him. Very much later, and in a completely different context, he referred to himself in a letter as having been 'one of those priests . . . whom women fall for'.[8] The assertion that Hope Patten did not like women is perhaps better put that he was frightened of some mature women and had rather old-fashioned views of the sex in general, apparently later saying that he thought that they should all wear a long skirt, a cloak and a large hat.[9]

Hope Patten lived at 2, Kingston Lane, Teddington, a substantial Victorian house not far from the church, but with the independence which came from not living in the vicarage. He had a local woman to help him with cooking and domestic chores, but she did not generally live in. The house was big enough for Father Roe, his former confessor who moved from St Paul, Brighton to be vicar of St Mary, Buxted, Sussex, in

6 W. H. Heather, letter dated 2 June 1981 (WA).
7 Letter from Phyllis V. Bishop, 19 January (?) 1962 (WA).
8 Letter to Raymond Raynes CR, 31 January 1947 (WA).
9 A view recorded by Enid Chadwick (WA).

1917, and the faithful Father Leeds, who was then in his first curacy, at Christ Church, Union Grove, Clapham, to visit.

After a time Hope Patten's parents came to live with him at Kingston Lane. This appears to have been because of the deteriorating state of his father's health rather than through any attempt to re-establish the family unit on a long-term basis. The daily lady began to stay more often in order to assist with Alfred Patten. Mrs Bishop thought Mary Patten 'very sweet but rather helpless', an observation corroborated by others who met her in later years.

It is not clear exactly when Alfred and Mary Patten moved to Teddington, nor whether they then gave up 31, Wilbury Villas. They were listed at the latter address in 1915 and it may be that they moved late that year or in 1916.

Alfred Patten was eventually unable to live at home, and he then died on 15 May 1917 at the Nightingale Nursing Home, Strafford Road, Twickenham. Hope Patten is described as being present at the death, which was due to cancer; the death certificate gives the cause of death as a malignant stricture of the oesophagus (i.e. cancer of the throat) with secondary deposits in the mediastinum (the space between the lungs) and in the liver.

Although Alfred Patten was not an Anglo-Catholic either by upbringing or by conviction, Father Leeds says that he died 'in good sacramental condition', which may indicate that he himself administered the last rites.

The death certificate again described the deceased as of independent means, but his will dated as long ago as 31 March 1897, leaving all his property to his widow or in the event of her predeceasing him to his son, demonstrated a rather different picture when proved by Mary Patten on 24 January 1919. The estate was a mere £156 5s 0d gross, £106 12s 0d net, a stark contrast to the sums left by his father a quarter of a century before.

Both Hope Patten's parents seem rather to have been left in the background as he came forward. He lamented in later years that he had never really known his father. It is not clear where his mother went to live after her husband's death and her son's later departure from Teddington, but it seems that she then lived with other members of her family.

Hope Patten left Teddington quite precipitately, because Father Cazalet moved on in 1918 and he was unable to get on with his successor, Revd Herbert Williams. It seems to have been a personality problem rather than a liturgical one, as certainly Father Williams thereafter had two curates who were both convinced Anglo-Catholics.[10] It appears that Hope Patten left without having a further appointment to go to, and so for a time in 1919 he assisted on a temporary basis at St Michael, Ladbroke Grove in West London. Prebendary H. P. Denison had recently retired from the incumbency of that church and been replaced by Revd W. H. J. Platts, who stayed for many years: he became a Roman Catholic layman in retirement. Hope Patten would no doubt have been pleased with the then most recent addition to the furnishings of the church, which was a late seventeenth-century reredos with a representation of Our Lady of Pompeii.

Having filled in some time at Ladbroke Grove, Hope Patten moved out of the London area for the first time, later that year, to the church of St Mary, Buxted, Sussex, the only Wagner church which was not in Brighton itself. Revd A. D. Wagner, the wealthy benefactor of so many churches in the town, had had a country retreat in the village of Buxted, acquiring a property called Totease House in 1873. In the same year he had built in the village a house which was named St Margaret's Cottage, which was for the use of the sisters of the Community of the Blessed Virgin Mary, which he had himself founded in Brighton in 1865. In 1878 he built himself a new house in Buxted which he named St Mary's and which had its own chapel, which he shared with the sisters. In due course the chapel was opened to the public.

Wagner was anxious to provide for the spiritual welfare of the inhabitants of the village: at that time they already had a mediaeval parish church, dedicated to St Margaret the Queen, but it was isolated from the area where a significant growth of population had taken place. Thus he financed the building of the church of St Mary, designed by E. E. Scott, who had been responsible for St Bartholomew, Brighton.

The new church was opened in 1886. The architect had made use of a great deal of symbolism within its building, such as constructing the sanctuary to the supposed dimensions of the ark (using Exodus 25.10 as the guide). There were seven lights in the west window and seven lancets in the north wall, again for symbolic reasons. More pertinently, the south aisle was enclosed by a screen so that the area within was 25 feet 6 inches by 13 feet 2 inches, the supposed dimensions of the Holy House at

---

10 Revd F. Nicolle was later one of the 21 who defied Bishop Winnington-Ingram's ban on benediction after the 1927–8 Prayer Book failure, and Revd A. H. Barlee was one of the victims of Bishop Barnes' persecution of Anglo-Catholic clergy in Birmingham.

Nazareth. Those same dimensions had been used for the mediaeval shrine of Walsingham.

Although Father Wagner clearly had the chapel built in this way to hark back to the Walsingham precedent, it does not appear that initially any great significance was attached to this. It was when Father Roe came to Buxted in 1917 that he appreciated the significance of the dimensions, and passed on this interest to Hope Patten when he arrived in the village. Under Father Roe's influence the parish became a powerful centre of Anglo-Catholic teaching. Unusually for a rural area, there were sisters in the parish: the Brighton-based Community of the Blessed Virgin Mary had withdrawn in 1912 and were replaced by the Wantage-based Community of St Mary the Virgin, which ran a home for girls there. In addition, the East Grinstead-based Society of St Margaret also had a branch in the village as a rest home for church workers, and this remained in existence until 1940.

Father Roe was himself an accomplished artist and he designed and painted the rood cross. The angelus was said daily at noon in the south aisle chapel. In 1932, a year after the opening of the shrine church at Walsingham, an image of Our Lady of Walsingham, similar to that in Norfolk and carved at Oberammagau, was erected and pilgrimages began to what was termed 'Nazareth in Sussex'. The previous year a gift of an icon was made to Walsingham by the Misses Hastings of Buxted, who later moved to the village, but it is not clear whether or not they had known Hope Patten when he was in Sussex. The screen of the chapel in Buxted was insensitively removed to the parish hall in the 1950s but has since been replaced and pilgrimages have continued over the years.

Little has survived of Hope Patten's stay of about 12 months in Buxted. He clearly would have found the religion practised there congenial, and he remained on good terms with Father Roe, who retired in 1935 and died in 1940; a monumental brass to his memory was provided in the Shrine at Walsingham. He knew Buxted already from his time in Brighton, and he undoubtedly used his period there to find out more about Walsingham, excited by the chapel and its connection. It may well be, however, that he found rural life boring after his time in London and its suburbs.

After leaving Buxted, Hope Patten may have had a short locum in 1920 at St Michael, Edinburgh, a lonely enclave of ultramontane spirituality in the Episcopal Church, but his next permanent move was to Carshalton in Surrey. This does not appear in some editions of *Crockford*, and it may be that it was an informal rather than a formal curacy. The vicar of Carshalton from 1919 to his death in 1957 was Revd W. Robert Corbould, a well-known Anglican Papalist who was prominent in many organisations. The old parish church of All Saints in the centre of the village had two daughter churches: the Good Shepherd, Stanley Park Road, Carshalton Beeches, a new suburb to the south of the parish and St Andrew, Wrythe Lane, to the north. It is not clear when St Andrew was built, but when Hope Patten moved to the area in 1920 there was a tin mission church in existence for Carshalton Beeches, and he was placed in charge of that area. Subsequently that church was demolished and in 1931–2 a striking church in the Spanish Mission style was erected to designs by Martin Travers and T. F. W. Grant. Father Corbould wanted to dedicate the new building to St Francis de Sales, but local opinion was strongly in favour of continuing the previous appellation and that was done. St Andrew became notorious because in 1927 Revd R. A. E. Harris, an uncompromising Papalist, was put in charge of it by Father Corbould. On the latter's death and replacement by Revd Leigh Edwards, Father Harris continued to use the Roman mass as he always had. His refusal in 1959 to cease to do so on the new incumbent's demand led to Bishop Mervyn Stockwood of Southwark causing the curate to be locked out of the church and a public furore. This episode led some Anglo-Catholics to look on in askance when some years later the same bishop was invited to become an Honorary Guardian of the Walsingham Shrine.

Father Corbould liked to run the parish himself and in later years resisted the Good Shepherd becoming a separate parish. He did not allow reservation of the Sacrament at the tin tabernacle, but he did allow Hope Patten to look after the sizeable congregation which had attached itself to the church. It is clear that during the relatively short period in which he was there, Hope Patten impressed some of his congregation: two sisters, the Misses Lloyd, were sufficiently taken with him to follow him to Walsingham, and one lady, Winifred Gotelee, remembered 40 years later how he captured her heart immediately when, on visiting her house, he took up her cat in his arms and exclaimed, 'Oh, you adorable person.'[11] This occasional spontaneity was an attractive feature of his personality, which was often hidden by the rather rigid face which he usually showed to the world, and which he thought was required of a priest.

---

11 See letter of 22 April 1961 from Winifred Gotelee (WA).

Colin Stephenson speculated that Hope Patten's Papalist tendencies were strengthened by this spell with Father Corbould. However, that is perhaps to underestimate the strength of those feelings even before then. Hope Patten demonstrated clearly at that time the characteristic thoughts of many in his position. He was entirely convinced of the validity of his Anglican orders. He was equally entirely convinced that the Church of England was not autonomous, but was a part of Western Christendom owing allegiance to Rome and that the breach which had been caused by the Reformation should be healed. He saw the adoption within the Church of England of Roman standards of moral and liturgical discipline as the precursor of the healing of that breach, but he looked to the Roman Church abroad and ignored those within this country almost completely. As with many other Anglican Papalists of his generation, Hope Patten actually knew very little of the Roman Catholic Church in England or indeed many if any Roman Catholics in this country. He was also, particularly in the early years at Walsingham, interested in the Orthodox Church, perhaps influenced by Father Fynes-Clinton, who was the founder of the Anglican and Eastern Churches Association and had many contacts in Russia and surrounding countries.

Hope Patten shied away, then and later, from the complete adoption of the Roman liturgy with the use of Latin, which was found as a liturgical language in some religious communities between the Wars and also in a few parishes, such as St Saviour, Hoxton, and St Alban, Fulham. It is interesting, however, to look at the touchstone of Papalism in the Church of England in the 1930s, the Oxford Movement Centenary Manifesto of 1932, masterminded by Fathers Corbould and Fynes-Clinton. Corbould and Fynes-Clinton were the first two signatories to what was a very uncompromising statement of the need for Anglo-Catholicism to realign itself in the direction of Rome. Not only did Hope Patten himself sign it, but Fathers Cazalet and Roe also did so, together of course with Father Corbould. Thus of the four priests under whom Hope Patten served substantive curacies, three were signatories and although Father Baverstock was the one exception, his brother had signed it.

Hope Patten's stay at Carshalton was again short, and he had come to the time when he was thinking of a parish of his own. He was 35, still at an age when some men were not given that chance, but with a strong personality and great charm.

There are at least two variations on the story of how Hope Patten was offered the living of Walsingham. The first is that the outgoing incumbent, Father Reeves, asked his former curate, Father Francis Baverstock, whether he could recommend anyone. The other is that the suggestion of Hope Patten came from Father Roe via his brother, who was the Rural Dean in north Norfolk. Both may contain an element of truth, although the Reeves/Baverstock connection is most usually given and seems the more likely.

Both stories were within the context of the living having been already offered to a number of others, perhaps as many as 20. One was certainly Revd (later Dom) Anselm Hughes, who turned it down because he had decided to try his vocation as a Benedictine, but most did so because the stipend was very low indeed, even by the standards of the time (about £224 per annum gross) and, unlike Father Reeves, most priests had no private means. Hope Patten certainly had no other source of income by this time. There was a substantial vicarage to keep up and run, and also, and unusually for that time, three churches to serve, namely Little Walsingham, Old or Great Walsingham (which, perversely is and was a much smaller settlement) and Houghton St Giles, with no curate to assist. Further, Walsingham was in a remote part of Norfolk (although then it still had a train service), and was far from London.

On the other hand, there was an established High Church tradition in the village, and, of particular interest to Hope Patten, there were the historical associations and the chance of restoring the devotion. There can be no doubt at all that it was the existence of the pre-Reformation shrine which caused him even to consider the offer of the living: without it he would in any event never have been recommended for it. He admitted on many occasions to Father Lingwood that he would never have accepted but for the chance to revive the pilgrimage.[12] He seems to have taken about three months to make up his mind, and finally did so only after taking advice from Father Paul Bull, the Superior of the Society of St John the Evangelist in Oxford. Quite why he asked him as opposed to the many other clergy he knew is not clear, as he had no close connections with

---

12 See Derrick Lingwood in a document entitled 'Rough Notes as they Come to Me', from which was adapted his article of recollections on Hope Patten in the memorial edition of *Our Lady's Mirror*, autumn 1958– winter 1959. Although there are some errors in relation to names, etc., in the early draft, there is more information than in the finished production and for that reason reference is made to it on a number of subjects. It is referred to as 'Rough Notes' hereafter (WA).

the Cowley Fathers. What is clear is that even up to the time he went to Norfolk he was not entirely sure: very shortly before he went to Walsingham he told his friends that what he really wanted was to be vicar of St Alban, Teddington.[13]

Apart from the questions of finance and location, however, there was no parish in England more attractive to Hope Patten. The prospect of reviving the Shrine, which was to be his life's work, was enormously attractive to a priest with his infatuation with all things mediaeval and his deep devotion to Our Lady. He also strongly supported the view, already mentioned in connection with Aelred Carlyle, that in order to show that it was indeed a true part of the Catholic Church, the Church of England should be able to manifest to the outside world the flowers of devotion: in other words, the shrines, religious communities, and the like which he had seen in Belgium and elsewhere on the Continent. That was one of the key strands in his thinking and that of many others of his religious inclination, and was perhaps the motivating factor behind all he attempted to do at Walsingham.

The other strength which Hope Patten had – a strength which was also to some extent a defect or weakness in his character – was that he had a very powerful but at the same time narrow focus. He did not concern himself with many of the preoccupations of the general population; he was uninterested in current affairs, sport, food and wine, or sex. He never drove a car. In due course the worry of money was taken from him also. He was thus able to devote himself without outside distractions to the promotion of the Catholic Faith in the Church of England, and in particular the restoration of the Shrine of Our Lady of Walsingham. His single-mindedness put some people off, but it enabled him to do that which others would not have done. Father Lingwood, who knew him better than anyone else, was later to write that 'his greatest failing was not being able to see another person's point of view; to him black was black and white white and there were no shades in between'.[14] While that was true, it was not, and was not intended by the writer to be, the whole truth about a complicated personality with many strengths.

Another characteristic of Hope Patten's which was to be demonstrated during the years ahead was impatience. Once he had made a decision, he

---

13 See letter from Phyllis V. Bishop, 19 January (?) 1962 (WA).
14 Lingwood, in *Our Lady's Mirror*, autumn 1958–winter 1959.

wanted to carry it through as soon as possible, regardless of practicality. Dorothy Bennett, a long-term resident of Walsingham, wrote after his death: '"wishful thinking" was his great weakness, and whatever he thought right must happen immediately without considering others' feelings'.[15] There was of course another, positive, side to this trait: he actually did things which others only thought about.

The Holy House, as drawn by Enid Chadwick.

15 Letter of 4 June 1961 (WA).

4

WALSINGHAM: THE EARLY YEARS AND THE RE-ESTABLISHMENT OF THE SHRINE OF OUR LADY, 1921–4

Hope Patten had strong foundations upon which to build at Walsingham. His position was very unlike those Anglo-Catholic priests who found themselves appointed to churches with an Evangelical or Moderate tradition and immediately imposed their own system of worship on the parish without any prior explanation or teaching. When, to take an extreme example, Father Sandys Wason arrived at the parish of Cury with Gunwalloe in Cornwall in 1905, he announced on the first Sunday of his incumbency that henceforth there would be daily mass at 8 a.m., and that on Sundays there would be sung mass at 11 a.m. and devotions to the Blessed Sacrament at 6 p.m. That approach, in a church hitherto untouched by the Catholic Revival, worked in only a very few cases, where the priest had the personality to carry his congregation with him, and ended in disaster for Father Wason.

Hope Patten certainly had a charismatic personality, but he had the great advantage of being able to follow on from the work done by his predecessors. The Lee-Warner family were the lords of the manor and had appointed him; they had absorbed the teachings of the Oxford Movement by the late nineteenth century, and although the services at Walsingham may not have been flamboyant, they were certainly far in advance of what was to be found in most country areas at that time.

Members of the Lee-Warner family themselves had held the living from 1807 until 1870, and in 1882 they persuaded Revd G. R. Woodward to accept the incumbency. George Ratcliffe Woodward had been a curate at St Barnabas, Pimlico, one of the early pioneer churches of the Revival in London, but was said to have been persuaded to move out to Norfolk because he was a relative of the Lee-Warners, although this has been doubted. The parish church was rearranged on Tractarian lines, a sur-

44

pliced choir was introduced, and once Woodward arrived he placed six candlesticks on the high altar and began wearing vestments to celebrate the Eucharist. He was a very talented musician and taught the choir plainsong; indeed, for some years there was a daily sung evensong, which was very unusual away from a cathedral setting. In the adjoining parish of Houghton St Giles there were similar influences at work and the liturgical practice was thought to be ahead of that used at Walsingham. Father Woodward only stayed at Walsingham for six years, and was succeeded by Revd H. A. Wansbrough (1888–1904) and in due course by Father Reeves, as already described, who also had a background in London Anglo-Catholicism. During Father Reeves' time there was an early said holy communion on Sunday at 8 a.m. and then on alternate Sundays there was either sung Eucharist or choral matins. In the evening there was sung evensong, and there were also some weekday celebrations. Father Lingwood recalled that there was a long interregnum after Father Reeves left in 1920, during which time of course the search for a new priest was continuing, and various priests came over from Norwich to take the services; this in itself is significant in that it indicates that the patron was looking for a tradition similar to that which had been established to continue even during the period between appointments, and so like-minded priests were imported from some distance away rather than, as was more usual, the neighbours assisting.[1] Father Lingwood thought it was during this period that sung Eucharist became the main service every Sunday: he, as a young villager, thought the priests from Norwich were 'very High Church'.[2]

When Father Patten arrived in Walsingham (which he always pronounced as if it had a 'z' instead of an 's' in the middle), he made an immediate strong impact. He was very unlike the traditional Norfolk parson, and intended to be so. One of the most important objectives of the Catholic Revival within the Church of England was that the clergy should be seen as professionals, rather than as part of the village squirearchy. He

---

1 The *Walsingham Review* of 16 June 1965 carried an obituary notice for Ven. F. J. Bailey, who had been vicar of St George Tombland in Norwich in the 1930s and was later chaplain in Florence. It was said that he had been one of the priests who assisted during the interregnum, but in fact he had not been priested until 1926. It may be that he assisted unofficially at Walsingham for a period after that, as many priests did, and he was certainly not attached to a parish for a time in 1926–7.
2 Lingwood, 'Rough Notes'.

was relatively young, good looking and silver tongued. His evident charm was well deployed during his first months in the village, in which he introduced various changes to the liturgical practices at the church, such as the regular use of incense,[3] the observance of feast days of Our Lady, and midnight mass at Christmas. Some of his alterations, such as the unilateral decision to move the patronal festival of the parish church from 1 November to 15 August, were not greeted with universal acclaim. The church was originally dedicated to All Saints, but in the late nineteenth century this was altered to All Saints and St Mary, under the influence of the Tractarian vicars. Hope Patten abandoned the first part of the dedication completely, perhaps because he had formed the belief prior to his move to Walsingham that he wanted to carry on his ministry in a church of Our Lady. It was characteristic of him that he brought his desire to fruition in this rather convoluted way. It was equally characteristic that in his *Short Guide* to the parish church he averred that the dedication had been changed to St Mary many centuries previously.

At that stage, the liturgical regime in the church was based firmly on the Book of Common Prayer. The Gloria was moved to the beginning of the mass, and Hope Patten said audibly the Prayer for the Church Militant, the Prayer of Consecration and the Prayer of Thanksgiving, although he supplemented them with parts of the Roman canon said silently. He recited morning and evening prayer from the Prayer Book. Reservation of the Blessed Sacrament was introduced very early on, and a protest from Bishop Bertram Pollock of Norwich was dismissed with the assertion that Hope Patten was accustomed to work in churches where that practice was found and would not work as an incumbent without it. The Bishop backed away from conflict and did nothing at that time.

Hope Patten (who in those days was known to his parishioners simply as 'Father Patten') was assisted also by his ability to make use of the talents of others. He was particularly fortunate in having Oliver Richards living in the vicarage: he and Thomas Tapping had moved there with him when he arrived, but Tapping stayed only for a short time at that stage before coming back to Walsingham later, as will be seen. Oliver Richards, however, stayed for a considerable time and from the very early days was able to revive the tradition of music in the village church, which Hope Patten himself did not have the ear to do. He left in 1928 to become organist and

---

3 It may be that incense had been used occasionally before.

choirmaster of St Margaret, Princes Road, Liverpool, a church where one of the priests imprisoned in the nineteenth century under the Public Worship Regulation Act had served.

In addition to the choir, Hope Patten himself, with the assistance in the early period of Thomas Tapping, organised the servers. The young Derrick Lingwood, who was the son of the village baker and his wife and was about 11 when the new vicar arrived, was tactfully told that he had not much musical ability and moved to serve instead. H. Vaughan Hayler was the first regular thurifer in the parish, responsible for filling the church with as much smoke as possible from the incense, and Arthur Bond was his boat boy, holding the vessel with new grains to replenish the thurible. Bond looked back many years later[4] and recalled the servers and priest being drilled by Thomas Tapping from Adrian Fortescue's *The Cere-monies of the Roman Rite Described*. Hope Patten used the combination, familiar to many Anglo-Catholics of the era, of the Book of Common Prayer with Roman ceremony added around it to make it look unlike an Anglican service, whatever was said.

Ironically, Arthur Bond later became a Roman Catholic and wrote a book entitled *The Walsingham Story through 900 Years*, the first edition of which, in about 1961, determinedly omitted Hope Patten's contribution to the village and its tradition of devotion. Bond had set up the Guild Hotel in the village in 1957.

It is clear that Hope Patten had particular success with the youth of the village, not least because he not only taught them but also entertained them, and did not patronise them. He used to have the servers and their girlfriends round to the vicarage on Friday evenings, where they were fed well and played games, including mimes and 'murder', which sometimes became riotous and quite rough. As we have seen earlier, the carapace which Hope Patten put round himself on occasion when seen by the outside world sometimes fell away, especially when he was with those he liked and knew. It would also be fair to say that he relaxed in the company of those he did not see as intellectual rivals. He always retained something of an inferiority complex when dealing with those who were better educated than him, perhaps because of his experiences in his own schooling. Hope Patten was a very intelligent man and, within his own spheres of interest, perspicacious, but he was not, and never claimed to be, an intellectual.

---

4 In *Walsingham Review*, 38, 1971.

It will also be noted that it was not only the servers who were invited but also their girlfriends. The impression is often given that Hope Patten did not like the company of women. However, it would be nearer the truth to say that he found it difficult to cope with women who pursued him, as some undoubtedly did. He was perfectly able to relate to the adolescent girls of the village in a natural way, at any rate at this period. The older villagers were surprised, but at the same time excited, that their children were afforded such notice at a time when the word 'teenager' had not been coined, but they too were entertained at garden parties and the like in the grounds of the vicarage, which was a substantial property with stables and other outbuildings built by one of the Lee-Warner incumbents in the previous century and situated a little way out of the centre of the village, on the road to Great Walsingham. It was until recently used by Sue Ryder Care.

In later years the canard was put about that Hope Patten drove some villagers away from the church and into the hands of the Nonconformists. That does not appear to have been the case, save for a very few people, most of whom later came back to the parish church. He was careful also not to discourage national Anglican organisations, such as the Mothers' Union, which were not incompatible with his teaching. He was a very assiduous visitor around the parish and his charm was displayed to full effect on the parishioners, who may otherwise have felt alienated from what was going on. The impression has sometimes also been given that he was eccentric. That is entirely the wrong epithet to apply to him: in many ways he was very conventional, especially on moral questions, but he did have particular gifts, of which he made good use, and, as already described, he ignored many of the commonplace preoccupations of the majority of the population, although he did become president of the village football club and was pictured in clerical dress with the team in their playing kit.

The evidence that Hope Patten did have great success in those early years in persuading the villagers to accept the considerable demands of his system of religion is overwhelming. Other priests were astounded at the number who went to confession on Saturday evenings and who were prepared to watch before the Blessed Sacrament, as they were encouraged to do after reservation was introduced. Father Leeds, Derrick Lingwood and Sir William Milner, an important figure in the Walsingham story, all knew the parish at this early stage in his ministry and all testified to the effect which Hope Patten produced. He was attempting of course to recreate in Norfolk a Belgian country parish, and was surprisingly successful in that from very early on. Interestingly Milner cites actual figures, which are often otherwise hard to ascertain. He said[5] that at the sung mass the attendance was 100–150, which out of a population of fewer than 1,000 was a considerable achievement. An even more impressive testimonial to the parish priest's efforts is contained in a contemporary letter written by Canon John Blake-Humfrey, who had retired to the village and lived opposite the church. He wrote, on 19 June 1926:

> Since [Father Patten's] advent, Church doctrine, life and 'go' have grown enormously in the parish, and his teaching, both amongst the young and old, has sunk in and 'holds' them in their lives. What makes people 'catch on' with him, (humanly speaking) is his loving sympathetic manner; in spite of interruption, or being stopped, he is always ready to give a listening ear, always ready to give up his time for people ... The whole spiritual atmosphere of Walsingham and church life here is of the very highest order. I cannot speak of it too highly. To sum up: the congregations at all the services are always large and have vastly increased and are increasing. The attendances at Holy Communion are wonderful both by the old and young. Old men and women, and women, girls and boys: they all come. I should say that the influence of Church Life in Walsingham is very great, extending to the whole parish and in consequence the Moral Tone is high.

This letter is of course so valuable as evidence particularly because it was written at the time rather than with the rose-tinted spectacles of hindsight.[6]

Hope Patten never learned to drive a car, which was less of a handicap than it may appear as in his time Walsingham was still on the railway network, although trains were slow and infrequent. In and around the village he often cycled, using a lady's bicycle with a wheel guard so that his cassock was not caught in the spokes, or alternatively he tucked it up and revealed grey socks and knickerbockers. On other occasions he was driven around in a pony trap by one of the parishioners. He wore a soutane with

---

5 In 'Reminiscences of Father Hope Patten' in *Our Lady's Mirror*, autumn 1958–winter 1959.
6 It was reproduced in *Our Lady's Mirror*, autumn 1958–winter 1959. Canon Blake-Humfrey (1847–1930) is buried in the churchyard at Walsingham.

beaver hat on his rounds, but certainly on more formal occasions and when out of the parish he dressed in frock coat and top hat as he had when a very junior curate. He kept very detailed visiting books which recorded the names of all the parishioners and their religious inclinations.

When he first arrived at Walsingham, Hope Patten said mass in the parish church at 8 a.m. and sung it at 11 a.m. after saying matins. In the meantime he had cycled to Houghton St Giles and back for the 9.30 a.m. mass; he was fanatical about fasting before saying mass, and so he would not eat at all until after the late sung mass. He then took catechism at 2.45 p.m. and finally evensong, first at Houghton at 5.30 p.m. and then at Little Walsingham at 6.30 p.m. The church at Great Walsingham was little used and services were generally held in the summer months only, with assistance from visiting priests.

In addition to this parochial activity, Hope Patten arranged a number of conferences for local clergy in an attempt to win support for Anglo-Catholicism and also to answer some of the suspicions which were inevitably aroused by his ritual innovations. These were substantial enterprises lasting several days, and involved well-known speakers such as Father Alban Baverstock, who had created on a smaller scale in his tiny Dorset parish of Hinton Martel that which Hope Patten was attempting to achieve at Walsingham, and Revd A. E. Monahan, later Bishop of Monmouth, whose brother, Revd W. B. Monahan, was a leading Anglican Papalist apologist. The conferences undoubtedly clarified what Hope Patten was doing, but it is not certain that they had any long-term effect on the other local parishes. Hope Patten followed the Anglo-Catholic party line of the time in being unenthusiastic about representative bodies of the clergy or deanery meetings and the like, a course which tended to isolate him from the thinking of his neighbours.

In addition to the conferences which were designed to educate, Hope Patten organised a small local Congress, which took place from 18 to 21 October 1922. The first national Anglo-Catholic Congress had been held in London in 1920 and was followed by a Priests' Conference in Oxford the following year. From that idea a large number of provincial meetings were held, and one of the smaller of these was that at Walsingham, where a high mass was sung in the church after the priests involved had processed vested through the village.

Colin Stephenson's assertion that the tradition of the neighbouring parish of South Creake dates from these conferences can, however, not go unchallenged. The living of South Creake was occupied between 1926 and 1944 by Revd H. B. Ventham, an ecclesiastical stormy petrel. Ventham had eventually been accepted back into the Church of England after a long involvement with the wilder frontiers of Anglo-Catholicism, including a novitiate with Father Ignatius of Llanthony and with the Carlyle's Benedictines before they moved to Caldey, and then consecration as an irregular bishop, in which capacity he was party to the issue in 1905 of a manifesto of a body calling itself the Society for the Restoration of Apostolic Unity. This was then followed by conditional reordination by the Old Catholic *episcopus vagans*, A. H. Mathew. Ventham restored the beautiful church at South Creake and established a pattern of worship which was continued by his successor, Revd L. H. Michael Smith, who was far more congenial a neighbour to Hope Patten. The latter had no truck at all with irregular bishops, and the suggestions that have in the past sometimes been whispered to the effect that he had been secretly consecrated are completely groundless.

It had been Hope Patten's clear intention when accepting the living to revive the mediaeval pilgrimage. He pursued that plan in parallel with his efforts within the village, because he had the perspicacity to appreciate that a pilgrimage centre which attracted those from outside the area would be unsuccessful if it did not have support locally. In those early years Hope Patten joined together the two strands of his ministry in a way which it was not possible to do so easily after the establishment of a separate shrine outside the parish church in 1931.

The new vicar pressed ahead with great purpose to establish a focus for the renewed devotion which he was determined to establish. The parish church was already provided with the small statue of Our Lady, which he had seen while a curate at Holy Cross, but that was not suitable for what he had in mind. It is always said that Hope Patten found a copy of the seal of the Walsingham Priory in the British Museum, and had it copied from there.[7] However, in 1912 a parishioner called Thomas Armitage Bennett, who was still in the village when Hope Patten arrived, had written a pamphlet entitled *An English Churchman's Guide to Walsingham*, which must have been available to the vicar, and which reproduced the reverse of the seal, showing the chapel of the Holy House. A Victorian tract entitled *Shrines and Pilgrimages of the County of Norfolk* by Revd Richard Hart did

---

7 The usually reliable Lingwood certainly thought that was the case.

show the depiction of Our Lady on the seal which Hope Patten used but it is not clear whether or not he had seen that work. It would have been a supreme irony had he in fact found the seal in the museum, since 'British Museum Religion' was a term of mild abuse used by those who, like Hope Patten, drew their inspiration rather from modern Roman forms than from mediaeval English precedents which could only be discovered by extensive archive research and was applied to the followers of Dr Percy Dearmer, whose approach was exemplified by the services at St Mary, Primrose Hill, when he was the incumbent there.

It appears that Hope Patten started one of his many collections for money to have a carving made of the figure as depicted on the seal, which was done by Sister Catherine, a Roman Catholic nun from North Kensington, through a Mr Bartlett of the Art and Book Shop, just outside the main entrance of Westminster Cathedral. Hope Patten did not appear to have any scruples about using the services of an English Roman Catholic for this purpose, although as we have seen he otherwise tended at this stage to pretend they did not exist. The figure is of a design which has since become synonymous with Walsingham. Another source of inspiration for him at this stage was *Pietas Mariana Britannica* by Edmund Waterton, published in 1879 and subtitled *A History of English Devotion to the Most Blessed Virgin Marye Mother of God, with a catalogue of shrines, sanctuaries, etc.,* with which he had probably been familiar since his days in Brighton. It contains a wealth of information about the mediaeval shrine, which he read and reread, taking copious notes and often scoring underneath and at the side of the text.

In essence, Walsingham had developed as a settlement purely to serve the pilgrims who visited the village to visit the shrine of Our Lady, which was described in the contemporary literature as being within a Holy House of similar dimensions to that at Loreto and as being adjacent or near to the very large Augustinian priory. The reason for the establishment of Walsingham's shrine was the appearance of Mary to a lady named Richeldis, which was said to have occurred in 1061. It became a very great centre of pilgrimage in the Middle Ages, and in addition to the priory a Franciscan house was also established there. After the dissolution of the monasteries and the split with Roman authority, the priory fell into ruins and no external trace was left of the Holy House. The village, however, remained particularly attractive, with many houses which had been constructed for the accommodation of the pilgrims, and this contributed to the success of the various events which were organised by Hope Patten, as well as encouraging visitors to what was still a remote area.

It is not clear whether or not at this stage Hope Patten knew of the erection, as early as 1897, of an image of Our Lady in the small Nottinghamshire village of Egmanton. The architect J. Ninian Comper, the son of the founder of St Margaret, Aberdeen, which had already featured in Hope Patten's life, recreated the image there from mediaeval precedents but without any specific knowledge of the original figure. The pilgrimage to Egmanton never developed to anything like the extent of that to Walsingham.

Hope Patten wasted no time in putting into effect the restoration of the shrine. He was instituted to the parish on 19 January 1921 by the local Rural Dean, Canon Gordon Roe, brother of his former vicar, acting for the Bishop of Thetford. In July 1922 he used the occasion of one of the local conferences described above to incorporate the re-establishment of the devotion to Our Lady of Walsingham. Hope Patten had always had a theatrical streak which had earlier manifested itself in his involvement in amateur dramatics. He was now able to harness that talent to the organisation of events such as this, and, importantly, to involve the parishioners in what he was doing. On 6 July 1922 the image was set up in the Guilds, or north, Chapel of the parish church. Father Alban Baverstock, who was in Walsingham for the priests' conference, assisted by blessing the image, which had initially been placed on a litter near the font. It was then carried into the chapel accompanied by some of the village girls in white dresses and veils and carrying branches of syringa (mock orange) to the accompaniment of the church bells, and placed on a pillar, looking towards the ruins of the priory from which its predecessor had been removed in 1538. The image was carried by two servers, Frederick Shepherd and George Howe. The sermon was preached by Revd Archdale King, then curate of St Saviour, Poplar, and later vicar of Holy Trinity, Reading, who subsequently seceded to Rome and wrote a number of very learned books on liturgical matters.[8] The following year Hope Patten started a local guild, which was later to be transformed into the nationwide Society of Our Lady of Walsingham.

---

8 During the Second World War, Archdale King lodged in Walsingham with Frederick Shepherd's mother-in-law, who herself went over to Rome in 1938. It was while he was living in Norfolk that he said his first mass as a Roman Catholic.

The use of the Guilds Chapel for the revived shrine was at the same time inspirational and tactless. It was inspirational because it provided an effective setting for the image, where it was possible for a small number to gather around without being lost in the main church. It was tactless because the stalls in the chapel were regarded by the lords of the manor as their family pew, and they were not consulted in advance. The chapel also contained the very fine Sidney tomb, in front of which a side altar had been erected some years before. Hope Patten also erected an altar of St Hugh of Lincoln to the north of the chancel arch.

The next step was to organise a pilgrimage to the church. There were at this time and later a very great number of societies on the Anglo-Catholic wing of the Church of England: Hope Patten's friend Father Fynes-Clinton was an inveterate founder of such bodies and revelled in meetings of their councils. Hope Patten, on the other hand, frequently joined such organisations but with his other commitments, and a lack of flair for administration, was reluctant to become involved in their running. He was an early member of Fynes-Clinton's most important foundation, the Catholic League, which was set up in 1913, but was barred from its affiliated body, the Sodality of the Precious Blood, membership of which was restricted to celibate clergy and which was instituted the following year, because his knowledge of Latin was too limited to allow him to recite the breviary in that language. He was, however, also a member of the League of Our Lady, which he had come across through Father Francis Baverstock when at Holy Cross, if not before. The League was under the Presidency of the revered Lord Halifax; it had been founded about 1904 and in fact was the most recent of three Marian societies in the Church of England. The first was the Confraternity of the Children of Mary, founded in India in 1880, which was later known as the Confraternity of Our Lady Help of Christians and after 1903 as the Confraternity of Our Lady. The second was the Union of the Holy Rosary, founded in 1886, which merged into the Confraternity of Our Lady in 1920. In 1931 all the streams came together in the Society of Mary. In addition there was in existence the Guild of the Living Rosary of Our Lady and St Dominic, which was set up in 1905 and also is still in operation.

It was decided that the first pilgrimage to the restored shrine should be under the auspices of the London branch of the League of Our Lady and should take place between 24 and 26 October 1922. This arose from a meeting of the League which Hope Patten had attended, and at which he met for the first time William (later Sir William) Milner, who was to be one of his greatest supporters and benefactors and was then the secretary of the League.

Hope Patten enlisted the assistance of his parishioners in offering to put up the pilgrims for the two nights they were to spend in the village. The programme was printed in advance and included solemn vespers on the first evening, high mass at 7.30 a.m. on the second day and low mass with music the next morning. Miss Elsie Lloyd, one of the sisters who had followed Hope Patten to Walsingham from Carshalton, was appointed as honorary pilgrimage secretary in the village.

Unfortunately this pilgrimage turned out to be little short of a fiasco. The dates fixed were from a Tuesday to a Thursday, which was not a convenient period for most people and was only chosen because the pilgrimage encompassed a visit to the Abbey grounds, which were then open only on Wednesdays. The organiser had noted down as definite travellers anyone who had expressed the vaguest interest in the project, and had failed to supply a list of who was coming, which was of some importance bearing in mind that sleeping accommodation had to be provided. When the train pulled into Walsingham station after the long journey from Liverpool Street, complicated by changes en route, a very tall priest (Revd Gordon Hibbs) and two elderly ladies stepped off.[9] It is not clear whether this failure of organisation was the personal fault of William Milner, who was not himself known for administrative competence, or whether it had been delegated to someone else. The position was further complicated by the last-minute illness of Milner himself, who was stricken with influenza and unable to travel.

Hope Patten was faced not only with a potential financial disaster but also with personal loss of face. He reacted with characteristic flair and decisiveness by transforming the occasion into a village pilgrimage, with all the services taking place in accordance with the agreed pattern and involving as many villagers as were free to attend. His reputation for resourcefulness and charm was saved and, perhaps more importantly, the

---

9 The priest has normally been identified as a Father Head, but in fact it was Father Hibbs, then parish priest of St John, Balham, Assistant Chaplain-General of the Catholic League and a prominent supporter of the time, and Head was a misrecollection by Father Lingwood (WA); the elderly women were sisters named Constance and Emma Baily.

parishioners became involved in the pilgrimage idea from the commencement.

After that unfortunate experience, the next pilgrimage, from 22 to 24 May 1923, also under the auspices of the League of Our Lady was much better organised and about 40 people made the trip from London. The starting point was the Wren church of St Magnus the Martyr, London Bridge, of which Father Fynes-Clinton had become parish priest in the same year that Hope Patten moved to Walsingham. It was largely the financial and other support of Milner and Fynes-Clinton which enabled Hope Patten to drive forward the revival of pilgrimages to Walsingham from outside the area. An anonymous pilgrim sent an account of his experiences to the *Church Times*,[10] and described a similar pattern of devotions to that which had been planned for the first pilgrimage in 1922. This publicity of course was all to the good so far as Hope Patten was concerned, although it also alerted the ever vigilant Protestant societies to what was happening in this corner of Norfolk.

Sir William Milner is readily recognisable in all the photographs of events at Walsingham for many years because of his great height. William Frederick Victor Mordaunt Milner[11] (1893–1960) was a bachelor from a wealthy Yorkshire family and was educated at Wellington and Christ Church, Oxford, with a period of military service. In due course he inherited a baronetcy but then, although he qualified as an architect, appeared to leave all the work to his partners: he himself was an extraordinarily talented gardener and also, incongruously, a very able knitter. His architectural firm, Milner & Craze (at one point Milner, Craze & Urquhart) became well known for its ecclesiastical work, but that was largely through the efforts of Milner's longstanding business partner Romilly Craze. Like Hope Patten, Milner was enthralled by the Middle Ages and the religion of that era and he was captivated by what he saw happening at Walsingham. Because he had financial resources which he was prepared to devote to furthering the cause, he was a valuable ally to Hope Patten, who had no money of his own and in any case was spending at this time very much more than his meagre stipend was paying. He became one of his few close friends, and addressed him as 'Pat', a privilege accorded only to those very near to him.

---

10 25 May 1923.

11 Despite all these Christian names, he was known by his friends, confusingly, as Derrick.

Father Fynes-Clinton was an enormous influence on Hope Patten and the two also became firm allies. It was he, with his network of contacts in Russia and Eastern Europe, who encouraged Father Patten to look with more favour upon the Orthodox Church, in which the latter had shown no great interest before then. Fynes-Clinton was, like Patten, convinced that the Church of England had to demonstrate to the Roman Church and others that it had within it the spiritual resources which could produce manifestations such as a shrine of Our Lady, such as had occurred at Lourdes and was in the process of occurring at Fatima. One of the enormous number of enterprises which he established was the Walsingham Clergy Fund, which was designed to supplement the stipend and to provide funds for a curate. He was assisted in this by Miss Alice Doyle-Smithe, who was the secretary of the Fund.

Early on in his time at Walsingham, Revd F. H. Williams assisted Hope Patten on occasion, although it is not clear how if at all he was paid. He was certainly there at the time of the pilgrimage in May 1923, as he is recorded as preaching to the visitors. Frank Hiram Williams had been trained for the priesthood at the somewhat unlikely venue of Wycliffe Hall, Oxford, and his churchmanship must have risen up the scale with some rapidity thereafter. He was a curate at St Augustine, Grimsby from 1921 to 1922, but is then described as having permission to officiate in the Diocese of Norwich until 1924, when he returned to more regular duties as curate of St Augustine, Highgate. It is not clear whether or not he spent the whole of the 1922–4 period in Walsingham, although Derrick Lingwood certainly recalled him as helping.

In 1926,[12] however, a congenial assistant arrived in the form of Hope Patten's old friend and follower Father Leeds. He had served a long first curacy at Christ Church, Clapham, from 1913 and had then gone to South Creake as a locum before Father Ventham's arrival, apparently when the previous vicar was in Australia. It was no doubt during that period that he re-established close contact with Hope Patten.

There was only one potential barrier to the renewal of their former intimacy, which was that in 1922 Father Leeds had married Doris (Dolly), the attractive daughter of his vicar in Clapham, Revd P. D. Hedges. In general terms of course Hope Patten strongly disapproved of clerical marriage. It

---

12 *Crockford* says 1926, but Father Leeds' own reminiscences give the date as 1924.

was Hope Patten's practice at this period to answer questions from the pulpit after benediction and on one occasion, when asked whether it was lawful for priests to marry, Hope Patten answered quickly and unequivocally that it was not, despite the presence in the front row of the nave not only of Father Leeds but of his wife, his son Peter and his daughter Joan.[13] Despite that answer, in practice he was welcoming to Mrs Leeds and enjoyed her company. Father and Mrs Leeds lived in the parsonage at Houghton St Giles and stayed until 1932. He later wrote of the warmth which Hope Patten extended to them at Christmas and of how he used to read ghost stories to his guests.

The parsonage at Houghton had also been built by the Lee-Warner family in the nineteenth century and it had generally been used to house any curate which the vicars of Walsingham had. It continued, however, to be owned by the family.

In 1922 Sir Eustace Gurney and his wife Agatha (née Lee-Warner) took up residence at the Abbey. Sir Eustace was a member of one of the best-known Norfolk families, who had originally been Quakers. He took over the estate from his wife's relations after very substantial debts had been incurred by them, at least in part in the earlier restorations of the parish church and at least in part owed to Gurney's Bank. His wife of course had known Walsingham from an early age through her relatives, and she was in principle not unsympathetic to what Hope Patten was trying to do. Sir Eustace, however, despite being the brother of Samuel Gurney, the well-known benefactor of Anglo-Catholicism, was strongly Protestant in his outlook and boycotted the parish church after complaining that matins was not the main Sunday service. The institution of the shrine in what was regarded as the family pew upset Lady Gurney and the result was that frostiness, rapidly turning sometimes to overt hostility, grew up between the patrons of the living and the parish priest.

This hostility had several unfortunate consequences. Sir Eustace died in 1927, but his widow outlived Hope Patten and, although they remained on polite terms she did not always give him the support and encouragement which might have been expected. The more immediate effects of the breach were financial. It had been customary for the priest to receive any rental income from the Houghton house when there was no curate in

---

13 I am indebted to Paul James, who knew Father Leeds in later life, for further information on what is a well-known story.

residence, but Sir Eustace ended that practice. On Hope Patten's arrival he had been receiving £60 per annum from that property, paid by the tenant who was a Miss Parry Oakden. It had also been the tradition that the patrons paid £90 per annum as a donative to the vicar to compensate for the fact that the benefice of Great Walsingham had no income. Eustace Gurney ceased that, further reducing Hope Patten's income, which in any event was being far exceeded by his spending at that time. Another consequence of this was that, out of respect for his relatives, Samuel Gurney, who might have proved a useful benefactor of the shrine as he was of so many other projects, kept away.[14]

These unfortunate events did not deter Hope Patten from proceeding along the path upon which he had determined. Once the first successful pilgrimage had taken place in May 1923 they became regular events, albeit not frequent. The pattern for a number of years was for the League of Our Lady to come at least once a year, usually in May or October, and for other groups to come occasionally, sometimes just from Norwich. There was very little pilgrimage activity at the weekends, when parish worship continued in the usual way.

The shrine itself was progressively decorated in ways which Hope Patten had seen abroad, and in particular those whose prayers were answered were encouraged to leave tablets of the type often found at continental places of devotion. Every day at 6 p.m. 'Shrine Prayers' were said in the chapel: these consisted of the rosary followed by intercessions from a book which was kept for that purpose. Hope Patten retained letters and other testimonials to the answers to the prayers, including from those who claimed to have been healed following a visit to Walsingham.

It is clear that from the very beginning of his ministry at Walsingham, Hope Patten looked upon the revival of the devotion to Our Lady as a long-term exemplar of the wider move to bring the Anglican Church into line with Roman standards of practice. However, while he undoubtedly wished his work in the village to endure, he also foresaw the difficulties that might arise if he died, especially if that death were premature, and for that reason he was frequently in a tearing hurry to put into practice his current idea, whatever it might be. As time went by, the fear that the tradition and devotion which he had established would be dismantled after his

---

14 Canon Blake-Humfrey was a relative of the Gurneys, and the letter quoted above was sent to Samuel Gurney.

death became almost obsessional with him, and explains a great deal of what occurred thereafter.

As early as the first half of 1924 Hope Patten saw an opportunity to develop the pilgrimages by providing hospice (hostel) accommodation for visitors; without such provision there was very little accommodation available, and the local people obviously could not give up their beds on a regular basis. It was a crucial step to be able to put up pilgrims, particularly with the remoteness of Walsingham, and immediately differentiated the position there from that at Egmanton when Revd Silas Harris began to revive the pilgrimage there after he was appointed to the living in 1927. No accommodation was ever provided at Egmanton, with the result that it remained a local devotion with visitors only coming for the day.

The accommodation on which Hope Patten had set his eye was 'The Beeches' in Holt Road, which was a substantial property with a barn, garden, cottages and outbuildings which was being sold by the Adcock Estate. William Milner agreed to lend the money for the purchase on the basis that it would be repaid in due course. Hope Patten went about acquiring the property with some cunning; he refused to acknowledge his own interest and entrusted the local grocer, George Back, who was also his organist, to bid at auction on his behalf. He succeeded in buying the property for £1,750, which was a very considerable sum of money for that time: a reasonably substantial suburban church could have been built then for much less than £10,000, which affords some comparison.

The auction took place on 21 March 1924. Hope Patten sent a telegram to Milner to tell him of the success, and followed it up by a letter the same night.[15] He explained that a higher price had had to be paid than had been anticipated because a reserve had been put on the property, but that eventually the entire property (which had been in three separate lots) had been knocked down to him. He went on: 'I hope you are pleased. Now we shall look forward to the Hostel of Our Lady Star of the Sea, the cell of St Benet and St Francis Borgia's Hostel for aged priests, etc., etc., etc.' From that extract it is clear that Hope Patten's mind was running on to new projects, even before the hospice was in operation. He did in fact in due course set up a home for retired priests, as we shall see, albeit not dedicated to St Francis Borgia; the very strong likelihood is that that reference to that patently unsuitable saint was little more than a joke between two men who

---

15 In the WA.

were both very pleased by their coup and shared a similarly ecclesiastical sense of humour. The letter then continued in equally characteristic mode:

> It struck me suddenly – last night in the chapel – if you get the property you must arrange it *in your will* at once. This sounds as if I have an assassin's design on you – but it would be dreadful if anything happened and it goes back to protestant hands – or got to the R.C.s. *That was frightening me all last night.* I will be writing to you in a few days and sending the deeds . . . I think Our Lady is pleased.

Having acquired the property, which clearly then required the expenditure of considerable sums upon it to make it suitable for its new purpose, Hope Patten looked to bring some sisters to the village to run the hospice. Undoubtedly he also saw the presence of religious in Walsingham as in addition assisting in his unspoken design to turn the parish into a spiritual powerhouse of the Church of England, from which others could take inspiration back to their own churches and gradually transform the Anglican Communion from within.

He approached Mother Sarah of the Community of St Peter, the mother house of which was then in Horbury, West Yorkshire, for assistance. Mother Sarah was a formidable woman with a will as strong as that of Hope Patten himself and she shared similar views as to the direction which the Church of England should take. At this stage all was well between them and Walsingham became one of the very few rural parishes in which sisters from any order went to work. However, their respective personalities were such that a conflict in the future looked even at that time to be very likely.

The first three nuns to arrive in Walsingham lived initially in a cottage attached to the Rectory. They were Sisters Veronica, who was in charge, Marguerite and Grace Mary. The village was somewhat wary initially, but were quickly won over, particularly by Sister Veronica, who was described by Father Lingwood as 'a saint'. In due course they moved into 'The Beeches', which had previously been occupied by T. A. Bennett, who had written the book on Walsingham, and his family,[16] and it was renamed the Hospice of Our Lady Star of the Sea. Money had been raised by an appeal

---

16 Dorothy Bennett, who has already been quoted, was his daughter.

sponsored by Lord Halifax and Sybil Thorndike, which also raised the possibility of adapting part of the premises as God's House of St John for retired priests, but nothing was done about that at that time.

As well as 'The Beeches', the property acquired included a house in Knight Street where the village schoolmaster lived, which was later renamed St Augustine's, and a barn, which had been used by the Salvation Army and was at the time it was purchased being used by the Society of Friends but in due course became the pilgrims' refectory.

Hope Patten continued to suffer breakdowns in his health, which meant that from time to time he abandoned the village and went on trips abroad, sometimes at quite short notice. When that happened, priests were sometimes brought in to assist, or else Father Leeds substituted: Father Lingwood recalled on one occasion as a youth having to serve for the extraordinary Father Wason, who by then had begun a long period of peripatetic existence after being deprived of his living. He remarked that the village thought that he 'was a weird bird', which is something of an understatement. Those who thought that Hope Patten was eccentric had clearly not met Sandys Wason.

In late 1924 Hope Patten went to Assisi. On 3 October 1924 he encountered Peter Anson there on one of his own many travels abroad.[17] Anson, who was never ordained as a priest in either the Anglican or Roman Churches, had been admitted as a Franciscan tertiary two days earlier and was at that point in his life entirely entranced by the experience of Assisi. He said that while praying he had been surreptitiously approached by a man who wanted to make his confession and had concluded that Anson was, like himself, an Anglican priest in mufti. Having explained the situation, he was surprised the same evening to be introduced to Mr Hope Patten (*sic*) at a friend's house and to recognise him from the morning. Apparently the friars at Assisi were impressed by Hope Patten's piety in having himself lowered into a hole in the rocks known as the bed of St Francis, which was a particularly difficult exercise attempted only by the very devout.

Hope Patten was anxious when abroad to acquire authenticated relics to add to the atmosphere of piety which he was promoting in the parish: his profound interest in such objects, uncommon but not unknown in the Anglo-Catholic Movement, has already been noted. While in Assisi he

---

17 The date comes from a letter from Anson in the WA dated 13 April 1961.

purchased a reliquary containing a relic of St Vincent, which is said to have been bought from an antique dealer who took it to the local bishop to have the required certificate issued: without it, he would have lost the sale. Hope Patten let it be known, with a degree of licence with the truth, that the Bishop of Assisi had provided it for the shrine, and began a Guild of St Vincent for the servers. The relic was an arm bone and an ampulla containing some remains of the martyred saint's blood, but there were also various other 'relics of famous early martyrs' which were removed from the main reliquary and transferred to smaller expositories in due course.

The first four years of Hope Patten's incumbency were remarkable for the impact which the new vicar's personality had on the village and indeed on the outside world, although it must always be remembered that the appeal of the devotion at that time was to a very narrow section indeed of the Church of England: many who called themselves Anglo-Catholics stood and looked askance at what was happening at Walsingham.

The reverse of the seal from which the idea for the image was taken.

The obverse of the seal, showing the depiction of Our Lady as adapted for the image.

5

WALSINGHAM: THE SECOND PHASE, 1925–30

Having established his position in Walsingham, Hope Patten wished not only to consolidate but also to move forward. He had succeeded in placing the village back within the consciousness of many on the pro-Roman wing of the Church of England, but his vision was to increase the influence of the shrine so that Walsingham was regarded as an entirely appropriate flowering of Anglicanism rather than a somewhat exotic offshoot.

There is no doubt that Hope Patten was, like many of his contemporaries, strongly influenced by the Society of SS Peter and Paul and by the advocacy by that organisation and others of the so-called 'Back to Baroque' tendency. He personally was besotted by the Middle Ages, a cast of mind which was becoming somewhat passé by the post-First World War period and was more commonly found in the late Victorian clergy. Although he had a beautiful mediaeval Gothic church, the decorations which he installed in it were strongly redolent of more modern Continental devotion, deriving from Counter-Reformation Baroque. Hope Patten followed rather than led this tendency, and almost its final flowering was the building of the Holy House and Shrine Chapel at Walsingham, but it had begun even before the First World War and reached its apogee in the ten years or so after the cessation of hostilities.[1] The model for many was the small and structurally rather dull brick church of St Mary, Bourne Street, Pimlico, which was skilfully adapted by the stained-glass artist and decorator Martin Travers in the 1919–23 period, so that the high altar resembled something from the Netherlands of the eighteenth century. In 1924 Travers carried out equally successful work to Father Fynes-Clinton's Wren church of St Magnus the Martyr in the City, with the

---

1 See Rodney Warrener and Michael Yelton: *Martin Travers (1886–1948): An Appreciation* (Unicorn Press, 2003).

result that it looked like an Austrian church which had been washed over by the Counter-Reformation. In 1927-8 Travers designed the huge reredos for St Augustine, Queen's Gate, South Kensington, reminiscent of Spain or its former colonies in South America. In other places, genuine rather than pastiche furnishings were imported and used to enliven otherwise dull suburban churches.

Along with the decorations, the Society of SS Peter and Paul promoted the further disguising of the Prayer Book. The undoubted master of this technique was Revd E. O. Humphrey Whitby, vicar of St Mary, Bourne Street, from 1916, who had a strong attraction to the 1662 Book although he overlaid it with elaborate ceremonial derived from Roman sources. Hope Patten became an enthusiastic devotee of this form of liturgy, eschewing the use of the Roman mass which was adopted by some parishes and in particular by religious communities which were hidden from immediate public scrutiny. He altered his early practice of saying large parts of the Prayer Book service out loud, and by 1931 had definitely adopted the Bourne Street practice of a silent canon, albeit using the words of the 1662 book.[2]

The effect of that change was something of a trompe-l'oeil, as indeed was much of the 'Back to Baroque' stream. Hope Patten actually used more of the Prayer Book under this practice than he had been doing previously, but it looked to the outsider as if it had less in common with a standard Anglican Eucharist.

Having built a considerable and exotically decorated superstructure on to the firm foundations of belief which he found when he arrived, there were two important developments in 1925 and a further two in 1926, all of which enabled the progress which had been begun to be maintained.

The first development in 1925 was the formal transformation of the local guild which he had set up in 1923 into the Society of Our Lady of Walsingham (SOLW). This took place formally on 20 August 1925 during a pilgrimage. The members were invested with a 'little blue scapular', on which Father Fynes-Clinton gave an address at that meeting, and their names were included in a bound book which was kept in a casket at the foot of the image in the parish church; the book had been illuminated by an artist who visited the shrine. This was the first organisation which Hope Patten founded with the intention of supporting his work in Walsingham,

---

2 See letter from Revd Frank Reader, 8 May 1961 (WA).

particularly financially, and further of bringing together the members. It was said[3] that the members' privileges were daily remembrance at the shrine, the offering for them of the Saturday mass, and the sayings of requiems. For the latter purpose a Chantry Roll was opened in 1926 for the names of deceased members and other pilgrims.

The second important development that year was the arrival at nearby Blakeney of Bishop Mowbray Stephen O'Rorke, who had retired from his Diocese of Accra in what is now Ghana. Bishop O'Rorke had been ordained as deacon in 1902 and priest the following year. He served curacies in the northeast of England – at St Paul, Jarrow (1902–5), then St Margaret, Durham (1905–10) – before a spell in Rockhampton, Australia (1910–12). From there he moved to Accra as bishop in 1913, so his time as a diocesan bishop was actually quite short. When he came to Norfolk and took on the parish of the small seaside village of Blakeney, he also acted on occasion as assistant to the Bishop of Norwich, but his views were far in advance of any English diocesan. From the very beginning of his time in Blakeney he was a strong supporter of Hope Patten and began visiting the shrine, especially on the Wednesday of the midweek pilgrimages. He was prepared to preside at vespers, which thus became pontifical vespers; in this way the pilgrimages were given an additional dimension and did not appear to be solely the creation of Hope Patten. O'Rorke, who as his name implies was of Irish origin, was strong minded and prepared to stand up for himself if necessary against Hope Patten, but equally he enjoyed being dressed up with an enormously tall mitre, in which he can be seen sculpted on his tomb in the shrine church.

In January 1926 Hope Patten started publication of *Our Lady's Mirror*, which ran for the whole of his life, and indeed concluded with the issue after his memorial number. It was a quarterly publication, intended for the members of the Society of Our Lady of Walsingham, and was largely the parish priest's own production, although the motif which appeared in every copy was the product of a local artist, Lilian Frances (Lily) Dagless (1902–94). It depicted the image with on either side the patron saints of Great Walsingham and of Houghton. Lily Dagless was one of a large number of people whom Hope Patten was able to encourage to develop artistic talents of which they were themselves previously unaware. She was

---

3 In *Our Lady's Mirror*, January 1926, and in literature subsequently produced for the Society.

also one of the few local adherents who in due course defected to Rome; she and her brother James were later instrumental in furnishing the Slipper Chapel at Houghton when it was rebuilt for the Roman Catholic Church in 1936 and for some time before the war Peter Anson acted as liturgical adviser to the two of them.[4]

Early editions of the newsletter carried the warning that they were private communications for members only, but in later years readers were encouraged to publicise the shrine by passing them on to friends.

It is inevitable that *Our Lady's Mirror* provides one of the principal sources for what occurred at Walsingham thereafter; it shows also sometimes that Hope Patten, so gracious orally save when he intended otherwise, was not always a great master of the written word. While his historical articles are interesting, his appeals for money and perhaps more so the lamentations when money was not provided for his latest scheme (or for the continuation of the newsletter itself) do not always show him in the best light. They reflect perhaps that single-mindedness which was his greatest strength and also his greatest failing. There were also many articles in the newsletter giving information about Marian and other shrines on the Continent, some of which were by Patten himself but most of which in the early days were subscribed 'A. C. L.' or 'A. L.', the initials of Alexander Cuthbert Lawson, who at that time was living in Oxford with Revd Roger Wodehouse, parish priest of St Paul, but was himself ordained in 1932 and, although still living at St Paul's vicarage, became curate at St Mary Magdalen, Oxford. In 1946 he was appointed parish priest of St Ives, Cambridgeshire, where he stayed for some 16 years. His Marian books and ephemera were left to Walsingham and form the basis of the library on the subjects covered in the articles.

The final development in this sequence was in the long term probably the most important for the future development of the devotion: this was the arrival as factotum and in particular financial secretary of the young Derrick Albert Lingwood. He had been a server at the church from the time of Hope Patten's arrival and had participated in the Friday evening

---

4 She did not, however, refuse to carry out work for Anglicans thereafter. In 1955, for example, she provided paintings for the interior of the apse of the remote Norfolk church of Marshland St James, of which the parish priest, Revd C. N. Bales, was a great supporter of Walsingham and led Fenland pilgrimages to the shrine. She is buried in the churchyard at Walsingham next to her parents.

games at the vicarage. In 1925, by which time he was 15, he was cycling back with Hope Patten from evensong at Houghton when he told him by the side of the River Stiffkey, with some trepidation, that he wanted to be ordained a priest.

Hope Patten has sometimes been criticised for being a snob. There was undoubtedly a somewhat superior attitude to be found in him on occasion, but faced with what to most priests would have appeared an impossible dream on the part of his young and ill-educated parishioner, he did not discourage him, but said he would give the matter further consideration. The next year he went to Derrick Lingwood and suggested that he move into the vicarage and start studying with a view to ordination in due course, but that in the meantime he could deal with all financial affairs of the vicar and of the pilgrimages. Once again, Hope Patten had seen a talent in another of which he encouraged the development. His sole expressed reason for putting the proposition to Derrick Lingwood was that he 'came from a business family', which in fact meant no more than that he was the oldest of the six children of the village baker.[5]

Not only was it extraordinary that Hope Patten was prepared to hand over all his financial affairs to a boy of 16, but it also appears that the vicar had at last begun to face the fact that his credit was running out and that fiscal reality would have to be faced. Derrick Lingwood found that Hope Patten's tiny income, set against expenditure on a large house with lavish entertainment both of servers, parishioners, pilgrims, and at the conferences meant that he was by then in a very dangerous cash flow situation. He had debts which exceeded £1,000, a huge amount for the time and more than three times his annual income, and even the gardener had not been paid for six months. It is no exaggeration to say that had the position not been addressed, Hope Patten's ministry at Walsingham could have come to an ignominious and early end as a result of a flurry of writs and even bankruptcy.

It seems likely that William Milner assisted with the settlement of some debts, and certainly the Walsingham Clergy Fund helped to supplement the income of the priest. However, Derrick Lingwood still had to negotiate with the tradesmen and in due course, after some forbearance on their part, they were all paid. He then clamped down on all unnecessary expenditure. He wrote later that Hope Patten 'never interfered' but thereafter

---

5 As has been seen, Hope Patten himself came from a family in trade.

'had no idea where his income came from or how much it was . . . It is true to say that if he wanted a half-crown for spending he had to ask . . . for it.' Initially, even his Easter offering was paid over to Lingwood, but once the situation was brought under control Hope Patten was given a separate account of his own into which it and any other legacies or personal gifts were placed. Even birthdays and Christmas presents for his personal friends were seen to by Lingwood and all Hope Patten did was to '[write] the names on them'.[6]

There is no doubt that this development enabled Hope Patten to devote even more of his time to the development of his ministry and of the shrine without being distracted by the more mundane questions of finance. Derrick Lingwood later wrote somewhat ruefully: 'I wonder if any person has been able to do his life's work and never had to bother about any financial matters connected with it.'

There is no doubt, however, that despite Hope Patten's readiness to accept advice from Lingwood, he remained financially incompetent and to a degree irresponsible. Later there were two small incidents which demonstrated this recurrent tendency, both of which Lingwood recalled.

The first occurred when Hope Patten wanted to buy what was then called a wireless. He saw one in Norwich which was for sale at £15. He had the money in his own account, but insisted on taking it on hire purchase and then, inevitably, did not pay the instalments. Equally inevitably, in due course the finance company pressed him for payment, whereupon he went cap in hand to Lingwood and asked him what he was going to do about it. After a brief outburst from Lingwood, Hope Patten was told that it would be dealt with: Lingwood was then able to pay it using his power of attorney over the personal account after the vicar had been given a timely monetary present from one of his admirers.

The second incident was some years later when Hope Patten was running two accounts, one of which was overdrawn by £60. When he was given a cheque for £100, Lingwood strongly advised him to pay off the overdraft and save himself the interest he was paying. Hope Patten insisted on paying it into the account which was in credit, so that he could spend it.

Hope Patten continued to have lengthy spells away from the parish when he disappeared abroad, usually after his health gave way after long periods of prolonged hard work or of pressure. The exact pattern is not

---

6 See Lingwood: 'Rough Notes'.

clear, but in late 1926 he was away for about two months in France; Derrick Lingwood recalled spending two months with Hope Patten in the south of France and Switzerland and that was probably this period. There is certainly a photograph of the two of them on a beach in Belgium, recorded as taken in September 1926; they both sport bathing costumes which cover much more than would be the case today. In 1928 Hope Patten undoubtedly went with Lingwood to Lourdes and Rome for three months (where the vicar changed his outdoor headgear after seeing what was worn there). He much enjoyed having a younger companion to lead, just as he had done in Brighton with Wilfred Leeds in the early years of the century. In 1930 the vicarage was advertised to let furnished from 24 June to 9 August and again from 25 August to November that year.[7] In that year also it was announced that as the vicar had been ill, the doctor had 'ordered' him to have a car and to get out more; one had been given and was being run free of charge for him for a year.

Despite the financial stringencies, Hope Patten showed no sign at all of becoming domesticated himself, in common it has to be said with most contemporaries in his position. In 1927 a Walsingham villager, George Long, who had risen to the rank of Captain in the Army in the First World War, began doing the gardening and also waited at table in the evenings. Hope Patten was indifferent to haute cuisine, although he ate heartily save on days of abstinence, but he liked atmosphere and he insisted that he and Derrick Lingwood ate by the light of candles in silver candlesticks. When Hope Patten was away and if Father Leeds was not available George Long and his wife moved into the vicarage and looked after the visiting priests, ensuring that they too did not break their fast until after the 11 a.m. mass.

There was a period or periods of time (the exact dates are not clear) in which Hope Patten's mother came to live with him at Walsingham. Derrick Lingwood remembered her as a 'charming little woman'; when she was there he was made to dress for dinner, which must have been entirely out of his experience of life at that age. It was also said that while she was there her son kept others from meeting her. The general impres-

---

7 See *Our Lady's Mirror*, spring 1930. The previous year it had been announced that Hope Patten was to act as chaplain to a pilgrimage to the Holy Land under the leadership of Major H. Adderley (later Lord Norton) in June 1930, but it does not appear that he was well enough to go. A later such pilgrimage was advertised with Father Fynes-Clinton as chaplain.

sion seems to be that Hope Patten's mother played little part in his life after he moved to Walsingham. However, he was certainly closer to her than he had been to his father; facially too he strongly resembled his mother.

On 4 March 1929 Mrs Georgina Sarah Routh Keith-Falconer died. She was a devotee of Hope Patten who had lived in grace and favour apartments at Hampton Court, probably obtained through family connections (her husband was killed in action in the Boer War and his mother had also lived in the Palace). Not only did she leave him some money but also passed on, as it were, her elderly and obese housekeeper Hannah Harrold, who moved to live in the vicarage. The pecuniary legacy to Hope Patten was the then very considerable sum of £1,500, which must have assisted with his financial problems; it was about five times his annual income at that time. She also left £1,000 to Hannah Harrold.

Hope Patten continued into adulthood the tendency which he had had when younger of becoming delirious whenever he had a temperature. Lingwood remembered one such occasion when he had taken to his bed, and Hannah brought up his supper with a cover on it. Hope Patten had mentally relapsed into the retelling of the martyrdom of St John the Baptist when he saw Hannah, who had bad legs in irons, stumbling across the room towards the bed with her tray. He called out, 'Is that you, Herodias?' and she replied 'Yes, Father.' His eyes then almost left his head as he saw the cover on the tray, but when she lifted it up there was only an omelette on the plate rather than the head of the Baptist he had by then convinced himself was to be revealed.

Derrick Lingwood was by then used to dealing with these relapses into the past. On one earlier occasion when the servers were in the vicarage for one of their regular entertainments, Hope Patten fell asleep on the sofa and in his sleep began describing in bloody detail the martyrdom of St Thomas Becket. Lingwood tried to get him to bed, but he refused and continued. The village lads were astounded, but Lingwood decided to try to bring him out of the scene by introducing an incongruous note. He suddenly announced that he was the Bishop of Norwich, which cut across the dream and woke up the vicar. John Shepherd, who was to succeed Lingwood as Hope Patten's local protégé after the Second World War, remembers episodes of this nature occurring later on more than one feast of St Thomas the Martyr, which suggests that they may not have been as spontaneous as appeared.

By 1926 the first stage of the conversion work on the Hospice[8] of Our Lady Star of the Sea was completed; although the first phase was limited in scope, for a short time there was a chapel in the cellar (characteristically referred to by Hope Patten as 'the crypt').

Originally the preacher at the opening was to have been Father Vernon Johnson SDC, then one of the most popular missioners in the Church of England; he later seceded to Rome after a pilgrimage to Lisieux. The dates were changed, and it is not clear whether he was there when the hospice was blessed on 11 June 1926. In *Our Lady's Mirror*[9] it was announced that the crypt chapel had two altars and a 'dim catacomb-like atmosphere and light'. In due course the damp drove the nuns out and back to the parish church for their devotions, but not before the emergence of a scheme, which appears to have been started but never brought to fruition, to construct an oratory for the sisters in the garden of the hospice. The building was to be dedicated to Our Lady of Pity, and the interesting feature of it, in the light of later developments, was that it was planned so that 'the total interior measurements of the chapel and its porch will be the same as the Holy House of Loreto, while the actual oratory will reproduce the exact measurements of the Holy House or Shrine of Our Lady of Walsingham'.[10]

Hope Patten's mind was like a Catherine wheel shooting out ideas, some of which were immediately put into effect and others of which never came to pass. At almost the same time as the Hospice of Our Lady Star of the Sea was blessed, he announced that 'through the generosity of an anonymous friend' (probably Milner again) it had been possible to acquire three mediaeval cottages in the High Street, which were to house a pilgrim shop and 'eventually' a chapel at ground level, with the Hospice of SS Michael and George on the first floor. Hope Patten believed that they had been a pilgrim hostel during the Middle Ages, another draw to him. This now forms the house now known as 'Shields'; although the cottages were purchased, the conversion did not in the event proceed as intended.[11]

The pilgrimages were steadily developing, but had little impact on the wider world. The pages of the *Our Lady's Mirror* show that during this

---

8 Hospice at that time was used in its mediaeval sense of 'hostel' rather than its more modern meaning of a place offering care for the terminally ill.

9 October 1926.

10 *Our Lady's Mirror*, autumn 1928.

11 *Our Lady's Mirror*, summer 1926.

period there were usually only four major pilgrimages a year. The League of Our Lady came at least once a year, and in May 1926 there was a priests' conference arranged, which was then cancelled because of the General Strike. In August that year Archbishop Seraphim of the Russian Orthodox Church in Exile was to come, but his visit too was cancelled, in his case because of a conference in Paris, where he was based. The following year Major A. F. Bowker, founder of the Society of Retreat Conductors, who was to play a significant part in matters at the shrine later, had arranged a pilgrimage which again had to be abandoned, as he was ill. There was, however, a significant event in June 1927 when Father Fynes-Clinton brought the first pilgrims from the Catholic League: that organisation thereafter became regular patrons of Walsingham, encouraged by the strong support of their leader. Father Whitby also came that year to preach to the League of Our Lady pilgrimage in May. In 1928 there were a larger number of pilgrimages, including from the local Anglo-Catholic Congresses held at Norwich and Kettering, two from the League of Our Lady, the Catholic League, and groups from London and Yorkshire, the latter led by Revd D. Ferrier, whose widow Dorothy was later to be prominent in Walsingham affairs for many years. In 1929, perhaps in reaction to this, it was announced that there would be four main pilgrimages only, namely the League of Our Lady, the Catholic League, the priests' pilgrimage and a Yorkshire pilgrimage, but an announcement was also made in relation to a group from Birmingham.

However, in 1926 Walsingham received considerable publicity, which in the long run may have been beneficial in raising the public consciousness of the pilgrimages, although undoubtedly it led to a difficult period in the short term. Bishop Hensley Henson, then at Durham, had been the subject of considerable protest from Anglo-Catholics upon his consecration as Bishop of Hereford in 1918 on the grounds that he was a Modernist. At this time he was, in turn, prepared to use his considerable powers of invective against those whom he saw as wishing to reverse the Reformation. He visited Walsingham on 17 August 1926 when staying in the area and wrote about his experience in the *Evening Standard* on 1 September that year. At this time it was still unusual to find Anglo-Catholicism in rural areas and certainly Walsingham was unique. Hope Patten, typically using an attack on him to his own advantage, reprinted the article in *Our Lady's Mirror* for October 1926, asking his readers to say their Our Father and Hail Mary for the writer and other Protestants in the country.

There was substance in much of what Henson wrote: he was actually putting forward the case that Hope Patten was succeeding in his endeavours. He wrote:

Walsingham is . . . as complete an example of triumphant Anglo-Catholicism as the country can present. The Parish Church might easily be taken for a Roman Catholic church: there was nothing Anglican about it except the fabric . . . Perhaps it is inevitable that the revival of pilgrimages should be included in the general policy of 'undoing the Reformation' which the Anglo-Catholics have adopted and are pursuing with such remarkable vigour, pertinacity and success, for the abolition of pilgrimages and the demolition of the Shrines to which pilgrims resorted were conspicuous features of the religious revolution which the Reformers effected.

After that setting forth of what Hope Patten was trying to do, however, he went on to pour scorn on the pilgrimages themselves:

It would probably be an error to attach much importance to the revived pilgrimages, which are rather 'pageants' than religious acts. The pitiable rubbish of the Walsingham processional hymn could only be intelligible as part of a 'pageant.' As an act of religion it would be profane.

Many years later Henson retired to Hintlesham, Suffolk, and visited Walsingham several times, adopting then a less censorious attitude to what he saw, which was perhaps in concord with a more sympathetic attitude on his part towards Anglo-Catholics generally.

The reference to the processional hymn refers to another new feature of the Walsingham pilgrimages. William Milner had written the words, which have often been criticised for their banality, and which were revised into their modern form by Colin Stephenson after Hope Patten's death, but which have endured while many such once popular devotions have disappeared. It is clear that as early as 1926 they were being sung to the tune used at Lourdes.

Henson's observations, and the generally higher profile of what was occurring at Walsingham, also incited the ultra-Protestant faction, led by J. A. Kensit, to come into the area. Although they made a great deal of noise and disrupted some services, they received no local backing. Whether or not the villagers supported everything which Hope Patten was doing, they resented the intervention of outsiders and many of them also were beginning to appreciate the economic benefits of having so many more visitors in a still very remote area of the country.

Until this time, it appears that, although Hope Patten received no support at all from the diocesan authorities, he had not received much overt discouragement either. This may in part have been because it was abundantly clear that what the new parish priest was doing was well supported within the village. One of the many ambiguities which have plagued Anglo-Catholicism over the years is the combination of elevating the importance of the hierarchy of the Church, while simultaneously defying the authority of the Bishops; Hope Patten was certainly not free from that apparent contradiction.

Dr Bertram Pollock, Bishop of Norwich from 1910 to 1942, was a member of a family of distinguished lawyers; his brother, later Lord Hanworth, was Master of the Rolls. He came to Norwich with no parochial background at all; he had been headmaster of Wellington College. His posthumous and unfinished autobiography, *A Twentieth Century Bishop*,[12] reveals him to have been utterly conventional in all his views and to have combined that conventionality with considerable snobbery, particularly in relation to the royal family, with whom he had close dealings because of their house at Sandringham. The reality may have been somewhat more appealing, but, for example, he was strongly of the view that all ordinands should have been to university,[13] which not only meant that, even apart from questions of belief, he had little empathy with Hope Patten, but also that he was most unlikely to agree to ordain Derrick Lingwood. The Bishop's late marriage in 1928 to a woman much younger than himself was also not likely to endear him to Hope Patten, who as has been noted disapproved strongly of clerical marriage, particularly, as in this case, where the wife was a considerable power behind the episcopal throne. It may not be a coincidence that the following year the Council of the Society of Our Lady of Walsingham resolved that from then on 'priests who enter the state of matrimony are not eligible for membership of the Society'. That very much reflected Hope Patten's attitude, although as we have seen it was coupled with his kindness towards Mrs Leeds and his acceptance of her husband's ministry after their marriage.

---

12 Published by Skeffington & Son, 1944.
13 See Pollock: *A Twentieth Century Bishop*, p. 29.

It is interesting that Dr Pollock's autobiography contains no specific references at all to Hope Patten or to Walsingham. He does make clear his view that Anglo-Catholics should be obedient to the liturgy and regulations of the Church of England, but that only shows his conventionality. He himself has been wrongly identified as an Evangelical, because he joined with many Evangelicals in opposing the revision of the 1662 Prayer Book, but in fact he was a central, backward-looking churchman whose opposition was based on conservatism.

It is sometimes overlooked that many on the pro-Roman wing of Anglo-Catholicism strongly opposed the new Books as proposed in 1927 and as reintroduced in 1928. Hope Patten was one of these, but he was certainly not alone. The Prayer Book of 1927 had been very long delayed in its formation, partly because there was disagreement as to whether any new use should be an alternative to the former Book or a mandatory replacement for it. The combination of a widespread feeling that revision should be attempted with an ineffectual and long outmoded system of discipline left a vacuum into which Anglo-Catholicism had moved with increasing boldness over the preceding 20 years and from which its supporters were unwilling to retreat. The real reason for the defeat of the Books was that even those who in principle supported that which was proposed were unconvinced that the bishops would be able to enforce any new scheme of liturgy. The Evangelicals opposed the changes because they saw the new Book as being too influenced by Catholic ideas: the Anglo-Catholics opposed them because they preferred the freedoms which they had to supplement the admittedly deficient 1662 Book. The Catholic League pilgrimage to Walsingham in May 1927 was specifically to offer reparation for the proposed new Prayer Book.

For these reasons, there were strange alliances formed between the various factions. The Anglo-Catholics were in any event handicapped because they did not accept that Parliament had any right to legislate for the Church and thus they were unwilling to lobby. Darwell Stone, the learned and much respected sage of the Anglo-Catholic Movement, writing from Pusey House to Hope Patten on 29 July 1927, made the position quite clear, saying: 'I do not think it would be wise or politic to take any public steps in the way of opposing the Measure in Parliament because any such step could be misunderstood as a recognition of the authority of Parliament.'[14]

14 F. L. Cross: *Darwell Stone* (Dacre Press, 1943), p. 191.

One of the strangest of these alliances was that between Hope Patten and Pollock; the former organised a number of conferences which, in company with the various national Anglo-Catholic organisations, urged rejection of the Books. Derrick Lingwood remembered Dr Pollock coming over to discuss the situation with Hope Patten, but because of his underlying distaste for what was happening at Walsingham he never actually went into the vicarage; rather, the two men paced up and down on the gravel path outside talking over the position.

There is no doubt that the Bishop of Norwich made himself somewhat unpopular with his fellow members of the episcopate over the Prayer Book issue. He was one of a small minority of bishops who opposed it, and in the course of the debates he was heckled in the House of Lords by peers who wanted him to take action about the 'excesses' at Walsingham. Those peers would no doubt have been even more indignant had they known that Dr Pollock was in the summer and autumn of 1927 writing privately to Hope Patten effectively inciting Anglo-Catholics to declare their refusal to co-operate with the new book, if passed into law.

On 11 September 1927 the Bishop wrote: 'It is very strange and very happy that you and I with such different views should write to one another in such a spirit of happy fellowship.' On 26 September 1927 he wrote again, asking Hope Patten to ensure that the English Church Union would say that if the new Prayer Book were enforced against a member, they would close ranks as if he were being martyred.

After the failure of the first Book, the Bishop wrote to Hope Patten asking about his attitude towards the second Book (which was far less palatable to most Anglo-Catholics) and told him that the steps which he had taken had been material in ensuring the rejection of 1927.

On 15 December 1927 and 13 June 1928 the two successive revisions were rejected by the House of Commons. The first rejection was a shock of the first order: the second was far less surprising only because of what had occurred the previous year. The main consequence of the failure of the Parliamentary process in relation to the revision was a dramatic loss of face on the part of the bishops. They were placed in the difficult position of having to enforce the use of a Book which most of them had publicly said was outdated and in need of revision, without any changes having been made to the antiquated disciplinary proceedings of the Church.

Dr Pollock at least escaped from the implied charge of hypocrisy levelled against most of the other bishops, but as a result of the events of those years Walsingham was projecting itself further into the public eye and there came a point at which he could ignore it no longer.

In the meantime, parish and pilgrimage affairs at Walsingham continued as before, and the opposition of the Kensitites did not dissuade either the parishioners or the pilgrims. Other innovations at this point were a journal-style pilgrims' almanac and an illustrated review, both one-off publications for 1928,[15] a Burial Guild of St Vincent, set up in 1928 to pray for all those buried in the village and restricted to men, and May Revels, which ran for a number of years from 1929 and included the boy bishop ceremony, in which one of the young male children was dressed as a miniature member of the episcopate.

Characteristically, in the pages of *Our Lady's Mirror* it was not said that this latter was a new development, but rather that it was a revival. The vicar asked for the loan of costumes for the pageant.[16] The May Queen was crowned in the garden of Hope Patten's vicarage and there were processions and a masked ball. It is interesting that among the festivities was dancing around the maypole, which was an activity much favoured among the adherents of the English Use and in particular the Christian Socialist wing of Anglo-Catholicism. The main exponent of this tendency was Revd Conrad Noel at Thaxted, Essex, with whom otherwise Hope Patten would have had little in common. The institution of this practice at Walsingham was another example of the vicar's deep identification with mediaevalism, despite apparent adherence to Counter-Reformation forms.

In 1929 also a temporary rood was erected in the parish church and later funds were sought for a permanent structure, after removal of the short-term model.[17]

Another development at this time was that in 1930 Hope Patten took a party from Walsingham on pilgrimage to Egmanton, and they presented the church there with a Marian banner. Revd Silas Harris had been appointed to that living in 1927 and the first organised pilgrimage took place there in 1929; Hope Patten was anxious that other places became centres of pilgrimage, provided of course they did not rival Walsingham

---

15 It was intended to continue with another edition of the almanac the next year, but this did not occur.

16 *Our Lady's Mirror*, winter 1929.

17 *Our Lady's Mirror*, winter 1929.

too closely. In return, Father Harris contributed an article on Egmanton to the autumn 1930 edition of *Our Lady's Mirror*.

The Bishop of Norwich, after some considerable consideration, determined in due course upon an inspection of the church to see exactly what was happening. The parish were asked in advance to pray and support their vicar. The exact date of his visit does not appear to have been recorded, but was probably in late 1930 or even early 1931. He arrived early in the morning and asked to see the interior of the church. What happened thereafter has been the subject of a number of reconstructions, no doubt added to over the years. Derrick Lingwood recalled the visit many years later, and he was on the whole a reliable witness, although of course he could not remember matters word for word. His account was that the Bishop first looked around the whole church. He immediately saw the confessional on the north side of the church. To this of course he expressed disapproval and the following exchange took place:

Bishop:	'How do you use it?'
Hope Patten:	'The priest sits here [showing] and the penitent kneels here [indicating] and then the penitent tells out his sin and if he is truly sorry for his sin absolution is given.'
Bishop:	'Do you make people go to confession?'
Hope Patten:	'It would not be of much use to them if I did, would it?'
Bishop:	'No, I suppose it wouldn't.'

The Bishop next went into the lady chapel to see if there was any justification for the complaints he had received that the Sidney tomb could not be seen behind the altar. He insisted that the frontal be removed and then got down on his hands and knees and put his head under the altar with his backside sticking up. The result of this close inspection was that he suggested to Hope Patten that the altar be moved forward so that people could have access to the tomb behind. The vicar had only just been able to restrain unseemly laughter at the sight of the episcopal posterior, but when the Bishop made this suggestion he replied that if the altar were moved forward it would mean visitors seeking to look at the tomb might inadvertently touch the tabernacle containing the Blessed Sacrament, which was then on the lady chapel altar. He said that he would be quite prepared to move the altar provided that the tabernacle could then be placed on the high altar and he would then be able to tell his people that it had been moved at the instigation of the Bishop. The latter was not to be tempted by the trap and said, 'Leave it where it is.'

The next questions, which followed from that exchange, went as follows:

Bishop:	'Do you have any services in connection with the consecrated elements?'
Hope Patten:	'Yes, we have the service of devotions.'
Bishop:	'What does this consist of?'
Hope Patten:	'We have two verses of a hymn in the beginning and then a litany, then two more verses of another hymn, an antiphon and prayer and an act of adoration to the Blessed Sacrament.'
Bishop:	'Hymns such as you could have at a Mothers' Union meeting?'
Hope Patten:	'Yes but it would all depend, wouldn't it, on the intention.'

After this, the Bishop appeared to be about to move into the nave without paying any attention to the shrine itself. Hope Patten pulled his coat and said, 'You must see this because it is a reproduction of the image which stood in Walsingham from 1061 to 1538.' The Bishop was heard to mutter, 'It is far worse than I had thought, far worse than I thought.'

When they did move into the nave, the Bishop told Hope Patten that all the innovations in the building must be cleared away and that all the services must be in accordance with the Book of Common Prayer. Hope Patten replied that everything which he had introduced and everything that was done in the church, with the exception of the image of Our Lady of Walsingham and the associated devotions, were common to Anglo-Catholics in the Diocese and that he would call a meeting of such priests and a common policy could be devised. However, he went on to say that the image never had been (i.e. historically) in the parish church and that if the Bishop liked he would see whether a chapel could be built to house the shrine, on private property. The Bishop appeared to welcome this idea, and before he left he agreed to give Hope Patten his blessing, which he did in somewhat faltering terms at the high altar.[18]

---

18 Lingwood: 'Rough Notes'.

In *Our Lady's Mirror* for spring 1931 Hope Patten wrote that 'the Bishop of the Diocese demanded that the images [*sic*] should be taken away and that many other matters should be "reformed".' He also referred to the Bishop's requirement that the image of Our Lady be replaced by a picture or icon.

It does not appear that there is any great discrepancy between the two accounts, namely whether or not the move was voluntary or under duress. Hope Patten clearly understood at the time that he was required to remove the image. His reaction to that demand, or perhaps anticipation of it, was the suggestion that it be moved to a new building, thus avoiding a head-on collision.

The suggestion of the image being translated to another place was, however, welcomed by Dr Pollock precisely because it got him off a hook. After returning to Norwich he wrote, 'I have not got it quite clear in my mind where the image would be placed . . . not, I suppose, in any consecrated building', and in that letter he refers specifically to being pleased that Hope Patten was prepared to fall in to his wishes over moving the image, which suggests that it was somewhere near a requirement by him. He had perhaps not perceived the potential of the idea which Hope Patten had formulated.

The latter was assiduous thereafter in oiling the waters, going to see the Bishop in Norwich and then telling him in his letter of 26 May 1931, after the second meeting between them, that 'we all hate and are grieved by the prospect' of moving the image, which again suggests that he did not agree to move it voluntarily. He also said, 'People who really mind and understand have all been very touched by your great kindness and consideration in this affair.' This was actually verging on the hypocritical, since in fact the Bishop had been neither kind nor considerate and had in effect made it entirely clear that he would not countenance the continued presence of the image in the parish church.

The suggestion that the image be replaced by an icon was typical of those distinctions without differences which some members of the episcopate were prone to draw in their dealing with Anglo-Catholics but was in fact what did happen: a new picture was painted by Clifford Pember.

Later, writing in *Our Lady's Mirror* for spring/summer 1947, Hope Patten gave a wholly different account of the facts, indicating that he had not told the Bishop that the image was to be moved into a separate chapel until after he had been assured of finance and then gone back to see him at

Norwich, but that appears to have been a complete misrecollection. In that article he also said that Bishop Pollock (who by then had died) was 'a very kind and considerate friend to the parish priest' and 'the revival [of the shrine] owes much to [him] for his patience and Christian toleration'. The objective reader might well think that his tongue was firmly in the side of his cheek when he wrote that. In his book *Mary's Shrine*,[19] written in 1954, Hope Patten went even further, saying that he moved the image not because of any problems with Dr Pollock, who, it was said, 'had always expressed a kindly and pastoral friendliness to Walsingham', but rather to forestall any potential difficulty with a replacement bishop in years to come. That version could reasonably be described as a comprehensive rewriting of what had actually occurred.

It is not clear whether any meeting of priests was ever called to work out a common policy over other matters, and it does not in any event appear that Hope Patten had many dealings with others in the Diocese. Nor is it clear whether or not the suggestion that a separate building be erected to house the shrine was or was not spontaneous. The probability is that it was not and that it was something about which Hope Patten had been thinking for some time, albeit without crystallising his thoughts; it is not apparent that he intended to house the image in the projected chapel for the sisters.

What is clear is that after the meetings with the Bishop, Hope Patten took up the project of a separate home for the image with characteristic verve and energy. The decision to go ahead with it was a turning point in the life of the parish, because it removed the shrine from its parochial setting and that was in turn to have many other consequences.

Before turning to the putting into effect of this idea, it is perhaps important to see it against the wider history of the Anglo-Catholic Movement. It is undoubtedly the case, on the one hand, that public consciousness of the Catholic Revival had been heightened by the series of national Congresses which had been held in 1920, 1923, 1927 and 1930, and by the planning for the Oxford Movement Centenary Congress of 1933, but, on the other hand, a certain coolness towards these manifestations was developing among the more Papalist clergy led by Father Fynes-Clinton, who continued to have a great effect on Hope Patten.

In earlier years considerable support had been given to the Congress by

---

19 Published by the Shrine.

Fynes-Clinton, and in 1927 and 1930, and perhaps earlier, Walsingham had had a stall of its own at the meetings. However, this developing coolness culminated in the 1932 Centenary Manifesto, in which excessive liberalism in the wider Anglo-Catholic Movement was condemned in strong terms. The decision to set up a separate shrine was a yet further demonstration of the desire among the Papalists to move onwards, whatever the rest of the Church of England thought.

These tensions showed themselves in other ways also. The Community of St Peter, from which the Walsingham nuns came, split in 1930 with a smaller faction reconstituted as the Community of St Peter's Chains at Rusholme, Manchester, and the majority, who favoured a more pro-Roman stance and liturgy, remaining under the leadership of Mother Sarah. In 1930 the larger group vacated the previous mother house at Horbury and took up residence at Laleham Abbey, Surrey, and the smaller group went back to Horbury and in due course adopted it as their mother house instead of Manchester.

By this time Hope Patten was beginning to develop the concept of Walsingham as a spiritual powerhouse for the Church of England. His old acquaintance from Caldey days, Denys Prideaux, was by the late 1920s well established as the Abbot of the Benedictine Community which had grown from the small loyal remnant of the organisation founded by Aelred Carlyle. The monks were by then at Nashdom, Buckinghamshire, and were another flowering of Anglican Papalism. Hope Patten was anxious that they too should be brought within the orbit of Walsingham, and in late 1929 he announced that in March 1930 the Benedictines were going to take over St Augustine's Hospice as a 'cell or rest house', but they would be prepared to accommodate male visitors during the summer. St Augustine's, which was part of the property acquired in 1924, and was originally the house of the village schoolmaster, had opened as a hospice in 1928.

There appears to have been some misunderstanding between Hope Patten and Prideaux: the brothers formed the impression that Walsingham was to be a respite or holiday centre for them, whereas Hope Patten wanted further monastic presence in and around the shrine, preferably under his control or direction. This fundamental misunderstanding was compounded by the extraordinarily primitive living conditions at that time in St Augustine's, which included no bath or inside sanitation. These conditions contrasted with those at Nashdom, an elegant Lutyens house adapted for the purposes of the Community. There were also problems because Hope Patten thought that some of the monks who came to Walsingham were not treating their religious state with sufficient gravity, something of which he himself could never be accused.

Following the Malines Conversations of the 1920s, the formation of a Uniate Church, in communion with Rome but retaining Anglican spirituality, had been seen by some as a solution. It originally surfaced in the paper presented to the Conferences by Dom Beauduin Lambert, a Belgian monk, and was taken up thereafter by others, culminating in the publication in 1935 of *Catholic Reunion: An Anglican Plea for a Uniate Patriarchate and for an Anglican Ultramontanism*, written by Father Clement, the nom de plume of Revd J. T. Plowden-Wardlaw, a well-known writer of the time and then vicar of St Clement, Cambridge.

It appears that Hope Patten himself flirted with this concept, as in 1930 he wrote to Revd H. K. Pierce, an American Episcopalian priest who was then living in Oxford; he later moved to Rome and in due course went over to the Roman Church. Father Pierce and three colleagues had founded the Confraternity of Unity in New York in 1926, and in 1929 the organisation was brought to this country and set up its English secretariat at St Saviour, Hoxton.

On 11 September 1930[20] Hope Patten wrote to Father Pierce, primarily in relation to birth control, of which he was a strong opponent. After condemning the attitude of the episcopate to that, he continued: 'I am more and more coming to the opinion that Catholics in communion with Canterbury must consider the example of the Wee Frees of the Scots – the day cannot be far off when some of us will have to go out into the desert – and there prove our catholicity – after which perhaps a united body may be formed as the link.'

This is an interesting letter and shows another aspect of Hope Patten. He is normally depicted as entirely loyal to the Church of England, but this shows that he was prepared to consider action by which that Church was fractured so that union with Rome could be brought about. He never, however, manifested to the outside world the slightest doubts about the validity of his own Anglican orders. On the other hand, his attitudes were certainly not those of mainstream opinion within the Church of England. His liking for relics has already been noted, and in *Our Lady's Mirror* for

20 WA.

spring 1930 it was recorded that he had been given 'several important relics', including those of St Peter, St Andrew, St Anthony of Padua and St Catherine. He assured his readers that 'they are all under proper seals and accompanied by letters of authentication'. It is not clear whether these were the result of another continental holiday, or had been donated to the shrine along with various other items such as ships, given in thanks for successful voyages, which were hung near to the image.

Hope Patten also took his opposition to contraception further at that time. He wrote to Bishop Pollock on 22 October 1930 to the effect that he had always taught his flock that birth control was wrong and asking how he should deal with local shopkeepers who were selling condoms. The Bishop said he should persuade, not condemn, them. Hope Patten replied on 30 October 1930: 'Your letter has both annoyed and dumbfounded me.'

The immediate preoccupation of the vicar of Walsingham, however, was the new shrine building. That and its consequences are important enough in his life to deserve a chapter of their own.

6

WALSINGHAM: THE TRANSLATION OF THE IMAGE, 1931

The translation of the image to the new chapel, an event which took place on 15 October 1931, was one of enormous significance in the life of Hope Patten and of the revival of the Walsingham shrine. Prior to its occurrence, what had been taking place in the church was based on the parish, and, crucially, was dependent entirely upon the continuance of the tradition of worship which Hope Patten had established. Had he died suddenly and the hostile lord of the manor replaced him with a figure of more central churchmanship, the shrine would have been regarded as a passing phase, of interest only to those who are fascinated by the minutiae of ecclesiastical devotion in the twentieth century.

The building of the new chapel, and the formation not only of trustees to hold the land upon which it was built but also of a College of Guardians, was specifically designed to secure the shrine from outside interference from the patron and from the Diocese of Norwich. The shadow of Caldey fell heavily across those on the Romanist wing, and Hope Patten was anxious also to avoid the shrine being lost to the Church of England by secession, concluding that it was unlikely that all the Guardians would go over at the same time. However, the new arrangement also meant that the shrine could in the future move forward and develop, outside the narrow parochial structure which would otherwise have held it back.

It was entirely characteristic of Hope Patten that the illness which had plagued him in late 1930 disappeared and that he threw himself into the new project with his usual energy and single-mindedness. It was at this time that the plan to convert the cottages in the High Street into the Hospice of SS Michael and George was abandoned; it does not appear that much if anything had been done since their acquisition in 1926, and the costs of conversion appeared too great, so they were sold and the proceeds used largely to pay off debts on the Hospice of Our Lady Star of the Sea.

Hope Patten no doubt also wished to concentrate on raising money for one cause only, particularly one which he saw as urgent.

The immediate problems with the project for a separate shrine building were the need for a site and, of course, finance. Within a very short time after the meeting with Bishop Pollock, Hope Patten attended a meeting in London with Fynes-Clinton, Milner (who had by this time succeeded to the family baronetcy), and others.

The decision to move the image was announced to members of the Society of Our Lady of Walsingham in *Our Lady's Mirror* for spring 1931. Hope Patten wrote that it was 'a very sad piece of news', but in fact covertly he appreciated that very great advantages could flow from it. Having announced that a new chapel would be built, he set out his vision for it in detail which is worth reproducing in full:

This chapel will be as near an exact reproduction of the original shrine – founded here by Richeldis in obedience to Our Lady's request – as it is possible without seeing the Sancta Casa in situ. But we have the Holy House of Loreto, which is claimed to be the actual cottage in which the Annunciation took place, where Our Lord was incarnate and lived his days on earth, and we know that the Shrine at Walsingham was supposed to have been a copy of this building, although – according to William of Worcester – slightly smaller in dimensions. So we have much to go on. In this little chapel was originally enshrined the image of Mary of Walsingham, and in this reconstructed sanctuary the statue we all love so well will find its new and, we hope, permanent home.

But at the time of the dissolution, this 'English House of Nazareth' was itself enclosed in yet another chapel, called variously 'The Church of S. Mary' and the 'Novum Opus'. It was only a small building, when all was said, but was sufficient to preserve the Sancta Casa and to enable pilgrims to circulate under cover from our variable and inclement weather. We propose erecting a similar building: similar, that is to say, in dimensions, although not in style, as we have no record of that, and moreover there is little doubt that it would be a chapel of great magnificence and totally beyond our wildest dreams at the moment. This building, enclosing the Sancta Casa, will be erected on private property – the ground has already been given – and will be held by a trust, drawn, we expect, from members of the Society, and so it will be an 'independent' chapel. Of course, unless the Bishop of the Diocese licenses it, we shall not be able to offer the Holy Sacrifice there. Our confession and communion will still have to be made in the parish church as at present. But we want all members of the Society to start prayers and request that the Bishop may grant us the privilege of having holy mass at the shrine – and this is not beyond possibility – as the outer building will serve as the chapel for the sisters. This little pilgrimage church will always be open to the public although on private property, and whatever the parish church may be in years to come, its doors will always be open to the servants of Mary who will seek her in the sanctuary of her choice.

The reasoning in the last paragraph, referring to whatever may happen with the parish church, shows the thinking behind what was happening very clearly. The newsletter went on to ask for funds, indicating that £700 had already been promised, but that much more was needed. The psychological approach adopted by Hope Patten in his appeal was very telling: he told his readers that 'this votive chapel is to be put up as an act of reparation for all the insults Mary and her divine Son have endured during the last three hundred years here in England and it is our privilege to be able to do something in this restoration'. He also announced another characteristic touch, namely that all contributors would have their names entered in 'The Golden Book of Our Lady's Friends', which was to be sealed in the altar.

In practice, the whole project was made much easier because there already was land available on the corner of Holt Road and Knight Street, which had been the kitchen garden of the house which had since been adopted as the nuns' hospice. Much has been written about the use of Hope Patten's supposed psychic powers to choose the site, but the underlying reality is more prosaic, namely that a sufficiently large portion of land was there to be used, and was undeveloped, in the centre of the village, and very near the former priory.

The architect chosen for the project was Romilly Craze, usually known by his second name of Bernard, who was of course Milner's partner. Craze was a man of infinite patience who was able to cope with Hope Patten's frequent changes of mind, coupled, it must be said, with flashes of inspiration over the design. It was the guarantees available from Milner which had in any event enabled the key decision to be made to go ahead not only with the Holy House but also with the outer building. Craze first produced two sets of plans: one for the Holy House with only a porch attached to it, which was estimated to cost £1,500; and the second with the Holy House protected by the outer building, which was to cost nearly £3,000. Hope Patten himself left a number of rough drawings which he himself compiled, showing various different ideas.

The architect's plans were the subject of extensive discussion one evening between Craze, Hope Patten, Milner and Lingwood, and they all went to bed after deciding that they had at least to start with the less ambitious of the two schemes. However, at breakfast the next morning Sir William Milner announced that he was prepared to guarantee the difference, so that the more ambitious building could be built immediately. Derrick Lingwood remembered this scene with some clarity, as it was the only time when Hope Patten showed caution and restraint in matters of that nature. He protested that Milner might lose his money: £1,500 was a considerable sum at that time, and the slump was almost upon England. Not only was it the only time when Lingwood saw Hope Patten so restrained, but also the only time when he saw the placid and agreeable Milner lose his temper. He retorted that it was his money and he could do what he liked with it, but in any event the money would not be lost.

In fact, this appeal seems to have produced the required sums with some expedition and in any event, because of the guarantees, work was able to progress with some speed. At the same time as he sought money from the members of the Society of Our Lady of Walsingham, however, Hope Patten asked lapsed members to return their scapulars, as he wanted the confraternity to be 'a living reality and a zealous body'.[1]

Prior to the commencement of work, Hope Patten arranged for the religious sisters and brothers who were in the village to meet at the site on a number of occasions and pray for a sign from above to confirm the choice; in particular, he wanted a water source to be discovered, as had been the case with the original shrine, which had a holy well. He then insisted that excavations were carried out prior to the foundations being dug, and enlisted the help of Jack Dewing, one of the choir, and his brother. They cut out trenches in the garden, and rapidly found the remains of a cobbled courtyard.

Hope Patten immediately leapt to the conclusion that this was the yard of the chapel of Our Lady, which had been recorded as being to the north

---

1 *Our Lady's Mirror*, summer 1931.

of the priory church. The site where the shrine was to be re-established was indeed to the north of the ruins of the priory, but there was some considerable distance between them, together with a road; even at that time his conclusion seemed somewhat specious to some. He claimed that the road had only been cut through after the dissolution of the monasteries. The workmen next discovered the base of a churchyard cross, and the vicar decided that was in the former burial ground of the Augustinian canons. It was, however, the third discovery which convinced him finally of the righteousness of what he was doing: water gushed out not far below the surface and further investigation showed that they had uncovered a disused well, which at some point appeared to have been deliberately blocked. Beneath a clay plug were found soles from shoes of some centuries before and in due course the well itself was identified as of Saxon origin.

The exposure of the well galvanised Hope Patten's already considerable nervous energy into further intensive hard work to forward the building of the housing for the shrine. He was now convinced beyond any doubting that its construction was blessed from above. He was further convinced that the site which had been chosen was the site of the original Holy House, a belief he retained to the end of his life but which in due course would not be supported by any reputable archaeologist or historian.

The discovery of the well also necessitated further alterations in the plans so that it could be incorporated within the structure. In due course, however, work on the construction did start and was well documented photographically. The vicar wrote a pamphlet entitled *Sanctuary of Our Lady of Walsingham described by Erasmus*, which set out the discoveries and described the new chapel as it was being built. The original building was of course very small. The outer building followed the dimensions given by William of Worcester: namely, 48 feet by 30 feet with a narrow nave containing an altar, behind which was placed the Holy House itself, built to the dimensions of that at Loreto, namely 23 feet 6 inches by 12 feet 10 inches. Erasmus had described the original Holy House of Walsingham as having two doors facing each other, so that feature too was reproduced. At the eastern end of the building the architects designed a porch with, on either side, small chapels.

The altar of the Holy House was formed largely of stones from the ruined priory nearby, but others came from other religious houses. In the walls of the Holy House were incorporated stones from Augustinian houses, in the south wall, and Benedictine, in the north. This idea was pursued further when in later years the high altar of the pilgrimage church was constructed.

Although the building was small, there was, fortunately in the light of later developments, considerable room for expansion. In addition, there was a considerable sized garden, hidden from the road, which was landscaped into a pilgrims' park. The idea for this, which involved the erection of stations of the cross to form an outdoor way for pilgrims to follow, was no doubt that of Hope Patten, but the design and execution of the work was largely carried out by Sir William Milner and William Frary. Milner was a garden designer of considerable talent, who created a fine garden at his house, Parcevall Hall, near Skipton, which had originally been part of the holdings of Fountains Abbey. William Frary was one of those villagers who, like Tom Purdy the builder, became devoted to Hope Patten and were always on hand to assist with the practical side of the shrine; his brother Ivan also participated. In due course William Frary became beadle of the shrine as well as gardener and carilloneur,[2] and Hope Patten was badly affected by his early death in 1953.

The layout of the Via Dolorosa has been altered since originally executed because of the later extensions to the shrine church, but it too followed a precedent. It was designed on the same course as the original in Jerusalem, and it featured a small chapel at station four (Jesus meets his Mother) which had to be demolished later. The fourteenth station was designed as a reproduction of the outer and inner chambers of the Holy Sepulchre itself, and was said to be of the same dimensions as the original (7 feet by 6 feet and 6 feet high). There were various additions to the garden area, including the Hatcham Crucifix: a large wooden cross with figure which was so called because it was said to have come from the church of St James, Hatcham, in southeast London, which had the been the parish of Revd Arthur Tooth, the best known of the so-called 'ritualist martyrs'. More recently doubt has been cast on its provenance. A statue of St Thérèse of Lisieux, a saint to whom Hope Patten had great devotion, and whose cult was enthusiastically promoted by the Vatican at this time, was also later erected in the garden.

At the same time as the report of the translation itself, it was announced

---

2 As beadle he led processions of the Guardians; as carilloneur he was responsible for the bells of the shrine, which became such a feature of life in Walsingham.

in *Our Lady's Mirror* for autumn 1931 that the sanctuary was to be placed in the hands of trustees and a body of Guardians. There were four original trustees in whom the land was to be vested, namely Hope Patten, Fynes-Clinton, Milner, and Revd Harford Elton Lury, then parish priest of St Peter, Limehouse.[3] The first announcement in the newsletter indicated that there were intended to be 24 Guardians, 12 clerical and 12 lay.

The Guardians were not properly organised as a College until 1932 and the constitution as eventually adopted restricted their number to 20, of whom not more than eight were to be laymen. Initially it may be that it was thought that the body would be somewhat less formal than was eventually the case: on 10 October 1931, only five days before the translation was due to take place, Fynes-Clinton wrote to Sir John Shaw, with whom it appeared he had only a passing acquaintance, asking him to join and referring to the Guardians as an 'honorary body of supporters round the shrine'.

The original announcement was that the clerical members would be Hope Patten, Fynes-Clinton, O'Rorke, Denys Prideaux, Alban Baverstock, Elton Lury, Humphrey Whitby, Roger Wodehouse and Reginald Kingdon (vicar of St John, Isle of Dogs), and all were duly instituted. They were a representative group around the obvious names, all of whom had been involved for some time with the growth of pilgrimages to the shrine. There was no doubt also when it came to the selection of lay members that Hope Patten and Fynes-Clinton appreciated the value to such an organisation of a title. Sir William Milner was an obvious choice and they also recruited Lord Halifax, then nearing the end of his very long life, the Duke of Argyll, a great proponent of Anglo-Catholicism in the Scottish Episcopal Church, and Sir John Shaw (later Best-Shaw), another devout Baronet. At the other end of the social scale, and with a commendable desire to continue the involvement of the parish in the affairs of the shrine, were Derrick Lingwood, still only 21 but now indispensable to the running of financial and other affairs, and the two churchwardens, Jack Banson and George Long. The fact that in later years Hope Patten was able to refer to the latter in his will as his 'devoted manservant' does, however, perhaps indicate his view of Long's ability to contribute independently to the affairs of the College. Two other outsiders became Guardians, namely

---

3 Four was the maximum number in whom land could generally be vested following the reforms of conveyancing in 1925, although there were exceptions where land was held for ecclesiastical purposes: see §34 of the Trustee Act 1925.

Mr (later Sir) Eric Maclagan, Director of the Victoria and Albert Museum and son of a former Archbishop of York (for some reason named as Eric McDyles in the first list), and Major Arthur Bowker, a distinguished engineer who had been an Anglo-Catholic since knowing Pusey in his youth.

When the constitution was adopted, it provided that the duty of the Guardians was to 'extend the honour of Our Lady and promote pilgrimages to her shrine at Walsingham and protect her property': hence the full title of The College of the Guardians of the Holy House of Our Lady of Walsingham. There were obligations to say or hear mass as the case may be. Under the constitution, the fellows were to elect one of the Priest Guardians as Master for renewable five-year terms and a bursar for similar periods. The fellows were empowered to appoint a priest administrator for the sanctuary, who need not be a member of the College and whose duty was the spiritual management of the pilgrimage church.

In 1932 when the constitution was passed, Hope Patten was appointed Master and Derrick Lingwood bursar. Hope Patten was also appointed as priest administrator and held both positions for the remainder of his life, as of course he had always intended.

What was to prove the most contentious section of the constitution was clause V of the section referring to Priest Guardians, which was in the following terms: 'Should any Priest Guardian marry (subsequent to his election to the Guardianship) he shall *ipso facto* CEASE FROM FELLOW-SHIP.'

It is often said that Hope Patten turned a blind eye to the fact that Father Lury was married when he was appointed to the fellowship, but that is an unjust charge. The fellows were free at the setting up of the College or at any time thereafter to invite any married priest to join, but a priest was not permitted to marry once he was a Guardian without then resigning. Derrick Lingwood, who was later to become the victim of the clause himself, wrote that Hope Patten 'took the view that it was not for us to inquire into what a priest had done in the past, but that on accepting membership of the Guardians he put himself under the discipline of the Western Church as opposed to the Anglican Communion'.[4] That was a characteristic piece of logic on the part of Hope Patten, producing a solution which looked anomalous but was in fact justifiable on those idiosyncratic lines.

---

4 See Lingwood, 'Rough Notes'.

The position was rendered even more ironic by the fact that after Father Lury died in 1940 his son, in preparing notes many years later for an obituary of him, wrote that his mother and father, having had four children and being over 50, decided when they moved to Limehouse to 'live as brother and sister' and to devote themselves to their parochial work.[5]

Having set in motion the erection of the framework under which the new chapel should be run, Hope Patten was able to concentrate on the translation itself. His hand was behind every feature of the day, which was designed to show the strength of the devotion to Our Lady of Walsingham and at the same time to demonstrate to the Bishop of Norwich that he had been in the wrong when he insisted on the removal of the image and had in effect been outmanoeuvred by the parish priest. Simultaneously, Hope Patten was asserting that the Bishop was 'very friendly disposed',[6] which was in fact quite untrue.

The first ceremony in relation to the new shrine was on Saturday 10 October 1931, when Bishop O'Rorke participated in what even Hope Patten described as 'an unusual scene in religious life': he blessed and 'baptised' the peal of bells in the sanctuary, anointing each bell on the exterior with oil of the sick and on the interior with Holy Chrism. The bells were dedicated to SS Alban, Andrew, Benedict, Francis of Assisi, George, Hugh of Lincoln, Patrick, Peter, and to Our Lady. The bell of St Andrew was given by Hope Patten in memory of his late father and the bell of St Patrick was given by Derrick Lingwood in memory of another who had died and named after the donor's patron. The original campanile was a temporary structure of wood, erected over the chapel at station four on the Via Dolorosa.

That was, however, only the prelude to the translation itself which took place on Thursday 15 October 1931, which by happy chance turned out to be a fine day. It is not now clear why that particular date was chosen: it was the feast day of St Teresa of Avila, a saint to whom, in contradistinction to her namesake, Hope Patten felt no great affinity.

The first act in the proceedings was at 7 a.m. that morning, when 'a few parishioners and others' were present at the new chapel. Hope Patten aspersed the building from the outside as he walked around it, and then

---

5 In the Guardians file in the WA.
6 *Our Lady's Mirror*, winter 1932.

as the litany was sung he entered and aspersed within on the gospel side, followed by the epistle side. A votive mass of the Annunciation followed in the course of which, just before the oblations were brought to the altar, Sir William Milner presented the conveyance of the site to Hope Patten, who handed it on at the lavabo to Fynes-Clinton, as representative of the trustees, who retained it throughout the service. Milner then served the lavabo himself, which Hope Patten recorded was 'an ancient privilege accorded to the donor of lands on which a church or chapel or monastery was founded'.

The second act was pontifical high mass sung by Bishop O'Rorke in the parish church at 11.30 a.m. A special train had been laid on from London, which arrived late, and the contingent from the capital had difficulty in finding places in the church; indeed, some were unable to gain entry at all and queued outside. The sermon was preached by the elderly Revd Ernest Underhill of St Thomas, Warwick Street, Liverpool, who was by then very infirm, but appealed to Hope Patten because he had been under episcopal ban for many years. He delivered a rousing sermon, which included the following sentence, which must have been music to the vicar's ears: that they were going to do something that day which would help towards making the worship of Our Lady of Walsingham no longer a parish matter, but something that would be national.

The third act for the day was at 2.30 p.m., when the church was again full to capacity and even Bishop O'Rorke and his party had to push their way through. Father Alban Baverstock, who had blessed the image when it was set up in 1922, preached, and there followed benediction.

The fourth act was the translation itself. This was one of the great manifestations of what Hope Patten had achieved to that date, and it is significant that, although many attended from outside, he involved the parish in what occurred. Bunting and flags were hung from the houses along the route, and local children were involved in the procession as they had been in serving at the masses. The description offered in *Our Lady's Mirror* is so vivid and so redolent of Hope Patten's thinking at the time that it should be quoted in full:[7]

Picture then a perfect autumn day with scarcely a breath of air stirring, the trees clothed in glorious tints, and in their setting of old Tudor

---

7 See *Our Lady's Mirror*, autumn 1931.

Houses and low, red-roofed ancient cottages, a procession with over a thousand people walking, each bearing his or her lighted taper; many women in blue veils, little children in white casting their flowers; dark habited religious, nuns and monks; over a hundred priests in cassock and cotta; the mitred Abbot of Pershore[8] and Bishop O'Rorke. Behind streamed the many hundreds of other people, all singing the glories of Mary, and in the middle of this throng, high and lifted up upon the shoulders of four clergy in dalmatics, and under a blue and gold canopy fixed to the feretory, sat the venerated figure of our Lady, crowned with the silver Oxford Crown and robed in a mantle of cloth of gold.[9] Around the feretory walked men carrying torches; in front the lay Guardians of the shrine who were able to be present; and behind five of the priest Guardians, and immediately following them a group of banners from various parishes and pilgrim banners . . . When the head of the procession, which was over half a mile long, arrived at the court of the Sanctuary, the bells of Our Lady's chimes rang out. The procession-ists [sic] formed up in semi-circular rows on each side of the porch – first the women in veils, then the nuns, then the monks and the clergy. Finally the Abbot and Bishop reached the entrance to the church, before which rested the image of Mary surrounded by torches and her attendants. The prelate intoned the Magnificat and incensed the Blessed Virgin, at the conclusion of which the feretory was again lifted, and to the strains of Salve Regina, passed into the Chapel and Holy House. Here it was enthroned in the niche prepared above the altar. The relic of the tomb of Our Lady was then placed on the altar, as well as the casket containing the Golden Book, which had been carried in procession by two girls veiled in white. Two deacons then came to the Bishop for a blessing. One remained in the Holy House, while the other went to the entrance of the church, and in both cases the Gospel for the Feast of the Annunciation was sung simultaneously. The function con-cluded with a solemn Te Deum sung by all within and around the shrine and those standing in the road outside.

---

8 This was Denys Prideaux, whose official title was Abbot of Pershore and Nashdom, although by this stage the Community was no longer at the former loca-tion.

9 It was termed the Oxford Crown because it had been donated in 1929 by the con-gregation of St Paul, Oxford, who came to Walsingham led by Wodehouse and Lawson.

Even that was not the end of the services for the day. The last act in the prolonged drama was that, for the first time, shrine prayers were said at 6 p.m. in the new building.

The day of the translation was one of Hope Patten's finest hours. He had stage-managed a powerful demonstration of witness and of the strength of Anglo-Catholicism and had done so with the support and active participation of the parishioners. The visitors no doubt appreciated that such an event was rare in the Church of England, even unprecedented, and no doubt they looked forward to similar such manifestations elsewhere.

It will be noted of course that a notable absentee was the Bishop of Norwich. He realised that he had been outwitted by Hope Patten when he saw the new building going up. He was, however, outraged when he found that the foundation stone of the Holy House recorded, in Latin, that it had been restored in the pontificate of Pius XI, the episcopate of Bertram of Norwich, and the incumbency of Hope Patten. There was perhaps no statement which more adequately set out the Anglican Papalist position with succinctness, and conversely no statement that was more alien not only to most Anglicans but also to virtually all Roman Catholics. The Bishop was not a man to tolerate the inscription, and he sent to Hope Patten a cutting from the *Catholic Herald*, which commented adversely on what had been done. Hope Patten replied in his own inimitable way:

[The inscription] has been inserted in the wall as a witness to the claim of Anglicans, which claim our English Roman 'friends' will not allow, namely that we (the donors) believe that in this year of grace 1931 the rightful parish priest of Walsingham is Hope Patten, *not* Fr. Grey of Fakenham – and that the true bishop of the diocese is Dr. Pollock and not the Bishop of Northampton. But while maintaining these facts we also record our belief and affirm that we are not members of a separate body, cut off from the rest of Christendom, and to emphasise this fact we state that in the year 1931 Pius XI was Chief Bishop. We Catholics are wearied at the perpetual jibes of English Romans and their taunt that we are no ministers of the church, just as in the same way our patience is almost exhausted by the agitation and blasphemy of the militant protestant section represented by Bishop Barnes and the followers of Mr Kensit. In years to come we hope that, whatever people may say of us, good or bad, they will be able to say 'Well, these "English Catholics" did believe profoundly in their own ministry and at the same time their place in the rest of Western and Eastern Christendom . . .'

The terminology used in the letter is itself interesting, with Hope Patten referring to Anglo-Catholics as he always did as 'Catholics' and Roman Catholics as 'Romans'. He was struggling with the dilemma which faced many Anglicans at that time: if the Church of England was the true Catholic church of the country, where did the recusants fit into the picture? The cast of mind which categorised the Roman Catholic Church in England as the 'Italian Mission' provided no sensible answer to the question.[10] The only honest solution which was equally compatible with the validity of Anglican orders was that provided by some Anglican Papalists of a scholarly nature who came to the conclusion that there had in fact been an internal break within the Catholic Church in England, which led to the existence of two separate streams.[11]

Whatever the theory behind what was said, it proved unimpressive to the Bishop, who insisted that his name be removed. The penultimate line of what was a fairly lengthy inscription was filled with plaster, to the detriment of the grammatical construction of what was left. It is perhaps surprising in the light of his views about the use of Latin that Hope Patten had allowed that language to be used in the first place. As well as being unwelcome to the Bishop, the inscription also proved less than popular with the more central strands of thinking within Anglo-Catholicism, whose view that the shrine was on the outer fringes of the Movement was confirmed by this episode, which was also the subject of adverse comment in the *Church Times*, always an advocate of moderation in such matters.

While the shrine was still being built, Hope Patten had led a novena of prayers with the intention that Dr Pollock should license the shrine for the saying of mass: this ran from 14 August 1931, including within it of course the feast of the Assumption.

As will have been appreciated, on the morning of the day of the transla-

---

10 That was the view expressed by Revd J. Embry in his book *The Catholic Movement and the Society of the Holy Cross*, which was coincidentally published in 1931 (Faith Press). He referred to Roman Catholic priests in this country as being 'in the position of schismatics' (p. 309).

11 This was a view expressed particularly by Plowden-Wardlaw (see above, p. 84), in his *Catholic Reunion*, p. 44, and by Revd Thomas Parker in *Reunion*, 21, 1939.

tion, Hope Patten had celebrated mass in the new chapel. He had actually written to the Bishop on 12 October, three days before, flattering him by saying 'you have been so kind all the time I have been in Walsingham and I hate not being quite open with you', which were both statements of doubtful veracity. He went on to explain that he intended to say mass at the chapel and hoped he would not be put under a ban as a result. The Bishop replied sharply, to the effect that he had made clear that he did not think it proper 'for the Holy Communion to be celebrated publicly except in a chapel licensed for the purpose'. He went on to say that he appreciated that in certain respects Hope Patten had conformed with 'the general worship of the Church of England, as set out in the Book of Common Prayer'.

The last comment is not easy to understand, unless it refers to how pleased the Bishop was that the shrine had been taken out of the parish church. The legal position of the shrine had, however, not been agreed, and the situation was left to fester.

One important consequence of the move of the shrine has already been noted, namely that the devotion now became less parochial in nature. In practice, pilgrimages could not take place over the weekends before 1931 as the parish church was needed for the village, and in any event Hope Patten himself was busy with his local duties. After 1931, however, the shrine was available for pilgrims; although Hope Patten himself tended initially not to say mass in the new chapel, in deference to the wishes of the Bishop, visiting priests did, save on Sunday when the vicar insisted on worship being concentrated at the parish church.

As part of that reaching out, a new organisation was set up in 1931,[12] known as the Priest Associates of the Shrine; members of the Society of Our Lady of Walsingham who were also priests were encouraged to say mass in their own churches for the shrine and in return they would be prayed for at Walsingham. One of the earliest members was Father Woodward, who had been vicar of the parish in the 1880s and was by then living in retirement in Highgate. The formation of this organisation was Hope Patten's own idea, and proved successful: within the first year about 125 joined, and the number of shrines of Our Lady of Walsingham in churches across the country and abroad began to grow. Fynes-Clinton set

---

12 Stephenson unaccountably gives the date of 1927, but, even if foreshadowed earlier, it was clearly organised at the same time as the translation, and the contemporary records in *Our Lady's Mirror* show this.

up one of the first in his Wren church of St Magnus in 1931, and others followed.

In Hope Patten's fertile mind the new chapel was only the start. He envisaged a substantial expansion of the building, and his mind too ran on to various other enterprises which he saw radiating out from Walsingham.

7

WALSINGHAM: THE THIRD PHASE,
1932–7

Hope Patten was at a high point in his ministry at the end of 1931. He was, however, at this stage never a man to stand still, and the experience of being concerned with the erection of a building had a profoundly addictive effect on him. Thereafter he was constantly thinking of or carrying into effect extensions or alterations to the shrine chapel or of other new construction projects, his vivid imagination restrained only by fiscal reality, usually conveyed to him by Derrick Lingwood.

It is also important to stress that the Walsingham shrine at this time was still a very small-scale affair, which barely registered in the national consciousness or even in that of much of the Church of England. The first edition of *Our Lady's Mirror* for 1932 recorded that on average there had been 80 to 90 pilgrims a week visiting, which is not indicative of widespread outside interest.

However, the number of pilgrimages did definitely increase. In May and June of that year there were five, including the recently formed Society of Mary and the Catholic League, and the first weekend pilgrimage, from SS Peter and Paul, Teddington, near Hope Patten's old church, and St John, Isle of Dogs, of which Father Kingdon, a Guardian, was the priest. The party drove up from London on Saturday by coach, arrived at 8.30 p.m. and made a 'first visit', and then the next day attended at parish mass, intercessions, benediction, the sprinkling at the well, and a talk, followed by a 'last visit' before leaving for town. For the feast of the Assumption in 1932 a large marquee, soon nicknamed 'the cathedral', was erected on the lawn so that the devotions could take place within private grounds and so demonstrators could easily be excluded; this followed Kensitite attendance at the Catholic League pilgrimage which led to what Hope Patten referred to as 'a very disgraceful and sacrilegious brawn [*sic*]' in the parish church. At the same time the village was decorated again for the patronal

festival of the church. Then the anniversary of the previous year's translation was marked in October by three days of prayer in both the parish
church and the shrine, and the first children's pilgrimage took place.

Despite these positive developments, the financial position of the parish
and shrine was, as ever, under strain. On the one hand, Hope Patten
was appealing in the newsletter in early 1932 for funds to build a sacristy
adjacent to the new chapel: the required money was not forthcoming and
a temporary wooden building was erected later in the year. On the other
hand, the faithful Father Leeds had to leave because the money to pay him
was being used for the shrine. Father Leeds featured little or at all in Hope
Patten's newsletters, perhaps because he was embarrassed at the presence
of a married priest on the staff, although personally they remained on very
good terms. Leeds also said to an outsider that he himself was not especially interested in the restoration of the shrine, but what held him in
Norfolk was the manifest Catholic life among the parishioners.[1] He went
initially for a short further curacy at All Souls, South Ascot, and then the
following year became vicar of another All Souls in Clapton, East London,
where he stayed for many years.

This departure of course put yet further strain on Hope Patten,
who was, after the October 1932 meeting of the Guardians at which the
constitution was adopted, simultaneously parish priest, Master of the
Guardians, and priest administrator of the shrine. He advertised, optimistically and unsuccessfully, for a priest who would be prepared to work
in the parish and to take charge of Houghton with a free house but otherwise without stipend.

The evolution of the College of Guardians over the next few years was
an interesting one. In one sense they were a safeguard against the incumbent seceding to Rome and therefore they had no role save in those
circumstances; in another sense, however, they were a public demonstration of support for the shrine. While Hope Patten was alive he certainly
did not perceive the Guardians as having any management responsibilities
which conflicted with his own and he tended to disregard any expressed
views of theirs which did not accord with his own. However, in accordance with the outlook of himself and of his chief lieutenant, Father Fynes-
Clinton, the College gradually adopted a quasi-mediaeval tone. In 1933
Fynes-Clinton donated a silver gilt chain, cross and jewel, the latter

---

1 Article in *Catholic Standard*, February 1972, by Revd Frank Harwood.

depicting Our Lady of Walsingham, for the use of the Master of the College. In 1938 the Guardians adopted distinctive blue cloaks or mantles and in 1947 stars were added to these. A Guardian was expected to return his regalia when he left office.

In addition to any other support which they provided, the Guardians were generous with gifts for furnishing the shrine, as indeed were others. In 1932 an anonymous guardian (possibly Father Whitby, who was wealthy and well disposed towards the artist in question) presented to the shrine a crucifix by Martin Travers, which was initially hung in the Holy House at the west end.[2] The same year, a staff of Father Ignatius, the maverick predecessor of Aelred Carlyle in the foundation of male Benedictinism in the Church of England, was given.

Another gift that year was a feretory for the relics of St Vincent which Hope Patten had acquired in Assisi in 1924. In considering the life of any figure, there are some episodes and objects which sharply illuminate the personality of the subject of the biography. The manufacture and introduction of the feretory to the shrine throws a very clear shaft of light on Hope Patten's life and outlook at this time. In the winter 1933 edition of *Our Lady's Mirror* he described the reliquary, which was given by the mother of the late Lincoln Brett in his memory. The original reliquary of ebony was enclosed within the new; the description reads as follows:

> The shrine stands on a base coloured a dark green emblazoned with shields of those intimately connected with Walsingham. At the west end are the arms of S. Vincent, D. M., and the family of Brett, the donors. On the south side are the arms of Sir William Milner, the donor of the land on which the present Sanctuary of Our Lady stands, Edward the Confessor, who was lord of the manor when the Holy House was first erected, and Henry III, the first of the long line of royal pilgrims recorded to have visited the Shrine. At the east end are the shields of Walsingham and the first Administrator [i.e. himself], while on the north we have those of S. Augustine whose canons were the guardians of England's Nazareth for close on four hundred years. The next is a badge in a shield representing the Holy House; and the last on the base is the shield of the Clares, who were the patrons of the Priory and incidentally founders of the Franciscan house in the town. Over the base is

---

2 It was later moved to the Chapel of St Anne, and is now in the Hospice of our Lady Star of the Sea.

a wooden cover, similar to that depicted in Mr Charles Walls' *Shrines of British Saints* for the Venerable Bede; indeed ours was entirely suggested by the picture. The cover is painted in a dark green and is covered with a pall of silk. It is raised by means of a rope and pulley and rings attached to four iron posts which terminate in sockets for candles. When this cover is raised the actual shrine is revealed. It is beautifully made and is in colour and much gold leaf. There is a carved ridge on the top terminating in two crockets carved and gilded. At each corner there are pinnacles also carved and crocketed. On the east end is a panel with the figure of the saint holding his gridiron and a palm branch; he is vested in a scarlet dalmatic, and the back of this panel is diapered in gold and colour. At the west end the panel depicts Our Blessed Lady and the Holy Child vested in a similar way. On the sides are other panels containing heraldry repeating the shields of the base: the Holy House, S. Vincent and Brett, and on the other side S. Vincent, Walsingham and Brett. The west end is made in the form of a door and the whole of the south side wall can be removed to enable the relics to be exposed for public veneration. This was done of course on the feast of S. Vincent after the parish mass . . .

This shows a number of facets of Hope Patten's character: the looking back to the past; the ignoring of what had occurred at the Reformation; and an increasing interest in heraldry, fuelled by Father Fynes-Clinton, who was deeply interested in that subject and later devised armorial bearings for the College of Guardians, then obtained letters patent, and presented them.

At the first annual chapter of the Guardians in October 1932, it was decided not only to have a special pilgrimage the following year, for the Oxford Movement Centenary, but also to extend the shrine to include what was termed a choir. This proposal was to cost £3,000, and was to double the size of the pilgrimage church. Hope Patten reminded his readers that the great priory church was 408 feet long and all he was asking for was a choir some 54 feet by 30 feet. The response to this appeal, coming so close after the last, was not encouraging; in early 1933 the vicar rather optimistically suggested that the potential donors might be waiting until the Centenary year itself before putting their hands into their pockets. That particular project in the end came to nothing, despite printed material being prepared and distributed.

One way in which the message of Walsingham was being spread was by the establishment of shrines in churches in England and indeed overseas. As early as 1926, *Our Lady's Mirror* indicated that shrines had been erected in Nassau in the Bahamas, an unnamed place in Canada, and at Horbury for the sisters. In 1930 a copy of the Walsingham image was erected by Revd A. Parker Curtiss in Grace Episcopal Church, Sheboygan, Wisconsin, in the traditionally Anglo-Catholic diocese of Fond du Lac, and it was blessed the following year. This followed a visit to England by Father Curtiss, who had the image and special altar carved locally; it has remained a place of pilgrimage ever since and the building is now known as Grace Walsingham Church. Father Fynes-Clinton established a shrine of Our Lady of Walsingham in St Magnus in 1931, designed by Martin Travers, as already mentioned, and others followed these leads. On 16 December 1932 Hope Patten sent out a prayer card to those in charge of the various shrines with an invitation to pray for Walsingham.

He reported with some pride in *Our Lady's Mirror*, winter 1934, that many such had been established and in particular that the most northerly such shrine was at St Paul, Inverary, the Episcopal church near the Duke of Argyll's Scottish castle, and that the most remote was in the church of St Mary on the island of Tristan da Cunha in the South Atlantic, to which at that time the Anglo-Catholic Movement had reached out. Hope Patten undoubtedly saw the establishment of devotion to Our Lady of Walsingham as supranational, although he himself never seems to have visited what was then called the Empire, save many years later when he holidayed in Malta.[3]

---

3 It appears that the shrine on Tristan was erected there by Revd A. G. Partridge, who on the island from 1929 to 1932 and then returned the next year for about seven months. Augustus George Partridge was ordained in England, but then worked abroad, moving to Tristan from the pro-cathedral of St Laurence, Lourenco Marques, in what is now called Mozambique. While on the island he redecorated the east end of the church, which had only been erected in 1923, and although he does not mention the shrine in his book, *Tristan da Cunha, the Isle of Loneliness* (SPG, 1933), there is a rather indistinct picture in it which appears to show it on the gospel side of the sanctuary, as Hope Patten reported. There is no record of it in the best reference on this subject, E. Cannan: *Churches of the South Atlantic Islands 1502–1991* (Anthony Nelson, 1992), or in A. Crawford: *Tristan da Cunha and the Roaring Forties* (Charles Skilton Ltd, 1982), although in Cannan's book there is a later picture in which there is a space where the shrine had been. Despite that, the shrine was still recorded in the Walsingham literature as being in existence in 1960, shortly before the island was evacuated. The church has since been rebuilt.

Despite the failure to make any progress with the choir, other gifts were given to the shrine. Hope Patten was anxious that the sanctuary should be properly equipped so that what was required was not continually transported from the parish church and then returned after use, and he used his customary persuasive techniques to try to ensure that new candlesticks and the like were donated. He was also faced with the unfortunate problem that a number of pilgrims had fallen down the stairs to the holy well, usually because they had been concentrating on the imported stones in the wall and had not noticed the steps. When an 80-year-old woman fell down the entire flight head over heels and broke some bones, it was decided that an iron rail and gates were required, and they were erected in early 1934. It was a somewhat ironic sequence of events when Hope Patten was at the same time encouraging his pilgrims to report instances of cures which occurred after being sprinkled.

In 1932 another new organisation was commenced, which seems to have run until the outbreak of war. The Apostleship of Prayer was for inhabitants of the village: those joining agreed to spend half an hour each week in prayer before the Blessed Sacrament in the parish church, and half an hour in the shrine. The group placed itself under the patronage of the Sacred Heart, and observed the first Friday of each month with particular care.

Despite the failure to enlarge the shrine church at this stage, in 1935 a range of properties became available on the west side of Knight Street, consisting of a house with grounds and a row of dilapidated cottages, which had been condemned as unfit for human occupation. The Guardians bought them, with the aid of a substantial donation and a mortgage, thus consolidating their holdings around the new shrine church. Hope Patten asserted that it would have been a neglect of duty not to have purchased the houses, because otherwise they might have fallen into unfriendly hands or simply given others an unrestricted view of what occurred in the shrine grounds.

There were continuing problems after the erection of the new shrine with the presence of the Benedictines in Walsingham. The underlying problem, which was to recur in later years, was that Hope Patten really wanted a separate priory in the village under his control. He also objected to the brothers saying their office in the shrine in Latin, against which, as already described, he had a strong prejudice, and continued to be dissatisfied with their personal conduct.

Another involvement with the Benedictines, however, was the suggestion that a choir school be set up in the village to serve the shrine. Dom Anselm Hughes of Nashdom, a distinguished musician, who had of course been offered the living before Hope Patten accepted it, carried out research to this end in 1932, staying for a period of time in Walsingham. He recommended the establishment of such a school, on condition that high fees were charged so that the very best staff could be recruited. Hope Patten seized on the idea and asked Hughes to run it for him, and the latter was given permission to consider the matter by Abbot Denys Prideaux. However, while on a lecture tour in the United States Dom Anselm decided that he would not in the long term be able to work harmoniously with Hope Patten, a conclusion which would have been echoed by any objective observer. The choir school was, however, to be another idea which Hope Patten did not forget.

In 1934 Abbot Denys died and was replaced at Nashdom by Martin Collett, a far more able administrator. With Prideaux's death, however, the experiment of having Benedictines at Walsingham, which had been failing for some time, ended completely and Hope Patten was never on such intimate terms with his successor. No more was heard of the choir school for the time being.

The sisters of St Peter continued to work in the parish, but after 1932 were sent from Laleham rather than Horbury following the split in the community. At this stage there was no conflict between Hope Patten and Mother Sarah, although undoubtedly the vicar had at the back of his mind the prospect of a self-governing priory of nuns in Walsingham, with himself as the directing force.

One development of significance in the religious life at Walsingham was the decision in 1934 by Lady Phillida Shirley, daughter of Earl Ferrers, to adopt the name of Sister Mary Phillida and to live the life of a recluse within the grounds of the hospice. She was clothed within the Holy House and then ceremonially led to her cell, which had its own garden enclosed by wattle hedges. There she was to live for many years, often only a few yards away from the crowds of pilgrims. A stern warning was issued that anyone meeting a sister with grey habit and black veil was to respect her rule of silence and not under any circumstances to speak to her. To Hope Patten this was yet another example of the ability of the Church of England to produce the outward signs of Catholic devotion, and the mediaeval associations of the anchorite life were attractive to him as an ancillary to the worship at the shrine. Sister Mary Phillida was not a member of the Laleham sisters and had, as it were, an independent vocation. Initially Hope Patten himself directed her, but this task was later taken over by Father Raymond Raynes CR. On 29 June 1946 she took perpetual vows as an independent religious and she far outlived Hope Patten, as she did not die until 26 December 1989.

The Bishop of Norwich continued to be predictably hostile to the developments at Walsingham; he may even have appreciated that he was partly to blame himself for what had occurred. On 24 June 1932 he wrote to Hope Patten asking for an explanation of a leaflet which he had been sent asking for weekend pilgrimages, which included benediction as one of the devotions. Benediction of the Blessed Sacrament is now almost unknown as a popular service, but in the days of fasting communion it was regarded as de rigueur at evening services in advanced Anglo-Catholic circles, and equally as anathema by all diocesan bishops. The Bishop had been asked whether the invitation had been sent out with his sanction. An exchange of correspondence between the two followed, with the Bishop insisting that all leaflets should make it clear that they were issued without diocesan authority. A revised copy of the leaflet was suggested by Hope Patten, which omitted the reference to benediction all together and was headed: 'This paper is printed and sent out on the authority of the pilgrimage committee and the administrator of the shrine.' The Bishop, however, wanted added to that: 'and has no diocesan authority.'

In parentheses it might be remarked that this episode shows very clearly the difficulties in the disciplinary procedures of the Church of England: the Bishop was saying to one of his clergy that he could not stop him issuing leaflets inviting pilgrims to services of which he did not approve, but he must make it clear that the services did not have that approval. The correspondence rumbled on with Hope Patten using clever prevaricating tactics until finally his patience expired. On the feast of the Assumption 1932 he wrote to the Bishop saying that it was quite improper for a priest to have to send his notices to the Bishop in advance and concluding: 'I refuse to do anything more in the matter.'

Astonishingly, there was no reply to that somewhat peremptory letter, and the Bishop left the issue, although it was as clear as crystal by this time that he would not give any sort of approval to the shrine.

The main focus in 1933 was the Oxford Movement Centenary, which was celebrated in Walsingham despite the misgivings which had been expressed by Fynes-Clinton and his group over the direction in which the successors of Pusey and his colleagues were moving. There were in fact two celebrations in the village, which as always were orchestrated by Hope Patten with his usual attention to detail. The first was the midweek pilgrimage, which attracted about 500. This took place from 18 to 20 July 1933. Revd J. Lester Biddulph Pinchard, parish priest of St John the Baptist, Holland Road, Kensington, addressed the pilgrims at vespers on the evening of Tuesday 18 July and again at the pontifical high mass the following day, which was celebrated by Bishop O'Rorke with assistance from Hope Patten, Father Leeds and Revd A. F. Methuen. After the mass there was a procession through the village to the shrine, singing the rosary. The nonagenarian Lord Halifax was by this time too ill to leave his Yorkshire home at Hickleton to travel to the main celebrations in London, so he had had his own commemoration. An altar with pavilion above it, designed by Sir William Milner, was built especially for that one event but then donated to Walsingham, where it stood for many years in the shrine gardens. It was used for the first time after the procession through the village, when benediction was given from it, following another procession, this time of the Blessed Sacrament. In this Hope Patten carried the monstrance under a scarlet canopy born by Milner, the Duke of Argyll, Sir John Shaw and Captain R. Garrett[4] and the way was lined by scouts from Stepney. In the evening there was sung pontifical vespers at the pavilion, then a yet further procession, this time of Our Lady, followed by benediction again. The emphasis was, as can be seen, on public demonstrations of faith and certainly no one could accuse the administrator of not filling the visitors' time adequately.

Bishop O'Rorke participated despite a strong letter from Bishop Pollock to him a few weeks earlier. On 15 June 1933 Pollock wrote: 'It would be a help to me if your taking part in the services [at Walsingham] came as rarely as may be compatible with your wishes.'

On the following weekend a further group came, led by Father Kingdon, with a procession from the shrine to the church for the parish mass, followed by benediction and veneration of the relic of St Vincent.

Following Father Leeds' departure, Hope Patten was sometimes the only priest in attendance in the village, although he was assisted from 1933

---

4 Although not a Guardian, he was a supporter of the devotion and later treasurer of the Walsingham Fund.

to 1935 by Father Methuen. Allan Forde Methuen had served only one curacy, at St Mary Aldermary in the City, before being given permission to officiate in the Diocese of Norwich from 1933 to 1935, after which he took up an appointment as curate of St Silas the Martyr, Kentish Town, a church which strongly supported Walsingham. As with Father Williams earlier, he was not officially appointed as curate to Hope Patten.

The vicar tended not to say mass in the shrine, partly because of his parochial responsibilities but also because he had a certain deference to the Bishop's wishes in that regard. He also received a blow in 1934 when Bishop O'Rorke resigned the living of Blakeney to live in the West Country; his health was said to require a milder climate than was provided by the harsh Norfolk winters. His presence had given the early functions at the shrine considerably more credibility than had they simply featured the usual supporters of Anglican Papalism. He remained a Guardian and his commitment to Walsingham continued. On leaving the area, he gave to the sanctuary a tabernacle, which could also be used as a throne for exposition, and was placed on the altar of the Holy Cross, which itself was a gift from Canon Claude Powell of Ipswich and had originally been located in St Monica's Home, near St Alban, Holborn. The expositories containing the various relics which the shrine possessed were kept in this altar, and at this time also the sanctuary acquired relics of the Holy Cross, which were enshrined in a cross of silver with decorative jewels. This was placed in the Holy House amid great ceremony and following a procession through the grounds.

Our Lady's Mirror for late 1933 carried a notice which informed its readers of the intercessions which were being offered, one of which was for the formation of a body of priests who would devote themselves to the shrine. That objective was never abandoned by Hope Patten and the attempt to attain it caused him a great deal of anguish and many problems. At that time it appeared very far off, but the first step towards it, as well as the fulfilment of a promise made long before, was to attempt to procure the ordination of Derrick Lingwood. This was not made easier by the fact that in addition to dealing with all the financial affairs of the shrine, parish and vicar, Lingwood had taken on the task of pilgrimage secretary when Miss Elsie Lloyd relinquished it in 1932. Any absence on his part would necessitate those tasks being taken on by some other person.

Derrick Lingwood clearly had a vocation and a great deal of practical experience of the problems faced by the clergy. He had had, however, no experience of higher education, and he came from the sort of background which even at that time made ordination in the Church of England a hard road to pursue. It was clear by then if not before that the Bishop of Norwich would not ordain him, both because of his associations with Hope Patten and because he was opposed to the acceptance of those without university degrees. By this time the general system was rather less haphazard than it had been when Hope Patten himself was ordained. The Central Advisory Council of Training for the Ministry (CACTM) was set up in 1912 to give advice to bishops regarding candidates, but they were not bound by its recommendations.

Derrick Lingwood was ordained deacon by Bishop Alfred Blunt of Bradford in May 1934, and priest on 23 September of the same year. The circumstances in which this occurred have been the subject of a great deal of speculation over the years, with some even insinuating that Hope Patten had some sort of hold over the Bishop.

As with many aspects of Hope Patten's life, the facts are actually much simpler and more easily explicable. Blunt had been consecrated as Bishop of Bradford in 1931. He was a strong socialist and was thought of as a Modernist, although not in an extreme sense. However, shortly after he took office he began to feel a great deal of sympathy for the Anglo-Catholics in his diocese and moved into what can be described as a Catholic phase, in which he presided at the local Congress and also became the first diocesan bishop in England to have a tabernacle on the altar in his private chapel. In due course that phase too was to pass and he became somewhat disillusioned by what he saw as the excesses of the Anglo-Catholic Movement.

Blunt was, however, throughout his life scornful of CACTM and his biographer[5] says that he felt 'violent opposition' to it. He frequently ordained candidates who had not been recommended by the organisation, and from time to time he allowed his heart to rule his head and ordained those who were in fact unsuitable. Hope Patten's connection with Blunt was that Sir William Milner's house near Skipton was within the Diocese of Bradford, Milner was a generous local benefactor, and the two were friendly as a consequence.

In 1933 Hope Patten went to visit Milner at Parcevall Hall and carried

---

5 J. S. Peart-Binns: *Blunt* (Mountain Press, Queensbury, 1969), p. 126.

on to see a friend of his, Father Frank Harwood, who was then vicar of Oakworth, near Keighley, also in the Diocese of Bradford.[6] The Bishop was due to visit Oakworth on the following Sunday for a confirmation, and Hope Patten suggested that Harwood put the scheme for Derrick Lingwood's ordination to him at the meal before the service. Thus primed, Harwood did so and reported later that the Bishop 'took to it at once' and immediately suggested that Lingwood should serve his title at Holy Trinity, Leeds Road, Bradford, one of the strongholds of Anglo-Catholicism in his area.[7]

By this method, Hope Patten and Lingwood both got the result they wanted. The suggestion was that Lingwood would stay for about two years in Bradford, but in fact it was clear that he always wanted to return to Walsingham. He actually said his first mass in the village a few days after his ordination, an event at which his parish priest from Bradford, Revd J. G. Hardwick, was present. At the same time that Derrick Lingwood was priested, Bishop Blunt ordained to the diaconate Edwin Lee Hirst, who had acted as pilgrimage secretary for the summer in which Lingwood was away, and whose cause was similarly promoted by Milner. Hope Patten had told Lee Hirst that he would only support his ordination if he was not engaged or otherwise entangled with a girl.[8]

In fact, Father Lingwood, as he then became, stayed in Bradford for only a very short time. Hope Patten realised that he could not manage without his managerial and administrative competence, and in any event he wanted to realise his dream of establishing a community of priests at Walsingham, for which he needed Lingwood. He asked the Bishop to release him early, and Blunt agreed. In fact he was sympathetic to the intention of setting up a community, and wrote on 10 January 1935 to Hope Patten saying: 'I am quite sure that you are right to begin in a small way and to let things develop. I always believe that that gives a project the best chance.'

---

6 He was another priest whose marriage did not prevent a friendship with Hope Patten. He was pleased to be able to remain a member of the Society of Our Lady of Walsingham even after the ban on married priests, because he was married before the ban came into force. He may also have endeared himself to Hope Patten by naming his eldest daughter Richeldis.
7 Letter of 23 May 1961 from Father Harwood (WA). See also an article by him in *Catholic Standard*, April 1972.
8 Letter of 1 June 1934 (WA).

The Bishop of Norwich was then asked for his approval to Father Lingwood returning to Walsingham; he replied that he had no objection to him working with Hope Patten but that he would not give him his licence, because to do so would imply episcopal acceptance of the shrine. He said that Lingwood could go to work in the parish with his blessing but not his licence: this represented a characteristic refusal on the part of Dr Pollock to grasp the nettle. It was at about the same time that Father Methuen returned to London, but it is not clear whether his return was a consequence of Lingwood's homecoming or simply coincidental with it.

It was also convenient that the Bishop was able to replace Father Lingwood at Holy Trinity, Bradford with Father Lee Hirst, as he became. He stayed for about two years, before moving on to a variety of posts in Kent, ending with a long stint as vicar of St Mildred, Canterbury.[9]

Bishop Blunt's lack of discrimination in ordaining men became the subject of adverse comment among his fellow bishops, particularly when he agreed to accept as a candidate Harold Moxon, a protégé of Father Ventham of South Creake, who had a justifiably dubious reputation as described earlier. In the case of Fathers Lingwood and Lee Hirst, however, the faith shown in them by Bishop Blunt was amply repaid by their ministries.

It had been Hope Patten's dream for many years to establish a religious community, preferably in an Augustinian idiom, and he now saw that long-held ideal as being capable of realisation within the context of service to the shrine. He almost certainly appreciated also that there was no progress to be made in affiliating himself to one of the existing communities, because their own discipline and rules would conflict with his strong will. In other words, if he were to be a member of a religious community, it would have to be as its head. Undoubtedly he visualised himself as a recreation of the mediaeval prior of Walsingham.

The attempt to establish an Augustinian community in Walsingham was, bluntly, not successful in the long term, and the continuing failure to establish it on sound foundations after the Second World War blighted Hope Patten's later years. One assessment of Hope Patten's life was that 'the first half of [his ministry in Walsingham] could be called the years of

---

9 He died in December 1972; according to his obituary he had been offered the bishopric of the Windward Islands some years earlier but declined it because of ill-health (see *Catholic Standard*, February 1973).

achievement, the second the years of trial'.[10] The problem was perhaps that his greatest strength was the ability to focus his considerable talents and energy on one cause at a time, such as the initial attempt to win over the village followed by the refoundation of the shrine. Once that sharply focused energy was simultaneously dissipated into a number of different schemes, it was insufficient to carry them through successfully. From this time on a number of new projects were commenced, most of which did not come to establish themselves on a proper basis.

There was also another potential for division which was not apparent at that time. Derrick Lingwood modelled himself upon the exemplar of Hope Patten which had impressed him when he was growing up – a conscientious and charismatic parish priest whose services were rooted in the Prayer Book. He never really moved from that position, and was somewhat indifferent to the wish to commit himself to life in a religious community, whereas Hope Patten not only sought to move in that direction, but also moved progressively away from the use of the Prayer Book as time went on. He was far more influenced by Papalism than was Lingwood. It is of significance that when, in 1933, Hope Patten was appealing for new furnishings for the sanctuary one of his requests was for two copies of the *Anglican Missal,* edited by Revd H. W. G. Kenrick, parish priest of Holy Trinity, Hoxton, which was in essence a translation of the Roman rites: this shows the direction in which he was moving.

Initially, the Community of St Augustine consisted only of Hope Patten and Lingwood and they lived under the same roof at the vicarage much as they had done before. They took vows only of stability and obedience to the Chapter and said matins and evensong together, so the situation was in fact little different from that which prevailed in many clergy houses. In about 1936 they were joined as a laybrother by P. M. Harbottle, who was to play a significant part in matters at Walsingham for many years. He was generally known by his second name of Moses, but in religion he was known as Brother Peter, his first name. Harbottle came from a northern working-class background, about which he could be somewhat prickly, and, like Hope Patten, he found difficulties in coping with examinations. He went to Dorchester Missionary College in 1937 but could not complete the course and returned to Walsingham. The Community remained functioning on this low-key pattern until the Second World War, when, after a

---

10 See John Barnes: *Alfred Hope Patten* (CLA, 1983), p. 9.

break, it was in effect relaunched. During this period, little publicity was given to its activities and no public appeals were made for recruits.

Hope Patten had also set up during this period a Walsingham Ordination Fund, which was used to help Derrick Lingwood in Bradford and also to support Moses Harbottle when he was at Dorchester. The sums involved were very small.

A series called *The Walsingham Tracts* was begun, and there were at least three, which were published in two sizes. In 1928 Hope Patten himself wrote *Pilgrimage: Its history and purpose*, and this was followed in 1934 by *Our Lady in England*, which was unattributed, and *The True Church of England: Roman or Anglican?* by Revd R. L. Langford-James, a prominent Papalist apologist and the co-founder with Father Fynes-Clinton of the Catholic League.

Another project, dear to Hope Patten's heart, was the formation of a Shrine Crafts Guild, which was in operation in the late 1930s. He had a great ability to inspire artists and other craftsmen, while at the same time not being an easy man with whom to deal. It was really only Enid Chadwick who flourished consistently under his patronage and with his encouragement, although in the early days a Miss Martin had carried out a very great deal of high-class weaving and embroidery, making vestments and other items from an almost derelict cottage, and there were others who were also involved with similar work.

Enid Chadwick came to Walsingham in 1934 from Brighton, where she had studied at the Brighton School of Art. Very soon after her arrival she designed a typical map of the village with the religious sites marked on it, which has remained a popular icon; it was clearly derived from the plan of Oxford designed by Martin Travers for the 1921 Anglo-Catholic Priests' Congress, but nonetheless is an arresting image. She remained in Walsingham until her death in 1987, and her painting embellished the shrine church in many different respects. In addition she assisted later at the Sanctuary School. Her work outside the village was more limited, but she did paint some interesting figures on the screen of the mediaeval church at Kettlebaston, Suffolk, and also many images of Our Lady of Walsingham for other churches. Her drawings of the shrine buildings, which were often found in *Our Lady's Mirror*, were clearly influenced by the work of Peter Anson, whom she must have met when he lived locally. She was not always the easiest person with whom to get on, but Hope Patten managed to bring out the best in her.

It is undoubtedly the case that during the period after the building of the new shrine Hope Patten became more detached from parish life; he was too concerned with his other activities to have as much time for his parishioners as before, but after Father Lingwood's return the latter took on much of the visiting and the like, a task which was aided by the fact that he had been born and grown up in the village and knew everybody. In August 1937, for example, he and Hope Patten officiated at a double wedding in the village: one of the bridegrooms was Lingwood's brother, the best man was another brother and one of the bridesmaids was a sister. Moses Harbottle played the organ at the ceremony. One of the Lingwood brothers later assisted with financial matters until called away on war service.

A minor consequence of Lingwood's ordination was that he was transferred from the lay to the clerical section of the College of Guardians, although he remained as Bursar. The College had remained stable for the first few years, but in early 1934 the very elderly Lord Halifax died. He had never actually visited Walsingham, but his name added great weight to the College and he had encouraged the development of the shrine from on far. Abbot Prideaux died later that year as has already been mentioned, and in 1935 Father Wodehouse resigned after being convicted of a criminal offence of indecency with a male.[11] He resigned also from his parish of St Paul, Oxford, and was prevented from such work for three years, during which time he assisted at the ultramontane Community of the Holy Cross at Hayward's Heath. In 1938 he took up a curacy at St John the Baptist, Holland Road, under Father Pinchard, and in 1942 was allowed a parish of his own again, moving to St Thomas, Shepherd's Bush. He was re-elected to the College of Guardians in 1950 and the inscription on his stall did not record the gap. Hope Patten did not mention his resignation in *Our Lady's Mirror*: he appears to have been somewhat naive about matters of that sort.

The new Guardians, who were elected at the annual chapter on 16 October 1935, were Major Hubert B. A. Adderley (later to become Lord Norton), who had been connected with the shrine for some time and had considerable artistic and technical knowledge, having worked for Comper

---

11 Colin Stephenson was criticised by some for having mentioned this matter in his book of memoirs, *Merrily on High* (Darton, Longman & Todd, 1972), but it was common knowledge at the time it happened.

when he was a young man, and four priests: Revd Carrick Deakin of St Augustine, Queen's Gate, South Kensington, the originator of the Anglo-Catholic Congress Movement; Canon Claude Powell, vicar of St Bartholomew, Ipswich, who has already been mentioned as the donor of the altar of the Holy Cross; Revd G. R. Vernon, then vicar of Christ Church, St Leonard's on Sea and later Bishop in Madagascar; and Revd Sir Percy Maryon-Wilson, of St Mary, Somers Town, who was both a priest and a baronet and therefore possessed a particular appeal to Hope Patten's snobbish side. The following year Arthur Smallwood was elected as a lay Guardian, but his time in office was short as he died in early 1938. Smallwood was a layman and religious thinker who was Director of Greenwich Hospital, and in that capacity had overseen the building of the Royal Hospital School at Holbrook, Suffolk, a project which he had placed under the protection of Our Lady of Walsingham and to whom he dedicated the chapel. It had run vastly over budget (costing over a million pounds, a colossal sum for the time) but the result was a fine school with a splendid chapel.[12] What is perhaps surprising is that Hope Patten's sometime parish priest, Father Corbould, who was prominent in the many interlocked organisations supporting reunion with Rome, was never appointed as a Guardian.[13] Nor was Martin Collett invited to replace Denys Prideaux; Hope Patten was never on such close terms with the second Abbot of Nashdom as he had been with the first.

There was another important development at this time which affected the administrative framework of the shrine. In 1936 a private limited company was formed, Walsingham College Trust Association Ltd, to which the trustees transferred the land they held and which in due course held all the relevant property of the shrine and College. In 1941 it was recognised as a Trust Corporation able to administer funds for charitable purposes. It was clearly easier to have the property held in that way than to replace trustees whenever one died, and it simplified greatly the financial structure. All Guardians were members of the company (i.e. they were allocated shares in it) and some, such as Hope Patten and Lingwood, were directors. It seems unlikely that Hope Patten ever fully understood the

---

12 For more information on Smallwood, see Geoffrey Curtis: *Paul Couturier and Unity in Christ* (SCM Press, 1964), pp. 181ff.
13 On his death, shortly before that of Hope Patten, Corbould left three reliquaries to the shrine, but the administrator appears to have been somewhat doubtful about their authenticity, as there is no mention that they were certified.

consequences of the adoption of this corporate form and he tended to regard the shrine and all its activities as his personal fiefdom.

The somewhat ambivalent attitude which Hope Patten and many of his colleagues had towards the Roman Catholic Church has already been the subject of comment. On the one hand, they admired Rome from afar, particularly Rome as demonstrated in Belgium and Austria. On the other hand, they had next to no contact with, or even knowledge of, Roman Catholics in this country. The mirror was that the Roman hierarchy in England was very strongly opposed to any sort of fraternisation with Anglicans, or to the encouragement of quasi-Roman devotions within the Church of England. The development of the shrine of Our Lady of Walsingham as an offshoot of the established Church was incomprehensible to the Roman Catholic bishops.

Hope Patten had until 1934 had the pilgrimage field to himself. There had been some interest in Walsingham prior to that time from within the Roman Catholic Church but no steps had been taken because of a dead-lock between various factions. In 1896 Miss Charlotte Pearson Boyd, a very devout woman who was passionately concerned to further the revival of Benedictine life in the Church of England, attempted to buy the Abbey at Walsingham but in the end had to be content with purchasing the Slipper Chapel at Houghton St Giles. This small building had marked the place at which pilgrims to Walsingham had removed their shoes before walking barefoot for the last portion of the journey, but at this time it was being used as a farm building. Before the sale was completed, however, she was received into the Roman Catholic Church.

At that time, Roman Catholics were spread very thinly indeed across East Anglia. There was an established parish in King's Lynn, where the priest had ready revived the devotion to Our Lady of Walsingham and erected a chapel with an image. There was also an established parish at Bungay, just across the county border in Suffolk, which was run by the Downside Benedictines, whose spirituality tuned in exactly with Miss Boyd's own aspirations. However, the priest at King's Lynn was extremely anxious that the Benedictines should not obtain a foothold in his area of Norfolk, and obtained a ruling from Rome that Walsingham was within his parish and that mass should not be celebrated, nor any other public service held, in the Slipper Chapel. Miss Boyd made the chapel and the adjacent house over to the Benedictines who, because of the papal ban, were unable to develop devotion from it in any way. Hope Patten had asked the Abbot of Downside whether pilgrims to the Anglican shrine could pray in the chapel and was told that, regrettably, no permission could be given for public prayer; the letter was a great deal more civilised in tone than many exchanged at the time between the two churches.

There can be no doubt that many within the Roman Catholic community not only disliked that which Hope Patten was doing, but also wanted to outshine his projects. In 1934 the long-outdated papal ban was removed, the Slipper Chapel was made over to the Diocese of Northampton, and the decision was taken to develop it as the National Shrine of Our Lady. This development was reported by Hope Patten in *Our Lady's Mirror* with commendation, on the basis that it increased devotion to Our Lady of Walsingham and also because he had been told by an anonymous but prominent Roman Catholic that the pilgrimage would not have been revived by his Church were it not for what Hope Patten had done. However, there was an element of envy in his report that some 10,000 had attended at a pilgrimage led by the Archbishop of Westminster on 19 August 1934 to celebrate the rededication of the Slipper Chapel; the forms of service which he was encouraging were alien to most of the Church of England but second nature to those aboard the barque of St Peter.

For the next few years there was a regrettable degree of hostility between Anglicans and Romans. The latter opened a small chapel in the village, and circulated a great deal of literature which ignored or disparaged Hope Patten's efforts. The situation was certainly not assisted by the fact that the first Roman Catholic priest in the village was Revd Bruno Scott James, who was himself a convert from Canterbury and had been for a time a member of the Nashdom Community. He was tactless, abrasive and snobbish, as can be seen from his autobiography published some years later,[14] and in addition he was by this time strongly anti-Anglican, although he did commend Hope Patten and refer to him as 'a deeply serious and spiritual man'.

The writer, artist and sometime Caldey monk, Peter Anson, recounts in his autobiography how he went to Walsingham in the immediate pre-war years; he later stayed in the village while working with the Daglesses in the design of church furnishings. He wrote that in 1934, 'Few of the natives appear to attend the parish church, for they had been alienated by the unfamiliar type of religion introduced by the present incumbent with the

---

14 See B. Scott James: *Asking for Trouble* (Darton, Longman & Todd, 1962).

most laudable intentions.' He went on to say that the congregations were made up largely of pious old ladies attracted to Walsingham by the privileges available in the parish church.[15]

There was something in the latter point, in that there had been a number of such women who had moved to the village. Hope Patten at first encouraged them, but later regretted that encouragement, considering that they caused a great deal of trouble between themselves with internecine quarrels of labyrinthine complexity into which he was on occasion drawn. In autumn 1935 Our Lady's Mirror, for example, he reported that a supporter had purchased the Martyr's House and intended to run it as a restaurant. The purchaser, Mrs Payne-Jennings, then let the property to three sisters named Bloxam, with whom she then fell out and in 1938 expelled. Hope Patten took their side and was instrumental in setting them up in a rival establishment known as the Knight's Gate Café, which they ran until 1950, when it was taken over by the Roman Catholic Lady Pigott. The result of Hope Patten's intervention was that the original purchaser not only fell out badly with him, but also removed the shrine from the list of beneficiaries in her will.[16]

Other ladies who moved to Walsingham, but who did not fall out with the vicar, included Miss Doyle-Smithe, the secretary of the Walsingham Clergy Fund, the Misses Hastings, two sisters who had lived in Buxted, and Mrs Dorothy Ferrier, the widow of Revd Douglas Ferrier, formerly parish priest of St Paul, Shadwell, Yorkshire, who came to Walsingham on her husband's death just before the war and thereafter ran the shrine shop for very many years.

The general point made by Anson seems to have been considerably overstated and was no doubt influenced by his anti-Anglican views at that time, which mollified considerably as time went by.[17] Although there were difficulties with incomers, there were very many villagers in what was after all a small community who remained captivated by their priest and stayed loyal to him.

The more important point, however, was that after 1934 the pioneer

---

15 Peter Anson: A Roving Recluse (Mercier Press, Cork, 1946), p. 201.

16 Mrs Payne-Jennings subsequently, some years later, died in her bath, and was found by Tom Purdy; he broke in when her neighbours became worried. He was the undertaker as well as the village builder, so he then had to arrange the funeral.

17 Although when asked in 1961 whether he regretted what he had written on this subject, Anson replied in the negative (letter of 13 April 1961, WA).

efforts of Hope Patten in reviving pilgrimages to the shrine were some-what overshadowed by the ability of the Roman Catholic Church to mobilise, when required, very large numbers of pilgrims indeed, perhaps emphasising how far from most central Anglican thought Walsingham was placed. There was never the slightest danger that he would secede at this point, as had done so many other rising stars of the Anglo-Catholic Movement. His rigidity in these matters was a strength in this regard as well as a weakness in other respects. He did, however, tell one confidant that an approach had been made to him by Rome and that he had been 'quasi-offered' a monsignorship with the promise of remaining in Walsingham were he to have gone over.[18] It would have been an enormous publicity coup for the Roman Catholic Church had he succumbed to this temptation, and the fact that other such offers were undoubtedly made to some ultramontane Anglicans, coupled with the expansionist policy of Romans in this country at that time, suggests that this may well have occurred.[19]

Hope Patten's lack of interest in, or knowledge of, public affairs has already been the subject of comment. However, the outbreak of the Spanish Civil War in 1936 galvanised opinion in the Roman Catholic Church because the Republicans were seen as murderers of the clergy, and secularist murderers to boot. That antagonism was, not surprisingly, mirrored among Anglican Papalists, and on 17 November 1936 Fynes-Clinton, Corbould, Collett and the Duke of Argyll sent a joint letter to Roman Catholic newspapers supporting the anti-Republican stance of the Vatican. Although Hope Patten was not a signatory to the letter, he did institute a Holy Hour each week during the long conflict with prayers for the preservation of the Church in Spain.

The pilgrimages still continued to grow in number and in geographical scope. In 1935 it was said that 30,000 people in all had visited the shrine,

---

18 This was relayed by Revd I. H. Burton, who had a curious ecclesiastical career. After being ordained in the Church in Wales, in 1949 he went over to Rome. He then reverted to the Anglican Communion and was certainly at the shrine in 1955, before joining the Eglise Catholique Orthodoxe Orientale in Paris and adopting the name Father Barnabé (letters of 25 April 1961 and 5 May 1961, WA). Still later he joined the mainstream Orthodox Church. He once preached in Welsh at benediction at Walsingham.

19 The Sisters of the Holy Cross at Hayward's Heath, for example, were approached on three separate occasions.

including Princess Marie Louise, the only member of the royal family at that time to offer any public support for Anglo-Catholicism; her attendance no doubt pleased Hope Patten and probably more so Fynes-Clinton, who loved titles of all sorts.[20]

In 1935 Father Kenrick led the first walking pilgrimage to Walsingham from London since the Middle Ages, one of the participants being a young Colin Stephenson on his first visit to the shrine. In August 1936 the first Scottish pilgrimage arrived, led by Revd B. E. Joblin, who was then vicar of St Michael, Hill Square, Edinburgh, an ultramontane Caledonian outpost of Anglo-Catholicism. Joblin moved in 1939 to be chaplain to the Sisters of St Peter at Laleham and was thus to have further dealings with Hope Patten at that time. Conversely, in October 1936 Hope Patten led a party of over 40 members of his congregation on a pilgrimage to London, and in particular to the shrine of St Edward the Confessor in Westminster Abbey, although they also attended high mass at St Mary, Bourne Street and benediction at St Magnus the Martyr. In 1938 the parishioners of Walsingham went on pilgrimage to Lincoln, in honour of St Hugh.

The Bishop of Norwich had little to do with Walsingham during the years after 1932, and the parish was effectively treated as extra-diocesan. However, on 15 May 1936 Dr Pollock wrote to Hope Patten asking whether he was celebrating in the shrine chapel and if so how often, and for whom. Hope Patten's answers were revealing: in the preceding year he had said mass only 16 times in the shrine, but 380 times in the parish church. It is absolutely clear from those statistics that the use of the shrine chapel for the celebration of mass was only at times when pilgrims came, and then usually by the priests who accompanied them. The Bishop replied on 2 July 1936:

---

20 Princess Francisca Josepha Louise Augusta Marie Hélène Christina of Schleswig-Holstein-Sonderburg-Augustenberg (1872–1956), who chose to use the names Marie Louise in childhood, was the granddaughter of Queen Victoria; her mother was Princess Helena, daughter of the Queen. In 1891 Princess Marie Louise married H.H. Prince Aribert of Anhalt, but the marriage was annulled by a decree of her father-in-law in 1900, and she returned to England, where she had been born. In 1917 she relinquished her German titles and was thereafter known simply as Princess Marie Louise. She was a patron of the arts and of good works, especially ecclesiastical, and is frequently mentioned in connection with Anglo-Catholic enterprises.

I have been considering your letter, and from it it appears that though I have not licensed 'the Shrine' for the celebration of Holy Communion you are, contrary to my wishes, still from time to time celebrating the Holy Communion there. Obviously this does not come within the scope of the Communion of the Sick and the parish church is near. I therefore ask you to give up these celebrations altogether and to let me hear that you are proposing to abandon them.

This missive represented a harder line than the Bishop had ever taken before and was perhaps a belated attempt by him to deal with a problem which he had allowed to drift previously. Hope Patten pointed this apparent contradiction out in his reply of 15 July 1936, making the good point that the parish church had not been neglected, and ending with the request that 'if you cannot license the chapel just yet, I trust that it will be possible for matters to stand as they have in the past'. The Bishop was, however, not initially prepared to leave matters yet again. He replied in fairly strong terms on 27 July 1936:

Thank you for your letter from which I am afraid it is plain that you have acted upon my forbearance as if it had been an expressed approval of your celebrating the Holy Communion in a place which has not been licensed. What you tell me about the parish church in which there is, you say, a celebration every day, appears to show that there is quite adequate provision in the parish church for those who wish to attend Holy Communion. I cannot say that I think it is satisfactory to leave the matter as it stands: for your present practice seems to draw no distinction between a licensed and an unlicensed building, nor between a limited cognisance of what has been taking place and a sanction of it on my part. At the same time I do not wish to be inconsiderate or to hurry in the matter, and it may be that circumstances of which I am unaware would make it difficult for you to discontinue the present arrangements. I suggest therefore that you should gradually reduce the celebrations in this unauthorised building, and bring them completely to an end by the end of the year.

The correspondence continued, with Hope Patten first referring to the invalids who lived around the shrine and could not get to the parish church, then to the meaning of pilgrimages and the need for special facilities, including an occasion on which 30 masses had been said in the shrine chapel on the same day, which is not an argument which is likely to have softened the Bishop's mind. Eventually, on 19 November 1936, the Bishop reiterated his requirement that Hope Patten cease to celebrate in the shrine from the end of the year. Hope Patten neither replied nor ceased celebrating in the shrine.

On 24 February 1937 Bishop Pollock returned to the attack. He wrote asking whether celebrations of Holy Communion had indeed ceased at the end of 1936 and enquired as to the date of the last such celebration. By this point Hope Patten had circulated the Guardians with copies of the correspondence and replied to the Bishop the following day, somewhat disingenuously, that he had not in fact said mass in the shrine since the end of 1936, but that the Guardians were unanimous that celebrations in the chapel could not be allowed to cease. The Bishop took that letter, as perhaps was intended, as confirmation that Hope Patten intended to accept his ruling but he reiterated the position in a letter of 19 March 1937 written on Guardians' notepaper. There was then silence for 12 months.

The Guardians were caught on the same hook as Hope Patten: there was a clear contradiction between the emphasis placed by Anglo-Catholics on church order and the importance to that of episcopal authority, and the reality of dealing with hostile bishops. Various suggestions emerged, including one from the Duke of Argyll that he should use his ancient privileges to appoint Hope Patten as his private chaplain and then deem the shrine to be his private chapel.

On 2 March 1938 Dr Pollock wrote to Hope Patten asking whether he might take it that the celebrations in the shrine had in fact been discontinued for the preceding 12 months. By this time the extension, described in the next chapter, was under construction, something of which the Bishop obviously knew. Hope Patten, who as has already been made clear was convinced that the shrine was built on the site of the original Holy House, prevaricated again, saying that the discovery of further foundations might change the legal premises upon which they had both been acting. He meant by that that the shrine might be a reconstruction of an already consecrated building.

The Bishop was by this time beginning to lose patience. He caused a notice to be inserted in the *Diocesan Gazette* which read: 'The new chapel at Walsingham is not licensed by me and no priest in this diocese or any other has my permission to celebrate the Holy Communion there.' Hope

Patten was extremely angry at this, not only because of the contents but also because the matter had been put very clearly in the public arena, seven years after the erection of the chapel. He wrote to the effect that as parish priest he had the right to say mass wherever he thought fit within his parish. Fynes-Clinton commented that that was 'exactly the right way to write to a bishop', a comment which illuminates clearly the paradoxical attitude of Papalists to the Anglican episcopate. After further correspondence the two men met, without resolving anything, but Father Whitby then suggested obtaining counsel's opinion on whether or not the chapel could be regarded as consecrated because it was a rebuilding of the original.

The Guardians followed this course, and Hope Patten felt that his position was very much strengthened when counsel, Mr Marshall Freeman, agreed that as the original shrine had been a peculiar (that is extra-diocesan), a reconstruction on the same site might be considered to be in the same position. This was deployed to the Bishop when Hope Patten went to see him in May 1938; Pollock must have appreciated that he was being outmanoeuvred again and that if he persisted he would face a prolonged battle in the courts which would assist neither party. Although Hope Patten was not a legalist, and there were no lawyers among the Guardians, Fynes-Clinton loved litigation and had succeeded in a number of cases brought shortly after his institution to St Magnus. The Bishop's own failure to deal with the problem expeditiously in 1931, compounded by the fact that it was he who had asked that the image be moved in the first place, put him in a position where he was throughout on the back foot. After the raising of the legal issue, which was Hope Patten's strongest card, albeit one which he found only late, the Bishop made a graceful but undeclared retreat and ignored Walsingham thereafter. He was by then in any event an old man, and he was to retire in 1942. Hope Patten, however, became convinced that what he had been advised might be the case was in fact established, and thereafter frequently asserted that the shrine was indeed a reconstituted peculiar.

The further dispute with the Bishop was so far as Hope Patten is concerned only a distraction; his main preoccupation in the period 1937–8 was the extension of the shrine. To that we now turn.

8

WALSINGHAM: THE PRE-WAR YEARS AND THE EXTENSION OF THE SHRINE, 1938–9

The Shrine as built in 1931 was so small that it was clearly unsatisfactory as a venue for the numbers who gathered on certain occasions, and even more unsatisfactory as a long-term focus for spreading the devotion to Our Lady of Walsingham. On the other hand, the acquisition of the property in Knight Street in 1935 meant that it was possible to plan for expansion on a scale which would not otherwise have been possible. Hope Patten was himself a talented artist and he drew out many plans of his own, which must have made the task of the professionals working with him infinitely difficult. However, Craze was a tactful and patient man who appears to have relished his co-operation with this particularly demanding client.

The first attempt by Hope Patten to extend the building, the choir scheme of 1932–3, had proved abortive because the finance was not forthcoming, even after the printing of a leaflet which exhorted Catholics not to be less generous than were Protestants in supporting the Wycliffe Preachers; it was, after all, somewhat optimistic to launch such an appeal in the depths of the Great Depression. However, the need for additional accommodation became more acute, and Hope Patten was his customary impatient self, with an inability to see that others might have different preoccupations or calls on their purses.

In the summer 1935 edition of *Our Lady's Mirror* Hope Patten commented that more pilgrims and visitors than ever had arrived that year and that the restricted accommodation in the outer church had become a serious drawback on occasion. He continued: 'Somehow or other we must extend the present building or fasten three or four bays to the "East" and so make it possible for a modicum of comfort.' By this stage Milner &

Craze had drawn up preliminary plans (paid for by a donation in 1934 from a supporter, who died shortly thereafter) for an extension and Hope Patten asked for those who had 'a real love for Our Lady and her National Shrine' to come forward and give or loan the amount required. The costing at that stage, as shown in a leaflet which was prepared and distributed, was about £9,000, and the proposal then was to extend eastwards, but also to build what were described as 'domestic buildings to accommodate a small College of priests and laymen who will be in charge of the sanctuary'; these included six so-called cells and a cloistered court. A museum area was also included together with a brick tower and carillon, which was proposed for the liturgical south side of the building.

Initially, there does not appear to have been any great response to this appeal. However, one morning in 1936 Hope Patten, Lingwood and Milner were having breakfast together and the former was opening his correspondence. He suddenly announced that he had a cheque for £4,580 5s 2d.[1] The curious amount was explained by the fact that the donor (then anonymous but revealed by Lingwood in notes which he prepared later to be Revd A. M. Rumball, then curate of St John the Evangelist, Forton, Gosport, Hampshire) had rearranged certain investments, and that was the residue, which he specifically asked to be used for the building of the extension.[2] Lingwood, much more acute where money was concerned, reacted immediately by snatching the letter from Hope Patten, suggesting that he had misread the figures and that in fact it was £450. However, he then saw that the larger figure was indeed correct.[3] Father Rumball is one of the unacknowledged contributors to the shrine, but one whose monetary input was invaluable.

---

1 Stephenson says £4,578 4s 0d, which is a figure Hope Patten himself used; the difference is obviously inconsequential, and the point is that it was an odd amount. Hope Patten later said that it arrived on the fifth anniversary of the translation of the image, but that may be retrospective embroidery.

2 Arthur Milton Rumball was ordained deacon in 1928 and priest the following year. He served a curacy at Wymondham, Norfolk, 1928–31, and was then given permission to officiate in the Diocese of Norwich for the next year, when he may possibly have assisted at Walsingham. He then moved to Beeston, Nottinghamshire (1932–5), and Forton (1936–8) before becoming priest in charge of St Alban, Ventnor, Isle of Wight. He was extremely keen on Scouting. There is also a written reference to him being an assistant at Walsingham in 1935–6, perhaps between curacies, perhaps simply as one of the Chaplains of the Holy House; the shrine service register does not suggest that he was in residence for a long time.

3 See Lingwood, 'Rough Notes'.

This very substantial sum enabled Hope Patten to relaunch the appeal with a real chance of success, and of course by this time, although the international situation was deteriorating, the general economic state of the country was significantly better than had been the case some years earlier. The remainder of the money required did then begin coming in, and by 1937 work started. Hope Patten himself and Bishop O'Rorke were the trustees of the building fund, which was kept separate from other monies.

Hope Patten was anxious that the opportunity of further building work being undertaken should also enable archaeological investigations to be carried out, with the intention of supporting his theory that the shrine was built on the site of the mediaeval Holy House. He ensured that what was found on the site was photographed, and he set out his theories in a pamphlet which he wrote on behalf of the Guardians and was entitled *An Account of Some Recent Discoveries at the Shrine of Our Lady of Walsingham, Norfolk*: this is undated but appears to have been published in early 1938. The booklet is illustrated with some of the photographs taken during the excavations, and is also accompanied by a plan drawn by Major Adderley, who also contributed an addendum to the text. In the pamphlet Hope Patten sets out his interpretation of what had been discovered, and attempts with some ingenuity to reconcile the dimensions of the walls which were on the site with those described by William of Worcester as relating to the Holy House and its covering building.

His conclusion, expressed on behalf of the Guardians, was:

We . . . can say the dimensions, position and type of foundations discovered in 1931–7 seem to correspond remarkably well with the descriptions handed down concerning the ancient shrine, and there is adequate ground for believing that the site has a better claim than any other to be regarded as that of either the earlier building in which the Holy House originally stood (assuming, that is, that the legend which mentions two sites contains a background of fact), or the 'Novum Opus' described by William of Worcester and Erasmus.

That is not now a view which would be supported by any expert opinion, but it was certainly very influential in Hope Patten's own thinking, and he repeated it in different forms many times thereafter.

The first plans published after the receipt of the then anonymous donation were substantially different from the scheme which had been set forward in 1936, and of course the drawings were the subject of constant changes as Hope Patten's fertile mind thought of what was to be created. The plans in the 1937 appeal leaflet shifted the campanile to the liturgical north side of the shrine, with the sacristy under it, and provided for nine side chapels, most of which were the subject of individual sponsorship and dedication, rather than the four which had been envisaged in 1936. The 1937 leaflet also divided the project into two parts, with separate plans showing the chapel itself (for which, by that time, only £1,000 was said to be required) and the further development of the domestic buildings for the College. The museum remained in place to the liturgical south of the chapel, with the cloisters behind, but in place of the cell block shown in 1936 was a substantial library, and the accommodation for the College was envisaged as being in a converted St Augustine's, the house in Knight Street which now formed part of the holdings of the Trust Company. This scheme would have involved the demolition of the cottages on Knight Street and of the later administrator's cottage; the total cost of this part of the work was estimated at £4,740.

In fact, insufficient was raised to carry out any work on the 'domestic' buildings at this time. However, the plans both for the chapel and for the ancillary buildings became more elaborate almost by the day. In February 1938 Milner & Craze produced yet another scheme, which was released to the public with yet another appeal for money. By this time, the shell of the extension of the chapel was complete, but costs had escalated and it was said that £3,000 was required to free the building from debt. In addition, however, the leaflet asked for £7,000 to build a College to serve the shrine, and an additional £13,000 to convert other buildings.

This ambitious scheme envisaged the demolition of the barn behind the chapel, which had been used as a refectory for the pilgrims, and the erection beyond its site of a substantial College incorporating a library. The whole of the frontage to Knight Street was to have been reconstructed to provide for a new pilgrims' refectory, kitchens, a pilgrimage secretary's office, a gardener's cottage and other ancillary facilities.

The museum was retained in its original position and behind it was to have been a very substantial cloister in two parts, with an Orthodox chapel within one of them. Hope Patten's own knowledge of Eastern spirituality was not profound, but he was much influenced in that as well as other regards by Fynes-Clinton, whose learning in that field was extensive and who had many connections with the Eastern Churches. Hope Patten himself had annotated some copies of earlier leaflets to include such a chapel on the south side of the church, but this plan placed it a few feet away from the main building, although within the cloister.

In May 1937 the first visit of Orthodox clergy to Walsingham had taken place, during which a Russian prayer was sung. In November 1937 Archbishop Seraphim, who had been due to visit in 1926 but had been prevented from doing so, blessed the area of land near the shrine chapel designated by Hope Patten, to prepare it for the erection of the Orthodox chapel. He had brought with him a venerable and important icon, which indicated the importance which he placed on the visit. However, no building had taken place on the site by the time of the blessing of the extension.

The shrine church as completed in 1938 is a clear reflection of Hope Patten's own preoccupations and liturgical outlook. He was extremely anxious that the work be carried through as a whole in the shortest possible time: not, it would appear, because he foresaw the armed conflict which was then on the horizon, but because he was by nature impatient and in any event was anxious that the work be completed within his own lifetime, so that the shrine should not wither once he had died. The ever cautious Lingwood was among those who suggested that it would be more sensible to build half of a larger church, leaving it for further generations to complete the work if necessary, but Hope Patten would have none of it.

The number of chapels in what was not a large building even after it was extended had, as has been shown, gradually increased with each redrawing of the plans. Hope Patten had finally seized on the concept that there should be 15 altars within the building, one for each of the mysteries of the Holy Rosary. This was not an original concept: he had seen it used in the Rosary Church at Loreto and it was entirely in keeping with his thinking that he should import and adapt such an idea to Walsingham. The problem, which others could see but he refused to accept, was that the new shrine church was narrow and in many places cramped. The symbolic importance to him of fitting in all 15 altars was such that some were placed in unsuitable locations where some priests found it physically difficult to say mass. Hope Patten's vision was no doubt of the members of the College and the retired priests each using an altar for their private masses in the early morning, a pattern which would have replicated that found at that time at Nashdom and other such establishments.

One positive aspect of the multiplication of the number of altars was that many were sponsored by societies or individuals. Thus the altar of the Annunciation, which was the altar of the outer chapel as built in 1931, was linked to the Society of Mary; the altar of the Presentation was for the Society of Our Lady of Walsingham; that of the Agony was for Scouts and Guides (paid for by a priest particularly interested in those organisations, probably Father Rumball again); that of the Carrying of the Cross was for the Priest Associates of the Holy House; that of the Coronation for the Confraternity of the Blessed Sacrament; and that of the Ascension for the Seven Years Association.[4] In addition, the Chapel of the Finding in the Temple was a chantry chapel for Father Tooth, the so-called martyr of ritualism, who was also commemorated by the crucifix which was said to have come from his church at St James, Hatcham and for Father Wilmot Philips, a scholarly and holy priest who in 1898 had been ejected from St Ethelburga, Bishopsgate, after refusing to communicate the Protestant agitator John Kensit.[5] The Chapel of the Death on the Cross was the Fynes-Clinton chantry chapel, the Chapel of the Scourging was Sir William Milner's and the Chapel of the Crowning with Thorns was that of Hope Patten himself.

The influence of the administrator can also be seen in the erection of the statue of King Charles the Martyr, who would have not have been so commemorated by some of his Papalist friends because he was not recognised as a saint in Rome, and in the darkness which at that time was almost all-pervading; the church is now very different with more recent extensions having added cloisters and flooded much of the interior with natural light. Hope Patten thought that the dim corners which were everywhere added to the mystery of the building and created an atmosphere of devotion. The building was not of course in the Gothic idiom, which by this time was scarcely being used save in a most debased form, but rather took as its precedent the village chapels of Southern Europe with a Baroque air about them, and Counter-Reformation style furnishings.

There can be no doubt that Craze faithfully, and, in many ways,

---

4 A youth group under the auspices of the Church Union, which itself had been formed in 1934 by the merger of the English Church Union and the Anglo-Catholic Congress. The reference to seven years was to the period between the Centenary Congress of 1933 and the next planned Congress, which was to have taken place in 1940.

5 Father Wilmot Philips spent a long ministry thereafter at Plaxtol, Kent.

brilliantly, carried into effect the vision of his client, although he was of course constrained by finance. One of the most striking features of the extension was the row of columns which supported the gallery immediately behind the new high altar. They toned in perfectly with the rest of the décor, and few observers would have known that in fact they had been salvaged from the News Chronicle building in Fleet Street (very near to the offices of Milner & Craze) which happened to be demolished at a convenient time. Another typical touch was that on the ends of the roof timbers can be seen carvings of six of those who were involved with the shrine at that time: Hope Patten himself; Lingwood; Milner; O'Rorke; Frary; and, ironically in the light of what was shortly to happen, Mother Sarah of Laleham. A great deal of the internal painting was undertaken by Enid Chadwick.

The land upon which the extension stood was part of the area bought by Sir William Milner in 1924. He had donated to the Guardians the land upon which the original shrine chapel was placed in 1931, and had leased to them the remainder on a 99-year term. In 1938 he gave to the Guardians, or more exactly to the Trust Company, an additional area of land upon which the extension was built. At about the same time that the extension was constructed, the company also acquired a small cottage on Knight Street, just to the north of St Augustine's, which was the last remaining plot in the area west of that street not in shrine hands. A few years before, a range of six derelict cottages on the east side of Knight Street and opposite the entrance to the shrine church had been purchased, to prevent them being turned into garages and a fried fish shop. It was at first intended to use them for the home for retired priests, which remained one of Hope Patten's pet projects.

When the new high altar was built, Hope Patten continued the tradition which he had established in 1931 and which had been reinforced in the years after that when one of the original side chapels was established as the chantry of King Edward I, who was said to have visited the original shrine many times,[6] namely the use of stones from other foundations. The high altar contained stones from many cathedrals at home and abroad, and also from various religious houses both mediaeval and modern. Not only was this idea copied from that which Aelred Carlyle had done on Caldey 20 years before, but also the key to the stones, published in *Our Lady's Mirror*

---

6 This contained what was known as the altar of the Visitation after 1938.

for summer 1943, was very similar indeed to the key to the Caldey stones which was contained in the Abbot's explanatory book *The Benedictines of Caldey Island*, published shortly before the secession of the Community.

The shrine church (as it became with the new extension, crossing the subtle line from being simply a chapel), has not found much favour with architectural critics, but has an indefinable charm of its own, which was evident from its construction; in particular, it possesses an air of timelessness, as if it had always been there while on the other hand being alien to the landscape and surroundings. The editors of *Pevsner* are, however, predictably dismissive, saying: 'It is a disappointing building of brick, partly whitewashed, and looking for all its ambitions like a minor suburban church.'[7]

The blessing of the extension to the Pilgrim Church, as it was termed on the invitations sent out, was fixed for 6 June 1938, Whit Monday. From that arose the tradition, continued to the present day, of the most important pilgrimage of the year taking place on the Bank Holiday Monday, which followed Whit Sunday until 1970 and thereafter has been the last Monday in May.

Looking back at events at Walsingham with the enormous benefit of hindsight, it could plausibly be argued that the day of the blessing of the extension marked the highest point of Hope Patten's ministry. Although he was to remain in Walsingham for a further 20 years, his time thereafter was to be marred by the failure of a number of different initiatives and by increasing poor health. At the time of the building of the extension he was still only 52 and he could justifiably look around at that which he had accomplished in the 17 years he had been in Norfolk.

The arrangements for the blessing of the extension were not dissimilar to those which had been used so successfully in 1931. On Sunday 5 June 1938 Bishop O'Rorke, who returned for the ceremonies from his new home in the West of England, preached at high mass in the parish church and later consecrated the stones for the high altar of the shrine church, anointed them, and enclosed relics within as required by the Roman rite. Father Alban Baverstock preached at evensong, which was followed, as was the practice at Walsingham, by benediction. A deputation of Orthodox clergy led by the exiled Archbishop Nestor of Kamchatka and

---

7 N. Pevsner and B. Wilson: *The Buildings of England: Norfolk 1: Norwich and the North-East* (Yale University Press, 2002), p. 595.

Petropavlovsk attended the service and processed into the sanctuary, which was a sign of the increased interest being taken by Hope Patten in the Eastern Church.

The following day the village was again decorated with flags and bunting and a procession took place from the parish church to the shrine church. Hope Patten's genius for organising such events, together with his luck with the weather, made this another memorable day for the village. At 12 noon the Easter Angelus was said in the parish church, after which the procession to the shrine began. It was led by the Scouts, who appear to have played a considerable part in life at Walsingham during these years; Moses Harbottle was the local Scout leader at that time. They were followed by the cross and thurifer, then by a large number of religious including the Abbot of Nashdom. Next came girls robed in white carrying the banner of Our Lady of Walsingham with flowers and streamers of ribbon, and then about 150 Priest Associates of the Holy House[8] in soutane and cotta, after whom came the Orthodox delegation. The Guardians in their blue cloaks, lay followed by clerical, headed by William Frary as beadle, came after the Orthodox, and behind them Bishop O'Rorke in full pontificals with two priests from the Community of the Resurrection as his deacons of honour. After the Bishop came Craze, together with the wives of the married Guardians, and then between 3,000 and 4,000 other pilgrims who walked behind them: the procession took over an hour to pass any given place. John Shepherd, who had been born on 5 December 1932 and been baptised by Hope Patten on 31 December 1932, recalls sitting on the wall watching this procession and being frightened by the tall hats of the Eastern churchmen, as a young child might be.

When the Bishop reached the shrine church he sprinkled the interior and exterior with holy water, and blessed it, while litanies were sung, followed by the hymn 'Faith of Our Fathers'. He then presided at high mass, which was sung by Hope Patten, as if publicly to show his disregard for the Bishop of Norwich's injunctions, with Father Thomas OSB of Nashdom as deacon and Father Lingwood as subdeacon. The crowd was such, and even the enlarged shrine so small, that at the same time another high mass was sung at the Hickleton altar in the grounds by Revd P. Raybould of St Julian, Norwich, a staunch local supporter.

---

8 At this time there were about 250 Priest Associates, so the proportion present was very high.

During the afternoon the Orthodox clergy sang a solemn Te Deum in honour of Our Lady in the Holy House, and there was a sermon by Father Frank Biggart of the Community of the Resurrection. The Mirfield Fathers had become far less Anglican and more Roman in their outlook over the preceding 20 years, and this trend was to be accentuated when Father Raymond Raynes took on the leadership of the Community in 1943. Biggart preached a Mariolatrous sermon which was no doubt well received by his listeners, but would probably have been unacceptable to most of the diocesan bishops in England at that time. Benediction followed, which would certainly have been unacceptable to all the English diocesans.

The following day, Tuesday 7 June 1938, the Orthodox liturgy was sung at the high altar of the shrine church by Archbishop Nestor assisted by two Archimandrites, one of whom, Nicholas Gibbes, had been tutor to the Russian Imperial family. Bishop O'Rorke was present and it was recorded that one Prince Vladimir Galitzine, a connection of the Imperial family, acted as lector and administered the lavabo, an aristocratic presence no doubt inspired by Father Fynes-Clinton. The contact with the Orthodox at Walsingham at this time was exclusively with the Czarist Russian Church in Exile rather than with the rival state-influenced Church within Russia itself.[9] On 14 September 1938 Hope Patten was presented by the Orthodox with the medal of St Vladimir, struck to commemorate the passing of 950 years from the anniversary of the Baptism of Russia.

On 14 June 1938 the newly ordained Revd I. H. Vincent said his first mass in the shrine church.[10] Hope Patten remarked that it was the first time 'at least since the sixteenth century' that a first mass had been said at the sanctuary, an entirely predictable expression on his part since he believed firmly in the continuity of his building with that which had been destroyed after the Reformation.

---

9 Nicholas Gibbes (1876–1963) was born Charles Sydney Gibbes in Rotherham, and was tutor to the Imperial Court from 1908 to 1917. He later studied for the Anglican priesthood at St Stephen's House, Oxford, but abandoned that course and in 1934 was received into the Orthodox Church by Archbishop Nestor, taking the name of Nicholas after the last Czar; see C. Benagh: *An Englishman in the Court of the Tsar: The Spiritual Journey of Charles Sydney Gibbes* (Conciliar Press, California, 2000).

10 Ian Vincent was ordained in the Diocese of York and served his title at St Paul, Sculcoates, Hull. He then moved to the Caribbean and was eventually Archdeacon of St Vincent (appropriately) and St Lucia.

In the years just before the war, Hope Patten organised yet another group, the Chaplains of the Holy House. They were seen as an inner core of the Priest Associates and the obligation on members was to come into residence for at least four consecutive days each year and to officiate at the shrine. The first co-ordinator was Revd Patrick Lury of St Michael, Poplar, the son of Father Elton Lury. Hope Patten constantly complained in the newsletters about the strain on him and on Derrick Lingwood, and saw this as a means of relieving that. Although there is no doubt that they both worked hard, it may be that some of their readers became rather irritated by the constant references to the two priests requiring further assistance and time off; there were many parishes at that time, especially in the run-down inner cities, where the clergy were expected to work extraordinarily long hours without being able to take much by way of holiday.

The extension clearly raised public consciousness of the shrine and in the succeeding year Hope Patten recorded that there had been 32,000 pilgrims, which is not in fact a very great increase on earlier years. This success, and the fact that the extension had actually been constructed, spurred Hope Patten on to further schemes to widen the activities of the shrine, his vision being that Walsingham would become a spiritual powerhouse changing the whole of the Church of England from within through a range of institutions and initiatives.

Hope Patten was a gifted publicist, but his written output, apart from the newsletter, had tended to be of ephemeral pieces, although there were some short pamphlets and guides. In 1939, however, Revd Donald Hole wrote a much longer work on Walsingham, entitled *England's Nazareth*. After Hope Patten's death this book was updated and reissued several times, but it was then substantially reduced in content and was produced as a small paperback. The original 1939 version was also available in hard-back with a short but comprehensive account of the mediaeval pilgrimage and then what had occurred since 1921, but in addition it repeated the arguments which Hope Patten had set forward in relation to the place of the original Holy House. Donald Hole was a longstanding apologist for the Papalist position in the Anglican Church, and in 1942 he was to write an important tract actually entitled *Anglican Papalists*. He was the founder of the Actors' Church Union and at the time he wrote on Walsingham was chaplain to St James' House of Mercy in Fulham. His one drawback in Hope Patten's eyes was the fact that, as with a number who held similar views, he had married. He used the opportunity afforded by writing

England's Nazareth to press the cause of reunion with Rome, a chapter which was somewhat contentious and was omitted in the later reprints. There does not appear, however, to have been anything in the book with which Hope Patten would have disagreed, and it seems to have reflected closely his own views.

Hole does, however, provide one important piece of information which tends to show how far at that time the religious environment at Walsingham was removed even from that practised in most contemporary Anglo-Catholic parishes. He lists the relics in the shrine: not only were there those of the Holy Cross and of St Vincent, which have already been described, but also those of SS Andrew, Anthony of Padua, Benedict, Gregory the Great, Laurence, Louis King of France, Peter, Placida, Prosper, Ursula, Valentine and Victorinus. These had either been donated, or collected by Hope Patten on his continental holidays. The prominence given to veneration of such relics discouraged some from closer involvement with Walsingham.

One criticism that was sometimes made of the shrine at this time was that its adherents were insufficiently involved with charitable as opposed to pietistic matters. In 1928 a short illustrated *Review* of the years from 1921 had been published, which was intended to be the forerunner of more such publications but in fact turned out to be the only such. That recorded that a home for little boys had been opened under the patronage of St Hugh of Lincoln, who was described as 'a great servant of Our Lady' and to whom Hope Patten's devotion always remained undiminished. It was also said that this had been done under the auspices of the Holy Family Homes, which was a national organisation. It had grown from St Joseph's Home, established in Hinton Martel in 1903 by Father Alban Baverstock and a number of other such institutions were founded, mostly in the South of England: the largest was at Duxhurst, near Reigate in Surrey. Father Baverstock remained very involved with the homes and after resigning the living of Hinton Martel in 1930 he moved to Duxhurst to be priest director of the organisation. However, in 1932 there was a financial crisis and the parent organisation went into liquidation, although some individual affiliated homes continued to operate. It is not surprising, given the involvement of Father Baverstock, that Hope Patten was interested in this project, but it may be that the review was treating as done what was actually only a scheme, as it does not appear to have been mentioned or recorded elsewhere. Hope Patten's impatience sometimes led him to leap ahead of the facts in describing what was planned.

As with many of Hope Patten's projects, however, the establishment of a children's home was deferred rather than abandoned. In 1939 an opportunity arose to set up such a home in Walsingham, in somewhat unusual circumstances.

Revd Bernard Walke was a charismatic figure who, like Hope Patten, had succeeded in attracting to a country church an eclectic congregation which adopted wholeheartedly his uncompromising Anglo-Catholicism. He too was a signatory to the Centenary Manifesto of 1932, but unlike Hope Patten he was married and he was also a committed Socialist. He was particularly involved with the artistic community in Cornwall through his wife, Annie Fearon, after he became vicar of St Hilary, near Marazion, in 1913. Walke's ministry received attention nationally by the broadcasting by the BBC from 1926 onwards of *Nativity* and other plays written by him. Unfortunately, however, that very publicity attracted the Kensitites and they found a disgruntled villager who was prepared to bring proceedings against Walke in the Consistory Court. It is an interesting reflection on Hope Patten's success in Walsingham that the Protestant Societies were never able to attract any local support, even from Nonconformists in the village, perhaps because the vicar was respected even by those who did not share his ecclesiastical views and also no doubt because of the reluctance of Norfolk people to become involved with such outside organisations. Not only was Walke the subject of long-running litigation, in which he refused to participate on conscientious grounds, but on 9 August 1932 his church was wrecked internally by a group of protesters seeking to take direct action to enforce the orders of the Diocesan Chancellor. In May 1936 Walke had to resign the living because of ill-health, shortly after publishing his semi-autobiographical *Twenty Years at St Hilary*. He then retired to Mevagissey, where he died in June 1941. Shortly before his death he was received into the Roman Catholic Church.

Walke had founded an orphanage for boys and girls in a former public house in the village, known under its former name as The Jolly Tinners. In due course this was affiliated to the remaining Holy Family Homes. Once Walke resigned the living, however, the future of the home was not secure. There is no evidence that Walke and Hope Patten ever met, and in later years Walke rarely left Cornwall, but they had acquaintances in common, particularly Father Wason. However, Father Whitby did know and admire Walke and in January 1933 he had been to St Hilary to take services during one of Walke's absences through illness; he suffered from tuberculosis, which eventually killed him. It was Whitby who suggested to Hope Patten and the Guardians that the shrine might take on the home and this suggestion was readily accepted by Hope Patten and the others. Hope Patten, typically, saw it as a preliminary step towards a wider scheme with a network of such homes in various parts of the country.

In *Our Lady's Mirror*, spring 1939, Hope Patten announced the arrival in Walsingham of the children. He wrote:

> As we all know the church [at St Hilary] has suffered grave persecution and the impossible conditions of church life which have been introduced since the resignation of the last incumbent have made it out of the question for the children of the home to remain. We hope Walsingham will take them to its heart and that they will be real children of Our Lady. Two cottages have been bought for this home by Fr Walke's committee.

Initially there were five boys and six girls and as the cottages which had been acquired were not ready (and in fact never were occupied by the children), they were accommodated at first with a Miss Struggles[11] in the High Street. Their matron, Miss Treeby, came from Cornwall with them, and Hope Patten took on yet another position, as warden of the Home, with Derrick Lingwood as secretary. Once again, the burden of raising money for the feeding and clothing of the children fell on to the latter's shoulders. The St Hilary Home, as it was named, turned out to be one of the successful ancillary activities at Walsingham, although not without its early difficulties, as will be discussed later.

Although Hope Patten's attention was clearly being drawn away from the parish, he did arrange in 1939 for Revd Harry Howard of Goldthorpe, Yorkshire, to hold a mission in the village in the spring of 1939.

The long expected outbreak of war in Europe of course had very widespread effects on all facets of life in England. Walsingham was naturally not exempt from those disruptions, and the war years brought further problems for Hope Patten's visions and in some respects ended them.

---

11 She and a friend, Miss Cawdray, had recently come to Walsingham from the ultramontane church of St Thomas, Shepherd's Bush, and had intended to take in adult paying guests in their house, which was thus available at just the required time to house the children.

9

WALSINGHAM DURING THE WAR
YEARS, 1939–45

The Second World War halted any further development of the shrine itself for the time being, and in some ways the impetus for expansion was lost at that point and was never recovered during Hope Patten's lifetime.

Obviously there was no question of any extensive further building works being carried out during the war years, but, more significantly, pilgrimages effectively ceased for most of the war. It is interesting to see from reading contemporary accounts and records that in many respects church life continued amid the ravages of war and the destruction by bombing of so many churches: the campaign against the proposed united Church of South India, led by male religious of the Anglican communities, was vigorously promoted even while the great battles in Europe and elsewhere were being fought. Hope Patten was firmly behind that opposition, as might have been expected.

The very location of Walsingham, near the Norfolk coast and in an area where a plethora of RAF airfields were rapidly constructed, dictated that it was a restricted area and so for all practical purposes it was out of bounds for long periods during the conflict, although the Guardians were permitted to meet since they had business to transact in the village. In fact, the bans on travel were not continuous and there were several stretches of time during which Walsingham was accessible, but the very uncertainty made the organisation of pilgrimages very difficult and cancellations were often necessary even after a trip had been arranged. As the war drew to an end, the restrictions were gradually removed, although shortage of petrol remained an obstacle to travel by road.

The virtual cessation of pilgrimages had devastating effects so far as the income of the shrine was concerned, and put further pressure on the beleaguered shoulders of Derrick Lingwood. Hope Patten was extremely concerned that the shrine should continue to function in exactly the same way as before the war despite the absence of visitors from outside. He continued the Holy Hour which he had started during the Spanish Civil War, but now with the intentions of peace and of victory in the worldwide conflict. In addition, he held on occasions a Triduum of prayer, with daily an early low mass, a special mass in the Holy House, the rosary said one mystery at each altar, and benediction. Many who lived in the village joined in these services, not least because almost everybody had relatives in the services. Hope Patten was assiduous in that as in other respects in remembering the names of those who were away.

This war affected Hope Patten far more personally than had the 1914–18 conflict, which appears almost to have passed him by, because so many of the local boys, who had served at the altar and sung in the choir, had joined up. Later he was to regret that many of them, schooled in the somewhat idiosyncratic religious teaching with which he had imbued them, had found the Anglican services provided by the Army to be outside their experience all together. At the time he lamented the fact that they were no longer available to assist at services in the parish church. He was vociferous in his support of the Allied armies, and attributed successes in the field to the intercession of Our Lady. On the day after VE day he held a high mass of thanksgiving in the parish church.

Walsingham was the scene of a great deal of aerial activity during the war, both from attackers and defenders. In *Our Lady's Mirror* for spring/ summer 1947 Hope Patten looked back over the 25 years since the shrine had first been set up. He dealt with the threat from the German bombers in melodramatic terms:

Those dark and frightful nights, when almost without exception after the enemy aircraft started crossing our coast line they moaned over the Stiffkey Vale, constantly dropping bombs in places around the sanctuary. Every village was damaged by the enemy except Walsingham. By day they came over – hedge-hopping over the vicarage. Often and often, when the rosary was being said in the winter evening, the shrapnel would rattle on the roof and the Church rock like a ship at sea. But within the shrine there was always a wonderful peace and calm – Our Lady's Mantle was spread over it.

So far as the Guardians are concerned, they were able to meet only with difficulty, but did so. Father Lury died in 1940 and in the same year Father

Lester Pinchard replaced him, a logical appointment bearing in mind his close connections with the shrine. The following year another well-known London priest, Revd J. H. C. Twisaday, parish priest of All Saints, Notting Hill, from 1932 to 1961, was added to the College.

The informal Walsingham Clergy Fund which Fynes-Clinton had set up many years before had been able to supplement the stipend for Hope Patten and pay Lingwood: it raised about £200 per annum in the pre-war period, thus almost doubling the sum available for the priests, most of which was the product of an annual Christmas sale. Later this was being termed 'The Walsingham Fund' and had a council, still headed by Fynes-Clinton, and including Father Lury and Sir William Milner among the Guardians, together with others including Revd G. S. Dunbar, a well-known London Papalist priest, and L. Gray Fisher, the long-serving Secretary of the Catholic League.

During the war, the financial situation at Walsingham clearly deteriorated rapidly. The sales could no longer be organised and the outside interest in the work of the shrine had diminished by reason of the circumstances. A somewhat desperately worded appeal was issued, which was undated but certainly was in the war years and possibly in 1942. It was said to be from the Walsingham Clergy Fund and was signed by a number of the Guardians including Fynes-Clinton. It described an overdraft at the bank of £58 and a loan due of £43, with other debts owed to the indefatigable Miss Doyle-Smithe and another totalling £70. These seem very small sums compared with those which had been raised before the war, but the flier indicated that unless money was found urgently the two priests at Walsingham 'must resign'. That threat sounds entirely out of character for Hope Patten, and may have been received with some scepticism by its readers.

Also during the war, in June 1943, the Fund was reorganised and became known as the London Committee (later the Central Committee) for Walsingham. The chairman was Father Twisaday and other main participants included Revd W. G. de Lara Wilson, parish priest of St Peter, Acton Green, who, like Twisaday, is often referred to in contemporary accounts as being flamboyant in nature. In the years thereafter its main fundraising activity was an annual sale of work organised by Revd Ivan Whittaker, who later worked at Walsingham, and his wife.

In 1942 Bishop Pollock resigned from the see of Norwich and died relatively shortly thereafter. He was replaced by Bishop Percy Mark Herbert, who was translated from Blackburn and was a completely unknown quantity so far as Hope Patten was concerned. However, the cast of mind of Anglo-Catholics of Hope Patten's vintage was to be suspicious of the motives of bishops and so far as possible to manage without them unless, as O'Rorke had, they were prepared to co-operate almost unconditionally. Hope Patten wrote before Herbert's arrival that 'I fear that Catholics in this diocese are in for some stormy times',[1] a fear which was not in the event borne out. The new Bishop, however, made one immediate change of some symbolic importance: Derrick Lingwood had until this time simply been permitted to officiate in the Diocese of Norwich, but he licensed him as curate of the Walsinghams and Houghton, and the change was reflected in his entry in *Crockford*.

Under Bishop Pollock, Walsingham had effectively become extra-diocesan; he had eventually turned his back on the parishes and on Hope Patten.[2] Bishop Herbert took the view that that was not an appropriate policy and that he should visit the shrine to see for himself exactly what was happening, which Bishop Pollock had of course never done.

In early 1943 Bishop Herbert came to Walsingham, met the sisters, visited the shrine and stayed the night. He attended the 8 a.m. mass in the parish church the next morning, although no great encouragement was given to him to do so, perhaps because Hope Patten thought he might complain about the way in which the liturgy was presented. Certainly the vicar would not have been prepared to compromise at all in the way in which mass was said simply because the Bishop happened to be present. Hope Patten was publicly pleased and wrote in *Our Lady's Mirror* for spring 1943, after reporting the facts of the visit: 'This is the first time for over twenty-one years, that is during the present incumbency, that the Chief Pastor of this Diocese has attended a service of any kind in these parishes, and the first time since the sixteenth century he has visited the shrine.' The sentence quoted was characteristically hyperbolic: the first part was clearly accurate, but no Bishop of Norwich could have visited the shrine between 1538 and 1922 as there was nothing to visit between those years!

In private, Hope Patten was unconvinced of the sincerity of the Bishop, even though he was clearly far better disposed towards the whole

---

1 Letter of 7 May 1942 to Mother Dora CSPH (WA).
2 In the same letter Hope Patten wrote: 'he [Pollock] is ruled by his wife and pretends not to know of the shrine's existence.'

enterprise than had been his predecessor, and was ready to be constructive with advice when required. He was not asked back and did not ask himself back. It may be that that lack of trust by Hope Patten in his diocesan was not helped when the latter was asked by the former to consecrate the shrine. Hope Patten would have seen such a consecration as an endorsement of what he had effected during his ministry in Walsingham. The Bishop on this occasion saw the trap into which he might fall, writing to Hope Patten on 21 April 1944: '. . . I do not think I should find it possible to consecrate the shrine. It is obviously unsatisfactory to consecrate a place over which the Bishop has no control, as he could not in the case of a building which is private property, the owners of which would hardly wish to have its uses controlled by the Bishop.'

Even though no consecration took place, it was clear that the shrine was much more welcome, or perhaps less unwelcome, under the new regime than had been the case earlier.

On 8 December 1943 Hope Patten's mother Mary died at the age of 89. She was then living with her nieces, Ellen M. C. Sadler and Anne Oldfield, daughters of Revd William Sadler, at White Lodge, Northcourt, Abingdon, but died at Barton Court in the same town. Anne Oldfield was widowed by that time, but had been married to a priest. The cause of death on the certificate was cardiac failure, senility and bronchial catarrh. The impression given by the surviving documentary evidence is that, once he moved to Norfolk, Hope Patten had little time to spare for his family and that he had not a great deal to do with his mother as she grew older. It may well be too from the causes of death given that she had been unwell for some years before her death.

Mary Patten's will was dated 24 June 1936. It was drafted as if she was then living at Walsingham Vicarage, but had been witnessed by a solicitor's clerk and by Mrs Oldfield in Oxford, which suggests that by the time of signature she had moved permanently to Abingdon. Her testamentary dispositions were very straightforward, in that she left all her estate to her only son. A solicitor of the Hawks family from Hertford acted in the administration of the estate as had been the case with Mrs Patten's father-in-law's probate in the preceding century. The value of the estate was £2,500 odd, considerably more than had been left by her husband when he died almost 30 years before, and a substantial accrual to Hope Patten's means, which in due course when travel restrictions were lifted must have assisted him with his foreign holidays.

Another significant death at this time was that of Father Ventham of South Creake. A short-lived diary from the war years indicates that Hope Patten entertained Fathers Ventham and Moxon to tea on 21 March 1941, and Ventham also gave a vestment to the shrine at about that time. It does not appear that Hope Patten appreciated that his neighbour was an *episcopus vagans* until he refused his ministrations on his deathbed in 1944.

There was one relatively minor exception to the general statement that no expansion of the shrine itself took place during the war years. It was clearly impossible at that time to build a separate Orthodox chapel, as had been envisaged before the war, but, largely due to the efforts of Archimandrite Gibbes, a chapel was fitted out on the south side of the gallery of the shrine church, and in particular was provided with an icon screen and other requirements from about 1941 onwards. The chapel was blessed on Whit Sunday or Monday 1944 by Archbishop Savva of Grodno, who was a member of the small Polish Orthodox Church. For the next few years regular services were held there for prisoners and other refugees from Eastern Europe, and were usually conducted by Father Miodrag Najdanavic of the Serbian Orthodox Church.

The fact that no further building work could be carried out at Walsingham, even if the money had been available, meant that Hope Patten's still very considerable energy and creative impulses could be diverted into other enterprises. There were three different initiatives which commenced during the war, all of which led to very considerable long-term problems and in the case of the third to grave financial difficulties. These were: first, the attempt to take control of the sisters in Walsingham; second, the further attempt to establish the Augustinian College; and third, the renewed attempt to set up a school ancillary to the shrine. The story of the sisters and of the short life of the indigenous Community of Our Lady of Walsingham is too complicated to be dealt with here, and deserves a chapter of its own, which follows.

Before dealing with those new matters, it should be said that steady progress was made in relation to the children's home. It became clear fairly early on in the war years that Walsingham was to be a reception area for children evacuated from cities. Father Lingwood appreciated that the large Victorian vicarage would be used to house such children in any event, so it was decided to move the children from the St Hilary Home to part of the vicarage, with their matron, leaving the house in the High

Street free to accept evacuees. This arrangement did not last very long, as in 1944 a relatively modern property in Wells Road was acquired for the home and the children moved there. During the war years there was a rapid turnover in matrons and on occasion the villagers, and even at one time the two priests, had to assist.

The only problem with the children's home was that Hope Patten perceived it as a supply source for servers for the shrine. That meant that he was more interested in having boys in the home than girls, and by the end of the war, and against the objections of some of the Guardians, girls ceased to be accepted and only boys were admitted. Hope Patten's more spontaneous and kindly nature, which was largely hidden from the pilgrims, was shown to the children in the home and he was somewhat soft with them whereas he could be rigid in relation to the failings of others. It was also a symptom of his growing distance from village life that he no longer needed to recruit servers from among the villagers but could rely on those in the home. One of the boys at the home, Stanley Smith, arrived from Hoxton in 1941. He turned out to be of great assistance to Hope Patten in many respects; in due course he took over as Bursar and, after his mentor's death, was appointed a Guardian.

The Community of St Augustine (CSA) had continued to function in the limited respects set out earlier for some years, but there then appears to have been a hiatus, perhaps occasioned by Moses Harbottle having been called up for service with the RAF. Hope Patten also referred later to two other laybrothers having left for the services, and never returning. Although publicly Hope Patten continued to date the commencement of the College from the time of Derrick Lingwood's return to Walsingham after ordination, certainly in the later minutes he referred back to 'an earlier attempt to start the College', as if there had indeed been a gap.

In 1942, however, a serious attempt was made to relaunch the College and from then onwards its future occupied a central position in Hope Patten's thoughts. There is absolutely no doubt that, apart from his own fascination with monasticism, a fascination which went back very many years, he perceived the establishment of a College of priests serving the shrine as being another guarantee of its survival after his death. It is not easy to chart the life of the College over the next 16 years, despite the existence of the handwritten minutes of most of the Chapter meetings, because the rules were changed several times, and often amended in Hope Patten's almost illegible handwriting.

It is significant that Hope Patten had not fully absorbed the lessons which he had noted after the failure of the Aberdeen experiment in 1910–11. He never had any difficulty with the first problem he had identified then, namely having no definite leader: it was always clear that the College was under his personal direction. He also had an ideal in view, which was service to the shrine. He never really sorted out the basic question as to the nature of the Community, which veered from time to time between a loose association of those tending the shrine and a much more rigidly run order along more traditional lines. His greatest failure was not to heed the dilemma which he had clearly identified in Aberdeen of combining life within a religious community with parochial work. He never really thought through how the parish was to be run if both he and Derrick Lingwood were members of the College and had obligations in that regard which were time-consuming and onerous.

It also became clear as time went by that although in many respects Hope Patten was very acute in choosing and then encouraging men and women to assist with various activities in the parish and shrine, he was nothing like so gifted when it came to selecting those men who could form a community together. He was prepared to take many men in the hope that matters would turn out for the best, even when an objective observer would have warned him to be careful. Thus, a number of young men arrived in due course who were attracted by the more exotic flowerings of the Catholic faith which manifested themselves at Walsingham, and which were undoubtedly encouraged by Hope Patten, but found themselves unable to deal with the privations of quasi-monastic living and the strain of being in close proximity to the other members. The number who stayed only a very short time was quite high.

In 1947 Hope Patten wrote a long and learned article for *Our Lady's Mirror* which he had reprinted as a separate pamphlet under the title *On Colleges under the rule of S. Augustine B.C.D. in mediaeval times and a modern revival.* The essay described how in the Middle Ages there were in England many instances of groups of priests with laybrothers living together and saying mass and the offices in church. He went on: 'What would meet a great need in England today is churches staffed by Colleges of Priests living the common life in suitable surroundings which could form a religious, social and intellectual centre. Taking a small college quadrangle as a model with hall, library and common room, the right surroundings would be found.'

That extract shows Hope Patten's thinking on the College and is illuminated by the plans which he had devised at the time of the extension of the shrine in 1938 for accommodation for a college of priests.

There seems little doubt that Hope Patten's original plan was for a body which consisted only of priests, but fairly soon that was modified to encompass laybrothers; this development had the seeds of future difficulties within it, in that there was little defined scope for those who were not ordained in the running of the shrine. An undated set of rules was printed, which was clearly applicable to the ordained only and was almost certainly pre-war in origin. The order was then described as 'The College of Blessed Mary and S. Augustine, Walsingham'.

In 1942 Hope Patten wrote out in his own hand in a hardback notebook the rule which was to apply for the reorganised College, the name of which was very slightly modified so that 'Our Lady' replaced 'Blessed Mary'. In contrast to the complicated statutes which were by then in general use for the older-established communities, Hope Patten's initial basis for the re-established College was then little more than some rough jottings, which he had devised without outside advice. In January 1943 Father Frank Biggart CR is recorded as having made some suggestions to improve the rules, and in due course Hope Patten amended the handwritten copy in the notebook after the chapter agreed to his modifications.

As originally drafted, the rule was described as being that of St Augustine (of Hippo), adapted to the life of the College. Matins, chapter mass and evensong were to be said daily and in addition there was to be at least one half-hour's meditation each day. This is interesting, as one criticism sometimes made of Hope Patten was that he spent so little time in private prayer, while clearly being most punctilious and reverent in saying mass. The history of the CSA rule and the recollection of some who were members indicate strongly to the contrary, namely that he was rigorous about allotting time to be spent in private devotion and thought. In particular, he was very clear that save in the event of a matter of pressing importance, absolute silence should be kept in the sacristy and there was a notice to that effect below the clock; he prepared himself for mass with total concentration. It is also clear that, contrary to what has been written in the past, he did go into retreat on occasion as part of the life of the College.

One of the original provisions of the rules was that members must be in residence for at least ten months a year, and that midday and evening meals must be taken in common. The converse of the residence provision is the interesting aspect, since it enabled any member to be away for up to two months a year, which Hope Patten needed because of his recurrent health problems. It appears that he may have written that provision in for his own benefit; it was certainly very unusual in a community and his long absences were to be one of the main causes of the instability which plagued the College throughout its existence. It was also provided that there should be a holiday allowance of £6 per annum per member, and that there should be pocket money, originally fixed at 2s 6d per week but later at such sums as should be agreed. However, even then it was provided that there could be an augmentation of the holiday allowance to encompass personal gifts. This again was an unusual provision within the context and was to lead to problems later.

The rule so drafted ended with the defiant declaration: 'PRAISE BE TO JESUS AND MARY, NOW AND FOR EVER.'

The College as thus reconstituted consisted initially of Hope Patten, Lingwood, and Revd Derek White,[3] and as at the recommencement Hope Patten had no official title, although self-evidently he was the leader. The first chapter took place on 29 October 1942 in the sacristy of the shrine church, and this is referred to in the minutes as being the 'inaugural' meeting. At the meeting on 10 December 1942 it was noted that there was dissatisfaction that there was no Superior, and Hope Patten was elected to that post for 12 months retrospectively to the date of the first chapter meeting. Initially, Hope Patten and Lingwood had taken vows for six months, apparently as postulants, and Father White had been admitted for an initial three months' postulancy. On 29 January 1943, Moses Harbottle was admitted as an extern lay postulant of the College; he was still in the services, but was able to get to Walsingham from time to time. There is then a gap of several years in the surviving minutes, but it seems clear that Father White left at around that time,[4] and that on 4 March 1943 Hope Patten and Lingwood made their first six-monthly promises to observe the rule and customs of the College. It would also appear, from what is later written, that for a time up to July 1945 Anthony Turner was a

---

3 Arthur Derek White was priested in 1932 and had been curate of St Stephen, Clewer, from 1937. At some unspecified point at around this time another priest came, but only stayed for a week.

4 After leaving Walsingham he went over to Rome and died of tuberculosis in that city shortly thereafter.

lay member of the College, but then left to work in the School. At the end of the war, therefore, the College was still little more than a fledgling organisation, but then so had many successful religious communities been at an early stage in their development.

It was also characteristic that Hope Patten should establish a support group for the Community. The notebooks contain references and a list of members for a small group known as the 'Fellowship of the Servants of Our Lady and St Augustine', of which Hope Patten himself was of course the Superior and which dated from the reinauguration. That seems to have been largely a devotional group and a number of those in it progressed to try their vocation at the College. Their names were remembered on specific days of the week and there was an annual retreat for members. This group continued throughout the life of the College and typed newsletters were sent out at widely spaced intervals telling of what was occurring and asking for vocations.

In addition to the members of the CSA, Hope Patten encouraged the chaplains of the Holy House to participate more in the life and worship of the shrine, saying in the autumn 1944 edition of *Our Lady's Mirror* that at least one extra priest per week was required all through the year.

Hope Patten had never abandoned the idea that the shrine should have attached to it its own choir school. In his imagination he saw the shrine, which an objective observer at that time would undoubtedly have perceived as a marginal component of the Church of England, as taking its place with the great and well-established cathedrals of the country. The war years resulted in an opportunity arising for the development of such a school, an opportunity which was unfortunately not in the long term successful.

Quainton Hall School in Hindes Road, Harrow, was established under another name by Miss Agnes Elliott in 1897.[5] In 1901 Miss Elliott married John Eyden, a local builder and in 1903 they had a son, Montague John Eyden. In 1923 Montague Eyden (who was almost universally known by his pupils as 'Mont') began teaching at the school and during that decade its character changed. Whereas previously both girls and boys had been admitted, it transformed itself into a boys' preparatory school, feeding either the local grammar schools or public schools across the country.

---

5 Much assistance has been gained in relation to the school from the exhaustive history by Peter Milner: *Quainton Hall School: The First Hundred Years 1897–1996* (the School, 1997).

1. Hope Patten aged about 11 months, late 1886.

2. Hope Patten aged about 3, 1888–89.

3. Hope Patten at Christ's Hospital, aged 11, May 1897.

4. Hope Patten aged about 16, 1902.

5. Hope Patten aged 20, January 1906, in Brighton.

6. Alfred Patten, taken in the garden at Wilbury Villas, 1911.

7. Mary Patten, date uncertain but probably about 1911.

8. Hope Patten at Teddington, complete with biretta worn on the back of the head in accordance with the prevailing fashion.

9. A group at Lichfield Theological College, taken by Revd J. C. Spokes, 1911: Hope Patten on extreme right of picture.

10. The early years at Walsingham:
tea on the vicarage lawn.

11. The shrine of Our Lady
in the parish church. The
poor quality of the picture is
perhaps counterbalanced by
its historic significance: it was
taken on 6 July 1922, the day
the image was erected.

12. The second pilgrimage to Walsingham, May1923.

13. The church fete in the early years at Walsingham, August 1923.

14. A rare picture of Hope Patten (on left) in mufti: on holiday with Derrick Lingwood.

15. An early pilgrimage group outside the vicarage.

16. The shrine of Our Lady with banners adjacent, in St Mary. The original photo has written on the back by Hope Patten: 'With love and best wishes to Fr Wodehouse and Alec [Lawson] for Christmas from Derrick and AHP, 1929.'

17. The May Revels at Walsingham, about 1930.

18. Bishop O'Rorke blesses the bells for the new chapel, 10 October 1931.

19. The ministers at the mass on the translation, 15 October 1931. In the front are Father Leeds, Bishop O'Rorke and Father Hope Patten. Behind is Father F. H. Tatham, parish priest of Great and Little Ryburgh, near Fakenham.

20. The translation procession reaches the new shrine chapel.

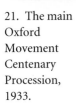

21. The main Oxford Movement Centenary Procession, 1933.

22. The afternoon procession for the 1933 Centenary celebrations is prepared. The enormously tall figure of Sr William Milner can be seen holding one pole of the canopy, and the guard of Scouts from the East End is in attendance.

23. The yard cottages (on the right) before their transformation in 1945 into the administrator's living quarters.

24. Hope Patten in his robes with his enormously tall CSA biretta, 1950s.

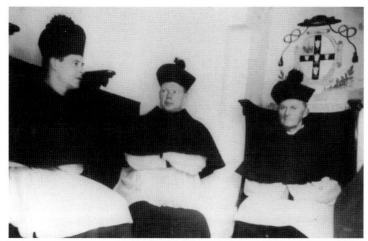

25. Three members of the CSA, Hope Patten on the right, Moses Harbottle centre.

26. Father Fynes-Clinton, in the van, leads a number of prominent devotees of the shrine: Enid Chadwick carries a banner, and on the far left is Mrs Payne-Jennings, with Mrs Ferrier following her next but one.

27. Father Roger Wodehouse with Father Fynes-Clinton on his right is followed by Father Hope Patten and then a youthful John Shepherd.

28. An archetypal Walsingham scene of the 1950s. The 21st anniversary of the translation was marked with a procession: the young John Shepherd leads his unsmiling mentor, flanked by the faithful Fathers Charles Bales (left of picture) and Michael Smith (right).

29. Hope Patten in an engagingly relaxed pose at the wedding reception of Stanley and Monica Smith, February 1958.

30. Hope Patten in his later years, in the sacristy.

31. Hope Patten at the high altar of the shrine church very shortly before his final collapse.

32. Hope Patten's funeral procession. Father Lingwood has Father Moses Harbottle on his left and John Shepherd, then still a deacon, on his right. The Guardians follow around the bier.

33. Father Hope Patten's gravestone in the parish church yard.

34. Niall Campbell, Duke of Argyll.

35. George Long, Hope Patten's faithful valet, in his Guardians' robes.

36. Father Francis Baverstock.

37. Father Reginald Kingdon, with his biretta at a rakish angle.

38. Sir William F.V.M. ('Derrick') Milner.

39. Bishop O'Rorke, pictured for once without a towering mitre.

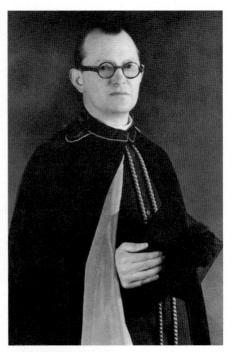

40. Father J. Lester Biddulph Pinchard.

41. Father Derrick Lingwood in his Guardians' robes.

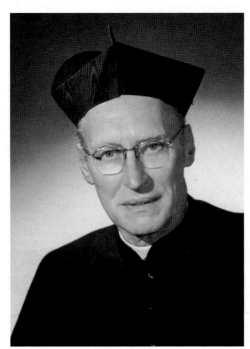

42. Father J.H.C. Twisaday.

43. Father Colin Stephenson at Oxford.   44. Revd Sir Percy Maryon-Wilson, Bart.

45. Father Edwin
H. W. Crusha,
who was to
witness Hope
Patten's death
certificate.

46. Father H. Elton Lury, the only married priest to be elected a Guardian during Hope Patten's lifetime.

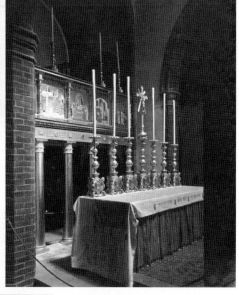

47. The high altar in the shrine church, a photograph commissioned by Hope Patten himself.

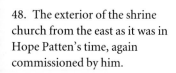

48. The exterior of the shrine church from the east as it was in Hope Patten's time, again commissioned by him.

Agnes Eyden came from a Low Church background but Montague Eyden was attracted by Anglo-Catholicism from an early age and in due course felt a strong vocation to the priesthood. He was ordained as deacon in 1932 and priest the following year and served until 1941 as a curate at St Mary, Somers Town, where he came into close contact with Father Maryon-Wilson, a Guardian of the shrine after 1935. Whether through that connection or otherwise, Father Eyden was himself attracted to Walsingham and got to know Hope Patten. He was a man of very considerable ability and enterprise; he was able for some years simultaneously to act as curate at Somers Town, to run the school and to be profoundly involved in Scouting at both places. He had a very strong belief in the virtues of the Scout Movement amounting almost to an obsession.

In 1935 Agnes Eyden died. Shortly after the war her son commissioned Martin Travers to decorate the Chapel of the Seven Sorrows in the garden at Walsingham in her memory. The artist produced a splendid representation of the Mater Dolorosa in place of a reredos in the small chapel, and also decorated the altar itself with a teardrop design on black. The work has recently been restored to its original glory.

On the outbreak of war, a minority of parents made it apparent that they favoured their boys being evacuated from the London area all together. Father Eyden wished to accommodate their wishes, and also to have available a refuge to which the whole school could in due course be moved if necessary. He therefore arranged to rent the vicarage at Long Marston, near Tring in Hertfordshire, to fulfil these purposes and asked Alfred Batts and his wife Winifred to become resident house parents at that address and also to take charge of the teaching of the boys who were there. Alfred Batts had been the organist at Somers Town and was a gifted musician with a particular talent for composition.

As time went by and the bombing in London diminished, it became apparent that not as much use was being made of the Long Marston annexe as had been anticipated, although there was a particular need for it from some boys whose families were abroad on war or other service. By the summer of 1943 there were only 16 pupils there, with all the teaching being done by the Batts.

As the war went on, Father Eyden became concerned for its future in the event of his own death, fears that were very similar to those which Hope Patten entertained for the shrine itself. He inaugurated discussions with Hope Patten and the Guardians with a view to the latter safeguarding the future of the school. This approach culminated in a draft agreement in August 1943 whereby the land and buildings would be transferred to an incorporated trust association in return for the payment of £8,000, and, importantly, that Father Eyden's own position as headmaster should be secured for at least 20 years. Hope Patten characteristically saw this as a first step towards a federation of schools connected to Walsingham which would have a strong Anglo-Catholic slant in their teaching.

Initially the draft was not made public, but in June 1944 a potential crisis occurred when it was learned that the vicarage at Long Marston was to be requisitioned. It was decided that the branch should move to Walsingham itself; Hope Patten thereby saw that through this transfer the shrine could at last acquire the choir school which he had wanted for so many years. This was his real interest in the matter.

The move from Long Marston to Walsingham took place on 9 and 10 June 1944. There remained 16 boys who all made the move.[6] The barn next to the shrine church, which in the pre-war period had been used as the pilgrims' refectory, was used for the next 12 months as the classroom, dining room and recreation area. The boys were initially boarded out around the village, with Michael Farrer and two or three others staying with the sisters in the hospice.

When the new term commenced in September 1944, a dormitory had been arranged in one of the houses on Knight Street, on the other side of the shrine church, and Alfred Batts had had time to practise with the boys; they sang their first mass as the choir of the shrine church on the feast of St Michael and All Angels, 29 September 1944. The sisters still cooked for the pupils at that stage. A pattern was then established in which on Sundays the boys attended the parish church as part of the ordinary congregation, since there was a separate choir there, but at the shrine church they sang at mass every Saturday morning and on any festivals which fell during the week, at benediction every Tuesday evening and at vespers of Our Lady and benediction on the day before any Marian festival. That year a number of boys from the locality joined the school and it appeared to be flourishing.

---

6 Fortunately one of them, Michael Farrer, now Secretary of the Anglo-Catholic History Society, has recorded his recollections of the school over this period, both in Milner's book (*Quainton Hall School*), in his own pamphlet *Alfred Hope Patten: His Place in the Catholic Revival* (ACHS, 2001) and in the appendix to Farrer and Young: *Faithful Cross.*

Hope Patten had always enjoyed the company of the young and, as has been seen with his early years as a priest, he was capable of relaxing in their company in a way which would have surprised those who thought of him only as unbending and humourless. At the end of the war demolition and rebuilding work began in the cottages on Knight Street, leaving ruins in which the boys played at soldiers in a recreation of that which had been happening all over Europe. They were surprised one day to see Hope Patten, attired as always in cassock, cloak and hat, suddenly emerge from one of the doorways making gun noises and pointing a stick to simulate a rifle.[7]

It had been agreed that as from June 1945 the ownership of both branches of the school should pass to the Guardians, but that thereafter the two should be separate; Father Eyden was clearly to remain in day-to-day control of the main school in Harrow, but was to have no more dealings with the Walsingham branch.

On 14 June 1945 Father Eyden wrote to all the parents with the information about what was occurring. An educational trust, Walsingham College (Affiliated Schools) Ltd had been formed in order to take over the two schools; the use of the plural in the title, signifying Hope Patten's view that this was only the start of something which would grow, was explained in the letter, which actually indicated that provision had been made for other schools to come within the aegis of the new company in due course.

The £8,000 was to be paid in four equal instalments over the 20-year period for which Father Eyden's position was guaranteed. He was also appointed as a governor of the school; Hope Patten was appointed Chairman of the Governors and all the others apart from Father Eyden were also Guardians. The founder governors were Fathers Fynes-Clinton, Maryon-Wilson and Lingwood with Sir William Milner and Sir John Best-Shaw, with the Duke of Argyll as President. The school had a proven track record of success under its previous management and it was clear from the outset that the governors did not intend to interfere in the day-to-day management. In the summer term magazine of Quainton Hall School, Hope Patten wrote a gracious letter of welcome to the parents and pupils. All seemed set fair in Harrow and was to remain so.

Beneath the surface, however, all was not well with the running of the new school in Norfolk even at that early stage. Alfred Batts, who had tech-

---

7 See Farrer in the appendix to Farrer and Young: *Faithful Cross*, p. 122.

nically been Father Eyden's deputy, appeared to be the obvious candidate to take the new venture forward. He had looked after the boys with exemplary care during the war and had supervised the removal to Walsingham. He was a committed Anglo-Catholic and a fine musician who had demonstrated that he was able to prepare the choir to participate in the shrine devotions as Hope Patten had expected. Regrettably, however, a dispute arose between Batts and Hope Patten which related to the music which the latter favoured; Batts, an acknowledged expert, looked down with disdain at Hope Patten's taste in baroque and rococo arrangements, while Hope Patten was angered by Batts having taught the choir a completely new repertoire while he was away. The result was that Mr and Mrs Batts left, although Alfred Batts was fortunate enough to obtain immediately a post at Berkhamsted School, not far from Long Marston. As with many other people, he did not fall out permanently with Hope Patten and came back to Walsingham in the early 1950s to run a summer school in plainchant.

At the first meeting of the governors of the new school, held at Father Fynes-Clinton's flat in Westminster on 22 June 1945, it was agreed after some discussion that the Walsingham establishment should be known as the Sanctuary School; it was under that title that it reopened in September 1945 as one more new venture in the very different world which followed after the struggles of the war years.

10

THE SISTERS IN WALSINGHAM, 1941–7

There is no doubt that Hope Patten had resented for some years the fact that the sisters in Walsingham did not owe their primary allegiance to the shrine and could be recalled or replaced at any time by the formidable Mother Sarah. Her Community of St Peter the Apostle, Westminster, which was the full name of the Laleham order, was in many ways a logical supporter of Hope Patten's work. The very full name of the sisterhood had been adopted in order to stress its continuity with a pre-Reformation community, a connection of which he must have fully approved. The establishment of the nuns at Laleham as recently as 1932 had marked a noticeable move towards a more Roman spirituality, which was accompanied by Baroque décor. The sisters worked in many parishes which also came on pilgrimage to Walsingham, such as St Mary, Bourne Street, St Mary, Kenton, and St Benedict, Ardwick, Manchester.

Mother Sarah had a personality rather similar in some ways to that of Hope Patten. Each attracted great devotion but each had detractors and those who were unable to see their charm. The handwritten correspondence between them, which survives in the Walsingham Archives, gives the reader an insight into why they each had such opposing effects on those with whom they came into contact.

By 1941, when the conflict between the two of them was about to develop, Sisters Marguerite and Grace Helen had been in Walsingham more or less continuously for many years. Hope Patten saw them as the nucleus of a new autonomous community which would be more directly under the control of the Guardians, or in practice under his own direction. They were both personally very devoted to him, and he acted as their confessor. Before the war there had normally been five or six sisters in Walsingham, but in 1940 Mother Sarah had reduced the number to three, including the two mentioned, because of the reduced workload attributable to the outbreak of hostilities. It may well be that Hope Patten resented that step and his note about it in *Our Lady's Mirror* for summer 1940 is somewhat tart in tone, although it is difficult to see that the extra numbers were needed during the war years.

The correspondence on this subject commences with a letter written by Hope Patten on 20 June 1941. He set out that the College of Guardians felt strongly that there should be a permanent community of sisters at Walsingham, and that that community should be from the Community of St Peter at Laleham. The stress in that opening paragraph was intended to be on the word 'permanent', as was made clear in the second, in which Hope Patten expressed the view that a new Mother or new chapter at Laleham might cause the withdrawal of sisters from Walsingham. His solution was to ask for 'this house to become a self-governing Community . . . with its own Mother, while at the same time it would be part of a Laleham, so to speak, congregation . . .' He went on to suggest that probationers wishing to enter the Walsingham house should commence their training there, then spend some time at Laleham, and finally be professed at Walsingham. He invited Mother Sarah to nominate the first Mother for Walsingham, after which the understanding would be that the sisters there would elect their own.

There was an ominous silence following this communication, and on 17 July 1941 Hope Patten followed it up, stressing the urgency of the situation as he saw it, not least because he then had in mind the simultaneous relaunching of the College of St Augustine.

These epistles resulted in an agreement to meet at Walsingham on 7 August 1941. A memorandum of what was agreed was prepared, presumably immediately afterwards, by Hope Patten, or more probably by Derrick Lingwood. It recorded that it had been agreed that there should be a permanent house at Walsingham under a prioress who was to be known as 'Mother Prioress', and to contain at least five sisters as a basis. For his part, Hope Patten committed the Guardians in principle to provide a suitable house in Walsingham for a priory.

On 4 September 1941 Mother Sarah wrote that following a meeting of her Council it had been suggested that the Guardians pass a formal resolution of their intent, but that as soon as that was done 'the details can be arranged and I will send the sisters'. It is not clear whether or not at this stage she had had the typed memorandum of what was agreed, but she certainly had had it by the time of her next letter, on 18 September 1941, as she refers expressly to it. That letter, however, still supports agreement to what was set out, although Mother Sarah was careful to make it clear that a priory would remain an essential part of the Community of St Peter and that the sisters would keep the same rule and wear the same habits.

The cordial tone continued into October 1941, and prior to a proposed visit by Hope Patten to Laleham, Mother Sarah sent back a signed response to the original request, in which she declared: 'I am willing to send a Sister in Charge to be called Mother Prioress and to send five or six sisters to try out with her the possibility of forming a permanent priory after the war, but our constitutions do not provide for this and it is not thought advisable to alter or add to them until then.' She went on to say that the sisters should have an external confessor appointed by the Abbot of Nashdom, Martin Collett, with whom, unlike his predecessor, Hope Patten was not on close terms. That letter was a cautious and sensible counter-proposal, but Hope Patten reacted badly to it, writing on 16 October 1941 that it was 'a bomb' and that it did not reflect what had been agreed before. His great wish was that the new arrangements come into force immediately, a wish which was a mark of his impatience with any project which he had in mind. He also reacted strongly to the inference that he should no longer act as confessor to the sisters. He indicated he was not willing to come to Laleham (where he was expected later that month) until basic agreement had been reached.

Although there are some gaps in the correspondence (and Hope Patten only kept drafts of his own letters), there was a meeting on 24 October 1941 at which he and Mother Sarah were able to come to an agreement, which he later sent to her for signature. The main terms were that there should be a permanent priory at Walsingham which was initially to consist of the two sisters already in the village together with Sister Helen, who was to be prioress. She was an elderly Laleham sister who had not worked at Walsingham before. The confessor for the sisters was to be appointed by the Abbot of Nashdom but was subject to the approval not only of the Reverend Mother at Laleham but also of the sisters concerned. Assurances were given as to the lack of need for financial support for the new priory and as to the intention of provision for a proper building for the sisters.

Once both parties had signed that concord, it looked as though the matter was settled. Hope Patten had a prearranged visit to Oxford at the end of October and combined that with going to Laleham, where the three sisters were blessed and commissioned for Walsingham on 1 November 1941.

It was not, however, to be so easy. In late 1941 an aspirant came to Walsingham and Mother Prioress Helen (as she was now known) wrote to Mother Sarah saying that she intended to receive the new recruit on 8 January 1942. Mother Sarah reacted strongly and Hope Patten wrote to her on 1 January 1942. The stress he felt can be seen not only by the fact he understandably misdated it 1941, but also that he drafted it at least twice. He sent a letter to be read to the chapter at Laleham and set out his clear impression that postulants would be accepted at the Priory at Walsingham if they presented themselves.

It was at this moment that the correspondence begins to become prickly. On 18 January 1942 Hope Patten wrote a strong letter to Mother Sarah and the sisters at Laleham asking for a clear statement as to their understanding of the status of the Priory, 'as it is evident that it is very different from that held all along by the sisters here and myself'. It is clear that, to put it neutrally, Hope Patten was not preventing discord between the sisters in Walsingham and Mother Sarah.

There was a long silence until Mother Sarah replied on 28 February 1942. Although there are conciliatory notes within the short letter, she indicated that she had had a letter signed by sisters Marguerite and Grace Helen 'asking for what really means an affiliated house, a completely different thing to a Priory'. She went on to say that there could be an affiliated house at Walsingham, but only if the Prioress agreed. Neither party was being entirely straightforward at this point. Hope Patten was inciting the two sisters he knew so well to something near rebellion by encouraging them to believe that they might be recalled from Walsingham. Mother Sarah, on the other hand, was saying she would accede to their demands if the Mother Prioress agreed, knowing that Sister Helen would not agree.

On 3 March 1942 Hope Patten replied, setting out what he regarded as a priory and as an affiliated house, and at the same time wrote to his second cousin in the Roman Catholic convent of St Scholastica at Teignmouth asking for her interpretation of the differences between the two. However, his letter to Laleham crossed with a letter of the same date from Mother Sarah in which she stated that, as a result of yet further letters which she had received from the long-serving Walsingham sisters, it was necessary to 'summon' them to the mother house for consultation. She went on to refer to the 'disastrous effect' on the sisters of the efforts being made at Walsingham to push forward with undue haste.

This provoked a letter from Hope Patten dated 6 March 1942 which began, with some considerable lack of tact: 'Your letter amazes me.' He went on to say that the sisters were not recallable as they were foundation members of the Walsingham Priory. He then continued in similar tone to his opening shot: 'The tactics of Laleham are truly amazing, they seem to be giving with one hand and taking back with the other.' He continued that the (that is, his) entire position would be given away if the sisters went to Laleham to meet the Council there. Hope Patten did not conceal in this communication his own support of the position being taken by the sisters in Walsingham, which was of course exactly what was behind that which was happening.

This letter was, within the context in which it was written, a declaration of hostilities. Worse, Hope Patten went on to say that if the two sisters did return there was a 'danger that the members may demand that they be submitted to [sic] the indignities concerning which the late and the present Bishop of London have knowledge – until they did agree'. Bishops Winnington-Ingram and Fisher had been and were respectively the Episcopal Visitors of the Community;[1] the oblique references to indignities can only refer to the fact that there had been a scandal, which was known in the circles in which Hope Patten moved, concerning the infliction on some sisters by Mother Sarah of corporal punishment, when she was at Horbury. It was not therefore a letter looking for a negotiated peace.

In any event, it would appear that the next letter in the sequence, from Mother Sarah on behalf of her Council, dated 7 March 1942, was written before receipt of Hope Patten's letter of the previous day. She made it clear that she would not agree to Walsingham being an affiliated house and that a priory would not have its own noviciate. She said, 'Our period of training extends over four and a half years at least; the meaning of the agreement you and I signed in October last is that of this period . . . two periods of six months should be spent at Walsingham by those sisters who are destined for the Walsingham house.' This was quite baldly stated, but she went on:

The fact that you announced in *Our Lady's Mirror* that the Walsingham

---

1 Laleham was in Middlesex until that county was absorbed by Greater London, when it was transferred to Surrey. Hence it was within the Diocese of London.

Priory would have its own noviciate is entirely the outcome of what we take to be your own misunderstanding of the agreement. What you and the sisters seem now to desire was never within the range of our thought as a present possibility, nor is it implied in the agreement. It may indicate a line of future development, but this may depend upon the experience and knowledge gained during this experimental period . . . We shall be grateful if any suggestion you have be made directly by you to me, and not discussed by you with the sisters of the Walsingham House, either individually or corporately. Such an action can have nothing but a harmful effect upon the sisters there.

This was not a suing for peace either: the use of the term 'House' rather than 'Priory' was a deliberate snub. She was of course correct about the announcement, which was in *Our Lady's Mirror*, autumn 1941.

Hope Patten wrote again on 9 March 1942 saying that the Abbess of his cousin's Benedictine house had assured him that a priory would have its own noviciate. His cousin, Mother Mary Scholastica Rayment, did not reply herself: she was by this time very old, and she died the following year.[2] Hope Patten then turned the argument on its head, asserting with the benefit of this information that a Priory would have more independence than an affiliated house.

The situation had been further complicated by this time because Sister Helen had returned to Laleham. It is not clear whether or not Hope Patten effectively forced her out, but he said in this letter that she could not do the work of a Mother and that the other sisters could not look after her because of all their other duties; she was said to be virtually blind.

Yet again, the letters crossed. Mother Sarah's letter of 9 March 1942 made the obvious point that the two of them had very different ideas on the status of a priory. She went on: 'We had not the slightest intention of granting the Walsingham Priory the measure of independence which seems to be the characteristic of your idea of a Priory.' She did, however, conclude by making three mutually exclusive suggestions for a way forward. Hope Patten thought these were important enough to copy out in his own hand separately, presumably in order to show the draft to the

---

2 She died on 19 November 1943. The entry in the books of the convent on her death reads: 'Her devotion to Our Lady was very great. In later years she showed particular interest in the Shrine of Our Lady of Walsingham as its Anglican custodian, Rev. Hope Patten, was a relation of hers.' I am grateful to Dom Geoffrey Scott OSB of Douai Abbey for assistance in relation to Agnes Rayment.

sisters at Walsingham. The three choices presented were: (1) the cancellation of the agreement and reversion to the status quo ante; (2) the recall of all the sisters from Walsingham, leaving Hope Patten to move forward as he saw fit; (3) the release of Sisters Marguerite and Grace Helen, if they so wished, from membership of the Community of St Peter for the purpose of founding a separate community at Walsingham.

The barbs continued. Mother Sarah stated clearly that Hope Patten had 'not any *religious* authority over the sisters' and to emphasize the point she told him she had summoned them to Laleham for consultation.

Hope Patten replied on 16 March 1942 that they had been keeping a Triduum about the issue and that the sisters would write to her themselves with their choice from what he called 'the three alternatives' (*sic*). The next day, however, he wrote himself saying that (1) was impossible since the Priory had been blessed and started and the ceremony of 1 November 1941 'either means *something* or it was a farce', that (2) was unacceptable since the sisters could not be recalled now that they were members of the Priory, and that (3) was a matter entirely for the sisters.

On 21 March 1942 Mother Sarah wrote yet again, saying that (1) was her proposed option and reiterating her previous view that Hope Patten had no religious authority over the sisters. Part of that letter is missing, but it appears from a summary that Hope Patten made later that the point was made that the sisters could only be released after an appeal to her and sanction by the Visitor.

Hope Patten's next letter, on 14 April 1942, is also missing from the file, but in it he said that the sisters were sending a formal request to be released.

By this time, Hope Patten had cast his net to see if the three sisters could be affiliated to any other Community, since looked at objectively there were not sufficient to form the nucleus of a new order; Sister Benedicta had joined the other two since the dispute had begun. He appears to have written to Fynes-Clinton raising the possibility of the Community of Our Lady of Victory, one of his many foundations, taking over the work at Walsingham. Fynes-Clinton wrote back on 20 March 1942 and was very happy with the concept of a move by them to Walsingham, but the reality was that that order was very small; it only had two members, and they were established in a small house in the grounds of the Sisters of the Poor at Edgware. The body had always been very small, and Mother Mary St John Watson was in poor health (although she lived for many years thereafter).

Fynes-Clinton's purpose in founding the order in 1915 was that they follow the rule and ideals of the former Order of Canonesses Regular of the Holy Sepulchre, with a life centred around the Divine Office from the Brevarium Romanum and the offering of intercession for the restoration of the Holy Places of Palestine to Christian Sovereignty. The idea of involving the Community of Our Lady of Victory led nowhere and appears only to have involved this exchange of letters.

The other approach which Hope Patten made was to the Community of St Peter at Horbury, a communication which could have been purposely designed to further antagonise Mother Sarah, bearing in mind the feelings she had towards those who had refused to follow her new initiative in 1932. In his letter to her of 14 April 1942 he also said that a request to return to affiliation to the Horbury foundation had been sympathetically received, as indeed it had since he had received a letter dated 11 April 1942 from Mother Dora to that effect, inviting him and the sisters to Horbury on 20 April 1942. Mother Dora wrote to him again, also on 14 April 1942, saying that she fully understood what the Walsingham sisters were going through as she had had a similar experience herself (meaning of course Mother Sarah's conduct at the time of the division).

The following day Hope Patten drafted a letter to the Visitor of the Community of St Peter, Geoffrey Fisher, a man who exemplified all the aspects of the Church of England which Hope Patten most disliked. Fisher had effortlessly moved to the episcopate from public school headmastership, omitting any pastoral experience. He was a narrow-minded bully who disliked and misunderstood Anglo-Catholics and in addition was a keen Freemason, which was another reason for Hope Patten to distrust him. However, in asking him for the sisters' release from Laleham to join Horbury, Hope Patten was duly deferential. He then had second thoughts, did not despatch the letter, and wrote instead to Laleham, asking whether the matter could not be settled without rancour.

Mother Sarah wrote again, on 29 April 1942, although this is missing from the file, but Hope Patten's answer to that letter finally indicated that there could not be any satisfactory arrangement with Laleham as too much water had flowed under the bridge. By her next letter, written on 15 May 1942, Mother Sarah accepted the inevitable truth that her Community could no longer work at Walsingham, and four days later she came to Norfolk to see the sisters. It is apparent from the next letter in this sequence, sent by Hope Patten late on 19 May 1942, that she deliberately snubbed him on this occasion by leaving the village without even speaking to him, while he waited for her at his desk. She never visited the shrine again, although the ill feeling between them dissipated itself somewhat as years went by.

The meeting with the sisters at Walsingham was clearly very difficult. Mother Sarah was as ill-equipped psychologically to deal with what she regarded as desertion as was Hope Patten. She had already written a letter to one of the sisters, on 29 April 1942, which began 'My dear Child'. It continued to demand a meeting and threatened that refusal would lay the recipient open to dismissal, emphasising that she was 'your Religious Superior responsible to GOD for your soul'. That set the tone for the visit to Walsingham, of which a note taken by Sister Marguerite and signed by the other two nuns records that the Reverend Mother said that they were very much in the wrong and had been stubborn, self-willed, obstinate, impatient, grasping and insistent on having their own way. Each side then accused each other of not telling the truth about what had occurred, although perhaps less directly than to use the word 'lies', the main point of dispute being the question of whether it had ever been agreed that there should be a novitiate at Walsingham. Then Mother Sarah is recorded as saying, 'None of this trouble is my fault. I wish you to know that it is entirely your doing if you are released from Laleham and the Community closes down the work here.' It would appear that much of the meeting was one-sided invective.

There could, however, be no doubt in the minds of any of the dramatis personae that after that meeting the Laleham Community was no longer to have any connection with Walsingham. It was a very unfortunate end to a long association. Neither party comes out of what occurred very well: Hope Patten was acting with great urgency to deal with a problem which only existed in theory, namely the desire of some future Mother to withdraw sisters from Walsingham. He did not clearly set out his real objective, which was to have a convent under his own control in the village. On the other hand, there seems little doubt that Mother Sarah went back on what she first agreed.

In the midst of the dispute, Father Alban Baverstock wrote to Hope Patten on 4 May 1942. He had just had lunch with Father Basil Joblin, the chaplain at Laleham, and recounted that he had told him that Mother Sarah was prone to forget what she had arranged. That is a convenient explanation for what occurred, but unconvincing in the light of all that had been written down. It is far more plausible to conclude that Mother Sarah was provoked by what she saw as the disloyalty of Sisters Marguerite and Grace Helen.

The episode did Hope Patten no good in the eyes of those who were devotees of Mother Sarah, who included Abbot Collett of Nashdom. Hope Patten gained the reputation among some who would otherwise have supported him of being devious and untrustworthy, which is unfair, although difficult and autocratic might not be. However, it may be that his critics did not know that some years later, on 27 October 1947, he wrote a letter of profound and unequivocal apology to Laleham, in which he referred to his 'very ungrateful and unkind actions at the time'. That missive is a salutary corrective to some perceptions of Hope Patten as being a man who always thought that he was in the right, and must have been a difficult one to send.

Once the visit to Walsingham had taken place, the field was entirely free for Hope Patten to continue his negotiations with the Horbury sisters, which had of course already started. He visited them as invited, and met there the Warden, Father R. L. Wrathall, from the nearby Community of the Resurrection. On 21 April 1942 a discussion took place at Horbury on their statutes on affiliated houses. While Mother Sarah's letters had been acidic, Mother Dora's verged on the glutinous. She saw her own Community's Visitor, Bishop Mouncey of Wakefield, who was very sympathetic; however, at this point she suggested that the Bishop of Norwich had better be involved. Pollock was in fact about to retire, and in any event had had no dealings with the sisters at Walsingham in any respect. He asked that nothing be done until his successor was appointed; Mother Dora suggested that in any interim period the sisters be members of her Community and Walsingham be treated as a mission house. This was not an acceptable solution to Hope Patten, who was extremely anxious to establish the proposition that there was, and had been since 1941, an established priory in Walsingham.

Hope Patten then wrote on 5 May 1942 to Fisher and the following day sent him a précis of the correspondence which had been passing. After the meeting at Walsingham, Hope Patten retold the story of what had occurred there to Mother Dora, who was duly sympathetic and suggested that the spiritual life of the sisters required their immediate release from Laleham. She was particularly scathing on the subject of Mother Sarah, going so far as to say that the Devil had got hold of her. In response, Hope

Patten wrote again to Fisher, who replied very expeditiously on 26 May 1942, which was after all only a week after the difficult meeting at Walsingham. Fisher said that his opinion was that release was the only option, but he could take no steps until the chapter at Laleham had ruled upon the application by the sisters.

The chapter was not to meet for some weeks, and the original date was then postponed. In the meantime, Mother Dora was very worried about Sister Grace Helen, whom she described as 'partly Irish and very highly strung'.[3] She was writing very frequently to Hope Patten at this time, and he replied although his own letters are not in the file. The generally friendly nature of the correspondence was disturbed by Mother Dora's letter of 16 June 1942, saying that a suggestion by Hope Patten for a separate title for the Priory at Walsingham would not be acceptable at all. She said, 'the minimum basis for affiliation must be similarity of *Title, Rule and Habit*'.

On 24 June 1942, however, Fisher was finally able to write to Sister Marguerite saying that he had heard from the Abbot of Nashdom that the Laleham Chapter had granted release to all three sisters, and that he had ratified that decision. Fisher was, for all his faults, an able administrator who dealt with this matter efficiently. At about the same time Mother Dora came to Walsingham, and was very impressed by the shrine.

Following that visit, on 20 July 1942 the chapter at Horbury amended their statutes in relation to affiliated houses, as had been agreed in April, and accepted the Priory at Walsingham as such a house. The amended statute provided that an affiliated house should elect its own Mother, Visitor and chaplain and could also establish its own noviciate. All seemed well again.

Yet again, however, the tranquillity did not last. In late August 1942 Sister Grace Helen was met at Peterborough railway station by Mother Dora en route to Horbury. On the platform she 'burst forth that she felt her soul was lost' and had to be comforted.[4] The Reverend Mother was surprised to find that the sisters at Walsingham had had no spiritual reading or mental prayer time for some years and had, she thought, insufficient foundation in faith as a result. She asked Hope Patten to come urgently to Horbury, and also wished to discuss Sister Benedicta, whom she described as being in an 'unsettled and unsatisfactory state'.

---

3 Letter of 29 May 1942 (WA).
4 Letter of 26 August 1942 from Mother Dora (WA).

Hope Patten did go to Horbury, only to find that by the time he arrived Sister Grace Helen had left and returned to Laleham. It may be that all the others involved had underestimated the effect on her of what had occurred in the previous two years. It is perhaps significant that in *Our Lady's Mirror*, autumn 1942, Hope Patten announced that he had been ill for two months and was convalescing. As always, the strain on him had resulted in physical symptoms.

There is a gap in the archive correspondence after that episode, and *Our Lady's Mirror* is very quiet about the sisters for the next two years. It appears that at some point the Horbury Community withdrew from the scene. The result of Sister Grace Helen leaving Walsingham was that there were only two professed sisters left in Walsingham, Sisters Marguerite and Benedicta, although by the autumn of 1943 four novices had arrived.

One of the consequences of what had transpired was that, when he had had a chance for reflection, Hope Patten appreciated that he had the opportunity to set up an entirely new foundation under his suzerainty. The new Bishop of Norwich was approached for assistance, and he, sensibly, suggested obtaining advice from Father W. B. O'Brien, the superior of the Society of St John the Evangelist in Oxford and Father Lucius Cary, a senior member of that Society who was instrumental in assistance with other such problems at the time. Hope Patten went to Oxford and met the two monks, and explained the background to what had occurred. A memorandum prepared at that time records: 'As a result of this preliminary exploration of the situation it was agreed that the best hope for the future lay in the formation of a new community having as its nucleus the two sisters resident at Walsingham who had recently been released for this or a similar purpose.'

A meeting took place at Norwich on 3 September 1943 between Bishop Herbert, Fathers O'Brien and Cary, Hope Patten and the two sisters, at which agreement was reached that the best way forward lay in asking one of the established communities to take novices in twos for a period of time, so that training could take place and their vocations be tested. It was also agreed that the developments should be supervised by a priest who was also a religious, or in other words someone experienced who would counterbalance Hope Patten's influence on the sisters. On 17 September 1943 Father Cary wrote to Father Raymond Raynes, the superior of the Community of the Resurrection, asking him to take on this commitment. He wisely said in that letter that the new order should 'be built up with such care and circumspection as may be available, in order to avoid a fiasco later on'. The letter also contains coded references to the need for external spiritual direction of the sisters, or in other words the situation in which Hope Patten was solely responsible for them was to be avoided.

Raynes agreed to take on this commitment and went to Walsingham on 30 November 1943. He then wrote to the Bishop on 10 December 1943 asking for his approval and saying that he had approached the Community of St Mary the Virgin at Wantage to ask whether they would undertake the task of training the novices. The Bishop wrote back six days later saying that Father Raynes' involvement gave him 'the greatest sense of confidence'.

On the same day that the Bishop wrote to Raynes, Hope Patten did likewise. It was a sign of what was to come: Sister Benedicta had complained to him that Mother Marguerite (as she had become) was telling the Community that 'Father Hope Patten has nothing to do with the Community now, and only has anything to do with the sisters who actually work in the shrine or church'. He said that the change in title from Sister to Mother had affected Marguerite badly and the village was complaining. The letter contains a plea that the Community should be of a type acceptable to the Guardians, and that he was the representative of the Guardians. Hope Patten's letter also said that two novices were about to go to Wantage.

It seems to have been in early 1944, shortly after that letter was written, that Mother Marguerite decided, even after all the years that she had spent at Walsingham, that her vocation was as a contemplative, and she transferred her allegiance to the Community of the Salutation of St Mary the Virgin, then at Cuddesdon, which had been founded only in 1941. That meant that of the three sisters who had been released for Walsingham by the Community of St Peter, two had since left the village. The only remaining professed nun was Sister Benedicta, who was temperamentally quite unsuited to be in charge of the house. Apart from her own personality problems, which involved rapid and unpredictable mood changes, it was very unfair on novices to try to stabilise themselves in the religious life when they had the distractions of the work of the shrine and little assistance from outside except that provided by Father Raynes, who was extremely conscientious but not of course near at hand.

On 9 March 1944 Raynes wrote to the Community that he thought all the novices should go to Wantage as soon as possible, and he repeated that in a letter to Hope Patten written on 18 March 1944. At about this time Wantage had sent one sister to Walsingham, Sister Marie Therese, who turned out to be a trial to everyone and to combine an alleged vocation to a solitary life with a tendency to complain about everybody and everything. The Reverend Mother at Wantage was asked to detach one of her number to become the Mother of the new order, but said she had no one suitable, and in any case the ethos of her community was very different. She then offered to intercede with Mother Sarah to see if she would provide a Mother from Laleham, which was not a very welcome suggestion to Hope Patten.

On 13 April 1944 Raynes came to Cambridge, where he met the executive committee of the Guardians and discussed the thorny question of the relationship between the new order and the shrine. The eventual conclusion was that an external religious should be warden, but that the administrator should be sub-warden and should have authority over matters connected with the shrine. The full constitution does not appear to have survived, but the rule of life has and is much fuller than that set out by Hope Patten for the Community of St Augustine (CSA), no doubt because it was drafted principally by those at Mirfield with knowledge of such matters.

On 29 June 1944 Fathers Raynes and Wrathall came from Mirfield to Walsingham to profess the sisters. Raymond Raynes suggested to Hope Patten in a letter of 15 June 1944 that the occasion be kept as quiet as possible, as he thought 'at this juncture we must move quietly and discreetly'.

Over the next period of time, there were difficulties with individual sisters, and Hope Patten continued to insist that the title 'Priory' be used, but in fact a number of novices arrived. Hope Patten had encouraged local girls to enter the novitiate, including Joy Long, daughter of George Long, who after leaving the Community later cooked for the CSA. However, they were allowed an afternoon off each week and it was said that some surprise was occasioned to visitors when they saw another local novice, in her habit, wheeling a much younger sibling around the village in a pram.

The vicar was, as always, looking for ways of adding to the influence of Walsingham and he devised rules for a group of tertiaries, but it is not clear that it ever came into operation.

Sister Marie Therese was still causing problems, although she had made a temporary profession at Walsingham, and on 26 January 1946 Hope Patten wrote to Revd Patrick Shaw, parish priest of All Saints, York, since

1904 and a well-known Anglo-Catholic, asking if his anchor hold cell in the church was free for her; he was told that it was already well occupied.[5]

In April 1946 the little Community had grown to 11, including novices, of whom it appears that a number had made annual vows. However, during the remainder of that year the order began to disintegrate. Two sisters did not renew their vows for health reasons, one did not do so for undefined reasons, and one (Sister Marie Therese) was asked not to do so by Father Raynes as he considered her unsuitable for Walsingham, which seems to have been the general view: she then went to the Servants of Christ at Burnham, Buckinghamshire. By the end of 1946 there remained only Sister Benedicta, five novices and one postulant, who eventually moved to South Africa, again at Father Raynes' suggestion.[6]

Hope Patten wrote shortly afterwards[7] that he had been unable to get to the root of the trouble all through 1946, but that eventually it was clear that the Superior (Benedicta) was the problem, as she was too temperamental and unstable. By the end of the year Benedicta was also ill, and went to live in East Dereham for a time with her family.

Father Raynes had a very great deal of experience of the religious life and he appreciated that a community which consisted of one very difficult and insecure professed sister with a number of novices was not likely to succeed. He coupled that perception with a high regard for the shrine and an understanding of Hope Patten's strengths and weaknesses. His solution was to appeal for help to the only other order for women in East Anglia, the Community of All Hallows at Ditchingham in southeast Norfolk. He therefore went with Sister Benedicta to Ditchingham and there met the Reverend Mother, who made some preliminary suggestions with a view to assisting.

The Mother Superior of Ditchingham came to Walsingham on 27 and 28 January 1947, and offered to take the novices. This precipitated a crisis. Hope Patten was pleased that an offer of help was being made, even if it might mean a loss of status for the Community and dashed off a long letter to Mirfield on 31 January 1947. One of the novices, Sister Mary Dorothea, was prepared to stay and help Sister Benedicta. The three other

---

5 Father Wason often stayed there.

6 The situation is summarised retrospectively in a letter from Raynes to the Bishop dated 29 March 1947 (WA).

7 The letter is addressed only to 'My dear Father' (probably Fynes-Clinton) and is dated 15 April 1947 (WA).

novices who were still there all said they could not remain with her, although one said she would stay on a short-term basis. One of the underlying problems was that Sister Benedicta had a form of schoolgirl crush for Derrick Lingwood, which did not make for easy relations, and Hope Patten had perceived that, referring to the fact that 'the infatuation . . . which *she* has for Fr. D. is known to all the sisters and is a cause of a lot of the trouble in the house'.

On 1 February 1947 Sister Benedicta wrote to Raynes to say that she thought it had been agreed that one of the Walsingham novices would be professed to help her, that the others would go to Ditchingham and that sisters from All Hallows would come over to visit. However, she had been told after the meeting that the others wanted to go elsewhere and would not go to Ditchingham. The letter continues: '. . . may I remind you that you gave me your word that you would stand by me through this difficult time. That you would not allow us to be absorbed by another Community, or made a branch house of it. We should be given the opportunity to build up the Community with the help of a well established Community, and be allowed to keep our own rule, constitution and customs.'

Raynes was beginning to be exasperated. He wrote back to Benedicta on 4 February 1947 saying that he thought that the novices were being ungrateful and self-willed and that what was being offered from All Hallows was sensible and generous. He talked of resigning and this precipitated a telegram from Hope Patten to Mirfield on 6 February 1947 saying that he was 'seeing a way out'. However, Raynes had had enough. He wrote to Hope Patten on 7 February 1947 that the proposals from All Hallows had not been received with appropriate appreciation and that he was not prepared to approach any other Community for assistance, since Horbury, Wantage and now Ditchingham had all been involved. He resigned saying, 'It is clear that I cannot carry on when everything I suggest or advise is rejected. I do not write in any pique and shall always maintain my love for Walsingham and my affection (and I hope friendship) for your own self.'

Hope Patten's rescue plan was that a full circle be turned so that Walsingham became a branch house of Ditchingham. The problem with that was that Reverend Mother Flora of All Hallows was insisting that the hospice be closed for the summer so that proper training of all those concerned could take place out of the public eye. Hope Patten thought that was 'just impossible' because it was of course the Jubilee of the shrine and they had pilgrimages booked every weekend. He was extremely anxious that the atmosphere of the Walsingham pilgrimages should not be adversely affected by the removal, whether or not temporary, of sisters from the hospice. However, the reality was that the Community had been reduced to Sisters Benedicta and Mary Dorothea with Sister Monica Mary only possibly staying.

On 15 February 1947 Mother Flora wrote that it was quite impossible for her Community to keep the hospice open for the summer, and an advertisement should be placed for persons not under rule to run it. A week later she wrote to Father Raynes following yet another meeting with Hope Patten. In her letter of 22 February 1947 she suggested that her community would take over the hospice as a branch house, but would not carry out the catering for the pilgrims and that in the meantime Sister Benedicta would be left at Walsingham.

Her letter was very clear: 'Sister Benedicta is the obstacle, she is quite determined to go on at Walsingham, although all the novices feel they cannot continue, as they have had no training in the religious life. She is quite clearly against this community ... In my opinion the present state of things should be brought to an end before a scandal happens. The reputation of the religious life has suffered considerably.' Hope Patten was caught in the crossfire between a number of strong-minded women. He approached Mother Dora of Horbury again, and she replied on 1 March 1947 that her community could not take over the work at Walsingham because of lack of sisters.

Hope Patten had roused a hornet's nest by his conduct over the sisters. He should never have interfered with the position as it was before his first letter in 1941; the question of a withdrawal from Walsingham was only a theoretical problem which did not require addressing. The establishment of the Community of Our Lady of Walsingham (COLW) was a disaster for almost everyone involved, and as Mother Flora commented openly and other people muttered, it did the religious life in the Church of England no good at all. Hope Patten's problem was that he was so devoted himself to the concept of the shrine and the promotion of all its ancillary works, that he could not see why everyone else was not as committed, and, more so, that they could not solve problems such as running a Community by such commitment. To be fair to him, he acknowledged as much, writing to Father Raynes on 14 March 1947 that 'I cannot but feel as the years go on that if Laleham and we at this end had gone about things in a different way it need never have happened.'

He was then left in March 1947 with a situation in which it looked as though there would be no sisters at Walsingham to look after the pilgrims, save possibly Sister Benedicta, and it was quite clear by then that so long as she was there no others would be prepared to work with her on anything but a temporary basis. Sister Monica Mary agreed to go to Ditchingham, and Sister Dorothea Mary was uncertain about how the future lay: she initially went to the Community of the Blessed Virgin Mary at Rottingdean for further thought.

It was at this point, however, that Hope Patten was rescued. One of the best-known stories about him concerns what happened next: he put it about that he had been told to go to the Priory of St Saviour in Haggerston, part of the Society of St Margaret (SSM), after hearing a voice repeating to him the name of the legendary Mother Kate of that community, the implication being that guidance from above was being given to his application for sisters, and that he jumped into a taxi and asked to go the Priory instead of returning to the railway station.

This story has been repeated and elaborated many times, but the truth is more prosaic, as it often is with Hope Patten.

The Guardians had an inner executive committee which met more frequently than the full College. On this occasion in early March 1947 Hope Patten had gone to London for a meeting of the committee, one of the members of which was the wise and experienced East End priest Father Reginald Kingdon. During discussion about the sisters, which was clearly the pressing topic of the moment, it was Father Kingdon who suggested that an approach be made to Haggerston, which was not far from his own parish.[8]

It was in those circumstances, and as a result of that advice, that Hope Patten went to Haggerston to put his request before the Reverend Mother. He knew that time was very short, as the pilgrimage season was to start at Easter, and it does appear that he went in person and immediately. What is clearly true is that he was given an immediate positive answer by Mother Cicely of the SSM, particularly that they would come with the idea of

---

8 Hope Patten wrote to Raynes on 5 March 1947, just after this had happened, saying: 'it was Fr. Reggie Kingdon's suggestion [to approach SSM] as they [the committee] all felt that Ditchingham was not the community for the job – on their own showing'. There could be few less supernatural presences than the bulky Father Kingdon.

building up a permanent Walsingham Priory, even though they were very short staffed at the time.

There remained the problem of Sister Benedicta. In his letter to Father Raynes telling him of the good news that assistance was to come from Haggerston, Hope Patten said that Sister Benedicta might join SSM if she were not rushed. He was becoming somewhat exasperated with her and the novices by this time and he added: 'Personally, the more I see of them all, the more difficult it becomes to sort out the rights and wrongs of the lot of them.'

By mid April 1947 final arrangements had been made for the arrival of the new sisters, and *Our Lady's Mirror*, which was always very quiet about difficulties and had been silent about the problems of the preceding years, announced the failure of the COLW and news of the new arrivals.

An agreement was also made with Sister Benedicta whereby she agreed to go to her relatives for a rest and would place herself under a priest nominated by Father Raynes for parish work. She expressed the view that she wished to return to Walsingham if the Guardians could see their way to her working there, and the Guardians agreed to be responsible for her maintenance. This agreement was, however, made with Hope Patten and was specifically subject to the agreement of the Guardians, which they did not then give, as they were unhappy with the prospect of a professed religious living out of community and in the world. This was a rare example of the Guardians not backing Hope Patten and put him in an embarrassing position.

The correspondence thereafter shows that Sister Benedicta was very obstinate. She believed that she ought to be allowed to stay in Walsingham and work at the shrine. If not, she should be maintained by the Guardians. She asserted in any event that it had been agreed that she would live away for two years and then could return. She went to see the Bishop of Norwich, who sensibly thought she was unfit physically and mentally for membership of any community at that time. There was a suggestion that Laleham take her back, but she would not go there or anywhere else.

In the meantime therefore Benedicta stayed either in Norwich, where she took an art course, or at Dereham, where she looked after her stepmother. The Guardians agreed to pay her £2 per week for 1948 only. She complained to Derrick Lingwood, who was quite severe with her. By 1950 she complained that she was in dire straits financially, writing to Lingwood that 'my medical condition renders life in a community impossible and that being a professed sister it is the responsibility of the church to maintain me, as indeed I was promised the Guardians would when I left Walsingham . . .' She then took legal advice and the prospect of proceedings being taken against him in a court of law began to haunt Hope Patten.

However, just before Christmas 1950 the monetary matters were agreed. Benedicta signed (after considerable prevarication) an agreement by which she accepted £200 for the furniture held by the COLW and also agreed that Derrick Lingwood be replaced as trustee of a fund of £500 held for the former community. She was the other trustee and the replacement was to be her nominee. The consideration for this agreement was that she abandoned any further claims against the Guardians and they agreed to give her an undefined number of orders for painting statues for the shrine shop.

Thereafter Douglas Purnell, who had been a pupil of Martin Travers, designed a plaster statue of Our Lady of Walsingham, the first one of which was for Quainton Hall, and it seems that Sister Benedicta coloured some and produced other objects for the shop.

Sister Benedicta's stepmother did not die until 1957. In the meantime she remained in a state of ecclesiastical limbo, still regarding herself as being the Community of Our Lady of Walsingham. There was some more correspondence in that later year when the suggestion resurfaced that she return to Laleham. There was by that time a new Reverend Mother, but there appeared to be no acceptable way in which she could join them, as she continued to say that she could not become a full member, and Laleham had no oblates. Oddly, it appears that Hope Patten was hearing her confession at that time, which required her to go to Walsingham; her very presence was a reminder to him of how matters had gone wrong.

Sister Benedicta outlived Hope Patten by many years. In 1971 she was featured in the *Sunday Times*, still habited and still engaged in sculpting and the like in Dereham, and she did not die until the twenty-first century. She was a living warning to others of the danger of meddling in the affairs of religious communities. Raymond Raynes, with his great experience, had appreciated that and on 20 April 1947, when writing to Bishop Herbert, he said that 'I am bound to say to you, frankly though *confidentially* that one of the difficulties in the situation is that Fr. Patten fails to realise some of the inevitable needs and complications involved in the internal administration of a religious community.' These words were apposite as well as prophetic, as the later history of the CSA was to show.

11

WALSINGHAM IN THE POST-WAR
YEARS, 1945–50

The end of the war brought a final end to the restrictions on travel which had largely prevented pilgrims from visiting Walsingham for the preceding six years. On the face of it, the shrine itself was in the same position as it had been in 1939, but of course the pilgrimages had to be built up again from nothing, and Hope Patten was impatient to implement the many unfulfilled ideas which he had developed during a time when it was impossible to put them into effect.

A less superficial look at the situation in 1945 revealed that there remained problems both with the sisters and with the College of St Augustine (CSA), and that the Sanctuary School was as yet an unproven quantity. The period from the end of the war to 1950 was to bring to a head the first of those problems and to illuminate clearly the fate of the school; the CSA, on the other hand, was to carry on without ever showing signs of being about to flourish.

Hope Patten himself began to show signs of those prostrating illnesses from which he had suffered in the past. The cynical might conclude that they reappeared only when foreign travel again became practicable, and certainly as soon as he could he was off. In 1948–9 he went on a very long break, described below, oblivious perhaps to the fact that, for entirely understandable reasons, Italy, one of his destinations, was at that time politically not very correct. He became fascinated by Malta after visiting it on the same trip, although he found long-distance travelling very difficult, particularly by ship. He struck up a friendship with an elderly Maltese Roman Catholic priest, Revd Francis Catania, a member of the Canons of St Paul of the Catacombs, a foundation of the Knights of Malta, the romantic associations of which were likely to appeal greatly to Hope Patten. His passport stamps show that he was abroad again in 1950 and regularly thereafter.

The Jubilee celebrations, to commemorate the twenty-fifth anniversary of the erection of the image in the parish church, lasted from 5 to 12 July 1947. The pilgrimage church was decorated for the occasion: in one of Hope Patten's favourite phrases it was festooned 'according to our custom' with evergreens. Hope Patten was extremely fond of this expression, and he filled notebooks in his almost illegible scrawl in which he set out what he called the customs of the shrine, to give a definitive account of how certain feasts were celebrated. It was sometimes said of him, with more than a little truth, that many of his customs were of his own invention and recent invention at that.

During the celebrations high mass was sung every day except Sunday in the pilgrimage church and on that day in the parish church. Hope Patten gave an address on the Sunday evening dealing with the restoration of the shrine. There was solemn benediction every night in the pilgrimage church, and pilgrimages were made by a number of groups. On the Wednesday of that week there was a social gathering aimed particularly at those who lived locally who had been involved with the shrine, which followed solemn vespers of Our Lady, a procession around the grounds, and then benediction. On 12 July 1947 a Jubilee procession around the village took place, which followed an oration by Father Pinchard. A number of the Guardians were present and took part in the procession; these included the indefatigable Fynes-Clinton and Milner, as well as George Long, Sir Eric Maclagan, Lord Norton, Sir John Best-Shaw, Father Kingdon and Canon Powell.

Hope Patten himself wrote a long article in *Our Lady's Mirror* for the spring/summer 1947, which has already been quoted in part. He looked back over the 25 years, often rewriting history somewhat as he did so and sometimes straining the credulity of his readers, as when he said that Bishop Pollock had been 'a very kind and considerate friend' to him.

Revd D. A. Ross had been parish priest of St Saviour, Hoxton, since 1928. The church had been made notorious by his predecessor but one, Revd E. E. Kilburn, who had made it indistinguishable from a Roman church both in appearance and in liturgy; although Father Ross had had to reintroduce the vernacular for services it remained at the ultramontane end of the Church of England. The church was badly bombed in 1940 and although temporary arrangements were made for services to continue, it became clear that it would not be rebuilt, standing as it did in an area with many churches and a declining population. Father Ross was therefore available to come and assist at Walsingham for a period during the long absence by Hope Patten in late 1948 and early 1949. He had assisted before and indeed in the procession on 12 July 1947 he walked on one side of the vicar with Revd John Oldland on the other. Father Oldland at that date held the position once occupied by Hope Patten himself, as curate of Carshalton in charge of the Good Shepherd, Carshalton Beeches but the following year he was appointed as vicar of St John the Divine, Balham. In 1949 Father Ross was appointed to the parish of Holy Trinity, Bradford, at which Derrick Lingwood had served his title, and left Walsingham for the North.

It is also interesting to see that the 1948 Whit Monday pilgrimage was defined as being one of reparation for the 'South Indian schism'. Father Howard, who had conducted the parish mission in 1939, preached. Although there were those who thought that the Anglican Papalists made too much of what was happening in India and Ceylon, in fact time was to show that that was the start of a series of initiatives in which Anglo-Catholics were always forced on to the back foot.

In 1946 the Guardians agreed that in addition to those actively involved they could appoint Honorary Guardians and also that those who no longer wished to participate in the day-to-day running of the shrine could be appointed as a Guardian Emeritus.

There were a number of changes in this period in the College, which had remained remarkably stable since the foundation. Father Whitby died in 1948, the Duke of Argyll in 1949, Father Baverstock and Major Bowker in 1950. The very wealthy Whitby, who had inherited substantial sums from his grandparents via his mother, rather surprisingly left nothing to the shrine and may by this time have become unhappy about certain aspects of its development.[1] In 1949 Father Kingdon retired from his active membership of the College but continued as a Guardian Emeritus, the first such. The departed were replaced within this period by Father Raymond Raynes CR (1949), Father Wodehouse, who returned in 1950 after his period of exile, and John Upcott (1950). Both the new appointments were of some interest: Raymond Raynes was a man of considerable intellect and drive who, like Hope Patten, attracted some but repelled others. He was certainly not a man who would accept what others said if

---

1 Father Whitby's own father, Edward Garrow Garrow-Whitby, had left his mother and subsequently been declared bankrupt. He had died in 1890.

he disagreed with them, and was not of the nature to rubber stamp decisions made by Hope Patten, as had often occurred in the earlier years. John Dalgains Upcott had been a housemaster at Eton; he had a deep knowledge of education and added an expertise otherwise lacking in that field to the College, which again acted as a corrective to some of Hope Patten's ideas.

There was no change in the liturgical regime at Walsingham, which was by now set. In any event, the five years after the war represented the final flowering of the introspective, rigid interpretation of Catholicism which had been emerging from Rome since the First Vatican Council; this culminated in the promulgation of the dogma of the Assumption of Our Lady in 1950, an announcement which was no doubt welcome to Hope Patten and those Anglicans of his way of thinking. Whatever his views about Roman Catholics at this time, he set his compass by the lodestar of the Vatican.

Hope Patten also continued his enthusiasm for collecting relics. In *Our Lady's Mirror* he wrote that one of his great ambitions had been to acquire relics of St Thomas Becket and St Hugh of Lincoln.[2] Within a few years, both had come his way, that of St Thomas from America in 1944 and that of St Hugh from a devout English client of the shrine in 1947. Readers were reassured that both were properly sealed and authenticated. The American donor was Canon Vivan Petersen, rector of St James, Cleveland, Ohio, who was then appointed as an Honorary Guardian in 1946 and who pressed Hope Patten to go to America to publicise the work at Walsingham. While Hope Patten expressed himself interested in that project, it never materialised. Father Petersen had been at Walsingham himself in 1937 and had celebrated mass in the shrine.

Some of the village festivities continued. There were two regular excursions a year. On the Monday in the Octave of the Assumption the servers and those learning their catechism were taken to Great Yarmouth for the day and over the Christmas period the servers were taken to the pantomime in Norwich. In the severe winter of 1947 Mrs Ferrier's car, which was being used for transport for some of them to the seasonal entertainment, boiled up; she then confessed that she thought that if she put anti-freeze in the radiator, water was not required in addition.

---

2 Autumn and winter 1947–8.

Towards the end of the war, work began on the cottages in Knight Street. Some had been acquired with the original purchase of the hospice, some had been bought in 1935, and one small plot of land was acquired later to complete the ownership of the area. No architect was prepared to say that the ramshackle collection of buildings could be salvaged, and it was suggested that they be demolished and a new start made. Hope Patten did not accept their view and in that he was showing his artistic flair and imagination: he could see that something could be made of what remained, and he persuaded the local builder, Tom Purdy, that it was possible. The unfortunate Purdy had an apparently impossible task having to deal with a particularly difficult employer who changed his mind frequently, almost daily, as to what he wanted. One of Hope Patten's phrases was 'Purdy must be told', used whenever something practical was required to be done.

Despite all these difficulties, over the next decade or so the buildings behind the shrine were restored, amalgamated and adapted. It was a practical solution which arose from the realisation that the plans set out in the pre-war proposals in relation to the domestic accommodation around the shrine were unlikely to be realised. As early as 1939, in fact, Hope Patten had appealed for money to convert the cottages, effectively appreciating that the money was unlikely to be forthcoming for extensive new buildings.

The financial position generally was not easy, although it was ameliorated in 1949 when Milner made over his estates in the North to the Guardians and yet another company was formed, named Walsingham College (Yorkshire Properties) Ltd, to acquire these. The purposes for which Parcevall Hall was to be held were limited to religious and educational objects and included its eventual use as a retreat centre.

Money could be raised on the security of that Yorkshire property and indeed the company was used as a vehicle for the acquisition of some properties in Walsingham itself. It does not appear that the passage of time had given Hope Patten any greater grasp of company law, and he remained of the view that the entire enterprise was under his own personal direction. That view, although legally unsustainable, did have the advantage that he was able to carry into effect schemes at which others baulked.

Work was able to start in 1944 on the first part of what became known as the College, and which eventually resulted in the reconstruction of a small quadrangle with a garden in the middle. This may have been eased in the first place in those years of austerity because building permits were available to assist with accommodation for the boys who had been evacuated from Long Marston. When that preliminary work was completed, Hope Patten himself and the other members of the CSA moved into the College, with the administrator himself occupying the cottage still used by his successors. This left the vicarage free, because of course the children's home had by then moved to its own property in Wells Road. From 1945 onwards the vicarage was therefore used as the main centre of the Sanctuary School, although that was supplemented by St Edmund's Cottage, and St Francis, a house built into the ruins of the old friary.

In 1946 it was proposed that a war memorial chapel be built on the north side of the pilgrimage church, with a new cloister and a library above the cloister. Plans were prepared and sketches drawn by Milner & Craze, but no work was ever carried out, presumably because the public response to yet another appeal was insufficient.

The children's home reached some stability after the war when its management was taken over by Mesdemoiselles Jessie Mary Bartholomew and Dorothy Williams (invariably known respectively as 'Barty and Miss Will'), who had met when in the Land Army together and then settled and ran it very successfully for many years. Although it is easy to refer to St Hilary as being a children's home, with the connotation that they were small children, in fact there were many teenagers and in due course a number left for National Service. The same edition of *Our Lady's Mirror* in which appeared the parish priest's recollections of the preceding 25 years also contained news of four of the boys who had been serving abroad and had returned to Walsingham on leave. In due course, after this period, a hostel for working boys was opened in the village with the laudable intention of providing stable accommodation for those who had been at the children's home and had moved on to employment. It did not prove successful in the long term, because of the scarcity of work in the area. It was run by Frederick Shepherd and his wife Pearl; their son, Frederick John Shepherd, always known by his second Christian name, was to become a protégé in the same way that Derrick Lingwood had been, and similarly was to proceed to ordination. Another former St Hilary boy, Theodore Williams, a nephew of 'Miss Will', lived at the College for some time after about 1949 and Hope Patten was his guardian, although it is not clear whether this was as a result of any court order. He assisted with secretarial and other functions; in due course he worked for Laurence King, who became architect to the shrine many years later and lived for a time in the clergy house at Holy Cross, Cromer Street.[3]

It does appear that a real attempt was made to develop St Hilary's as a home to which those who had lived there would return, rather than as an institution, although there were some typical touches, such as the veneration of a relic of the name saint on his feast day. It was a considerable achievement that such a home was run as well as was the case.

Hope Patten was always anxious to collect testimonies from those who believed that they had been cured at Walsingham, and to encourage them to leave small tablets recording their recovery as he had seen abroad. However, he never publicised the healing aspect of pilgrimages as much as other facets. On 5 June 1949 *The People* published an article on Walsingham after interviewing some of those who claimed to have had their health improved in that way, and the result was a short-term sharp increase in letters and in people coming to drink the waters. This was not the type of publicity for which Hope Patten was looking, but it did raise consciousness of Walsingham, and he was probably pleased with the headline, which read 'Duncan Webb [the reporter] investigates the English Lourdes'. The particular case most mentioned, that of a boy called Cyril Dawes who had been cured of ear problems after being bathed at the well, had already been set out by Hope Patten himself in *Our Lady's Mirror*.

The unhappy story of the Community of our Lady of Walsingham has already been discussed. After its collapse in 1947, the Society of St Margaret arrived and matters stabilised almost immediately. The triumphant note of earlier episodes was not reproduced for this arrival, and the young John Shepherd, then only 14, was deputed to meet the new sisters at the railway station. Hope Patten was wise enough to understand that after the experiences which he had had he must thereafter keep out of the internal affairs of the sisters and allow them to run themselves; this he did.

One of the minor consequences of the Second World War was that numbers in religious communities began to grow quite sharply in the few years after 1945. That was partly because those men who had a vocation to that form of life were being released from the services, and partly because some were turning away from a world which had produced such horrors.

---

3 Theodore Williams was received into the Roman Catholic Church some years later.

The College of St Augustine was not exempt from that trend, and the period between 1945 and 1950 was an important one for it.

The first member to be recruited was Moses Harbottle, who made his first six months' promise on 27 June 1946 and resumed the name of Brother Peter; he had by then been discharged from the forces. He was plagued by serious back problems over the next few years, but persisted.

On 30 August 1946 the chapter meeting agreed that any aspirant who came to the College should be treated as a postulant for three months and should then proceed to the noviciate for two consecutive periods of six months, before being professed. Harbottle was joined on 2 September 1946 by Leslie Oldroyd, who agreed to serve his three months' postulancy, and on 7 December 1946 was admitted to the noviciate under the name of Brother David. He too had been discharged from the RAF, and later left reminiscences of his membership of the College in the *Walsingham Review*,[4] in which he set out how Hope Patten made him revise and then re-revise the horarium. It was settled at that time as being matins and prime at 6.30 a.m., mass in the parish church at 7.30 a.m., then breakfast. After a period of mental prayer there followed terce, the chapter mass in the shrine church, and sext. From then until 12.45 p.m. there was work (which in the case of Hope Patten usually meant by this period that he disappeared to his study). There was then a visit to the Blessed Sacrament, followed by lunch at 1 p.m. At 2 p.m. none was said, followed by further work until 4.30 p.m., when it was tea time, and at 5.30 p.m. evensong, rosary, and shrine prayers. Dinner was at 7 p.m. and although life at that time in St Augustine's was not luxurious and there was no running water and very little heating, George Long served at table and the College had a housemaid called Mary Harrison. Later a steward named Harry Darnell worked in the College for some years. There was then recreation on three days followed by spiritual reading and at 9.30 p.m. compline was said. The Greater Silence was kept after compline until sext the next morning. There were variants on this at various times, including an arrangement whereby the private masses were said both in the parish church and the shrine church, and obviously from the chapter book there was prolonged discussion about insignificant details on many occasions, with frequent reference to 'the customs' of the College, especially when Hope Patten himself took the minutes, but that basic pattern remained the norm. Faults, that is

---

4 Numbers 65 and 66, 1978.

the public airing of the shortcomings of members, also became a feature of chapter meetings.

The difficulties of fitting in parish work within that framework are obvious. It is interesting that, in a foretaste of what was to occur later, on 9 December 1946 Brother Peter asked whether a hood could not be attached to the outdoor cloak as a skull cap was insufficient protection against inclement weather. It was recorded that Father Derrick objected, saying that this would savour too much of a monastic order, whereas they were a secular college. The problem was solved by Harbottle offering to buy a hat, but at the next meeting it was decided that hats or hoods could be worn according to choice. However, the basic issue raised by Lingwood as to what form of order was envisaged bedevilled the CSA throughout.

The dress of the members of the College was, and remained, somewhat idiosyncratic. Hope Patten had drawn for his interpretation of the rule largely on J. Willis Clark's *Customs of Augustinian Canons*, published in 1897, but he had also seen an illustration of an Augustinian canon in Sir William Dugdale's *Monasticon Anglicanum*, published in the seventeenth century, which showed him wearing a linen rochet[5] as normally worn by bishops with a black mozetta[6] and a long black cloak[7] for the winter with a very tall biretta. It was decided early on in the life of the reconstituted community that a cotta should be worn particularly for preparing or clearing the altar, which over a rochet was not a very sensible arrangement practically or aesthetically.[8] Most people who saw the members of the College remarked on the birettas, which were made so elevated as to be unique in the experience of even the most seasoned observers of ecclesiastical garb.

Although there were difficulties between the various personalities, and sometimes more can be read between the lines of the minutes than in the official record itself, there were lighter moments, despite complaints in the minutes from Hope Patten that there was too much laughter in the College. On one occasion[9] Peter Harbottle hid in the loft and used a microphone to simulate a radio broadcast in which he pretended to be a

---

5 A form of surplice usually worn by bishops, made of linen but with tightly fitting sleeves.
6 A short cape worn around the shoulders, in this case coloured black.
7 Referred to sometimes as a cappa magna.
8 Minutes for 12 November 1946.
9 See Leslie Oldroyd's reminiscences.

Roman Catholic spokesman who then referred to Hope Patten as 'the Protestant Minister Mr Patten'. Hope Patten and Fynes-Clinton, who were listening, were pictures of indignation, but both appreciated the joke when the truth was revealed to them. On another, Father Lingwood fell into an exposed manhole used for sewage disposal and was not much amused when it was discovered that the drain had been blocked by a pair of Oldroyd's underpants. This event was commemorated in a comic poem written by Leslie Oldroyd. There were also games at Christmas, including Monopoly, and Hope Patten remained fond of ghost stories at that season.

One character mentioned in a number of recollections of the period is Nicholas, the college cat, who was described by one of the schoolboys as being 'as big as a spaniel'.[10] He particularly disliked women, and was prone to attacking their stockinged legs with his sharp claws, but was tolerated even in the shrine church itself by Hope Patten, who was generally very punctilious about the saying of mass with decorum. One pilgrim recalled an incident in which the cat was about to jump on to the lectern just before Hope Patten said the gospel from it, and he gestured just in time but with his usual dignity for one of the servers to deflect Nicholas.[11] He died in 1952 and was afforded his picture in *Our Lady's Mirror*, but was replaced by a golden retriever pup.

The year 1947 was of particular significance in the history of the College. There was an important chapter meeting on 17 January 1947, at which it was decided (on the suggestion of the Superior himself) that he should be known thereafter as the Prior (more properly the Acting Prior, pending revision of the rule). It was then agreed that the noviciate should be extended in most instances to two years in all, after which vows should be taken for a three-year period before proceeding to final vows. Again, the movement was unmistakably towards a more monastic ethos. It was also agreed that the Prior, as he was now to be termed, would communicate with Father Raynes CR and Father Wrathall CR, the Warden of Horbury, over a more permanent form for the rule. He reported back on 3 February 1947 and the chapter were unimpressed with Raymond Raynes' suggestions, which it was recorded did not coincide with the objects and aim of the College. Those present then reversed the decisions they had made less than three weeks previously, and in their place agreed

10 By Major Patrick King in Milner: *Quainton Hall School*, p. 213.
11 Letter from Kathleen Blayney, 17 May 1981 (WA).

that an aspirant should stay for three months before proceeding to a noviciate of 12 months, which was extendable for another 12, and then renewable vows for three years should follow. A new constitution was then drafted for consideration, but on 10 April 1947 Hope Patten and Lingwood renewed their vows for six months only.

On 27 February 1947 Penry John Perry was admitted as a postulant and on 23 May of that year he moved on to novice and took the name Brother John. On 11 September 1947 Anthony Turner was allowed to return as a postulant, while continuing some work with the School,[12] and on 14 October 1947 Revd Frank Harry Reader was also admitted as a postulant. He was an important recruit: he had been ordained priest as long ago as 1932 and his last appointment before Walsingham was as vicar of St James, Walthamstow, from 1944 onwards. With his arrival, there were three priests and four laybrothers in the College and it appeared at last to be showing signs of steady growth.

On 3 November 1947 the revised constitution, which had had significant input from Mirfield, was adopted unanimously. Father Wrathall, who was then the Novice Master at the Community of the Resurrection, was appointed as Acting Prelate, the first external influence on the College. At the next chapters there was discussion on the name which should be adopted, and on 18 November 1947 it was decided to use the title 'Congregation of St Augustine, Walsingham' which was to be abbreviated to CSAW, although very soon this was reduced simply to CSA.

On 25 November 1947 Father Wrathall received the professions for three years, the length which had finally been agreed, of Hope Patten, Lingwood and Harbottle, who were of course the three pioneers of the venture before the war. Hope Patten wrote to the Fellowship that this indicated that the College had been 'officially established'.[13]

On 1 December 1947 Anthony Turner was admitted as a novice and took the name Brother Michael Anthony, and on 24 January 1948 Father Reader was similarly admitted under the name Father Lawrence. Also on 1 December 1947 Hope Patten was elected as Prior for a five-year term; although the result was as predictable as that of a Stalinist referendum, Father Fynes-Clinton was brought in as an impartial scrutineer of the

12 He signed as Fred Turner, that being his real Christian name; Anthony was simply a name by which he generally known.
13 Letter dated 30 January 1948 (WA).

votes and a secret ballot was held. The appointment was then ratified by the Guardians, again predictably, and the institution took place on 9 February 1948. The record of this institution was signed on behalf of the Guardians by George Long, who of course waited on the Community at table and who was sometimes referred to as Hope Patten's valet. He was a man universally esteemed, but whether he could stand out with independent judgement against Hope Patten in those circumstances must be debatable.

A great deal of chapter time in the months thereafter was spent in discussing the order of precedence applicable to the CSAW, and a complicated list was devised in which priests always came before laymen. Hope Patten was also very keen to ensure that the 'Augustinian bow' was used at all proper times. On 30 March 1948 it was resolved to adopt on a full-time basis the practice of reading at the midday meal, other than on feast days. This was another quasi-monastic development and Hope Patten was clearly beginning to see the Community moving in that direction.

The promising trend towards expansion began to unravel itself quite suddenly. The minutes record that on 26 April 1948 Father Lawrence (Reader) and Brother Michael Anthony (Turner) had withdrawn from the College. No reason was given. Father Reader went later that year to be vicar of Barney with Thursford, very near the shrine, and in 1956 he moved to the West Indies, where he later became a Canon. When material was being gathered in 1961 for a projected life of Hope Patten, he wrote some very critical letters from the Caribbean about the conduct of both him and Derrick Lingwood, complaining particularly about their holidays, and especially the fact that Lingwood had gone off to France for a month with the shrine car. Otherwise he did not specify his complaints in any way. Of all those who had been in close contact with Hope Patten, Father Reader was one of the most virulent detractors, although he attended at the shrine while at Barney. It may be that he was too experienced a man to fit into a regime which had been dictated by Hope Patten partly at least in accordance with his own prejudices and way of thinking.[14]

Anthony Turner, although clearly not suited to the quasi-monastic life, followed thereafter a path which has echoes of others connected to the shrine. He was ordained deacon in 1948 and priest in 1949 in the Diocese of Bradford, where Bishop Blunt was still in post and willing to assist in

---

14 Letter of 6 June 1961 (WA).

that regard, served his title at Holy Trinity, Leeds Road, in that city, where he was a curate under Father Ross for part of his time, and then went to the West Indies. He returned to Walsingham for a time in 1966 to assist. Later still he went over to Rome and was reordained in Canada.

Hope Patten wrote a somewhat defensive circular to the Fellowship dated summer 1948 in which he set out the numbers who had been members of the College and said, with some justification, that the assertion that a stream of men had been coming and going was unfair. He did also say that none of those who had left had had a real vocation to the life of the College.

In the later part of 1948, Hope Patten became ill again. Brother David (Oldroyd) was deputed at a meeting on 18 August 1948 to accompany the Prior on his holiday abroad to recover, and did so. They were away for a prolonged period in September and October 1948, and then returned to Walsingham. They attended chapter on 26 October 1948 at which Hope Patten asked for further leave from 18 November of that year to assist his recovery.

In his memoir, Leslie Oldroyd says that he left Walsingham in order to try his vocation in a more established order, but the contemporary record reveals that that was an economical account of what actually occurred. It seems strange that he was asked to accompany the Prior if his conduct had indeed been unsatisfactory, but the minutes suggest that there had already been problems before the trip. On 1 November 1948 he suddenly announced that he wished to withdraw from the College that week. Three days later a special meeting was called because he had asked to return. He apologised for 'deeply unsatisfactory behaviour' during the last three months, which must have included the time when he was away. It was decided to prolong his noviciate but to invite him to stay for three months with the Society of St Francis at Cerne Abbas before allowing him back to the College. After Hope Patten had gone away again, Oldroyd said he was no longer prepared to go to the Franciscans, and he left Walsingham. He eventually went to Nashdom.

During that short period when the Prior was back, the College agreed to try an idea floated by Bishop Vernon, who was then in Madagascar, for a Third Order attached to the College and with definite obligations, but this never seems to have been taken further. Hope Patten also suggested, presumably in the light of the problems they had had, that the novices should be kept separate from the professed, so far as possible. The positive aspect of this time was that Brother John Perry was professed for three years on 13 November 1948.

Hope Patten returned early in 1949, and at the first meeting of the year it was decided that proper and regular tuition should be given to novices and Brother John was appointed Novice Guardian. However, the Prior's health had still not recovered and he announced that he needed a further period away. It will be recalled that the rules provided for extra money left or given to a priest to be used for holidays, and clearly the time which Hope Patten had away in 1948–9 had involved considerable expenditure. This was not always appreciated by the outside world, especially at a time of great austerity, when he put it about that he was living only on the very small allowance provided. Before he departed, however, a special chapter was called for 14 January 1949 to consider a renewed application by Leslie Oldroyd to return. It was agreed that he should not do so before he had been somewhere else for six months or so, and he never did return as a member. However, he did come back to Walsingham many years later at the invitation of the then administrator and worked as the catering manager, with some success. He finally lived in an almshouse in the village and suffered from agoraphobia before his death in 2005. He had become a Roman Catholic, as did so many of those associated with the CSA.

Hope Patten was away until May 1949, in France, Switzerland, Malta and Italy. In effect therefore he had been absent from Walsingham for almost the whole of the preceding nine months. He wrote to the Fellowship on 11 June 1949 explaining what he had been doing and describing with enthusiasm his visits to various Colleges in Italy including that at Pavia, where he had seen the tomb and relics of St Augustine of Hippo himself. During his absence two new postulants had arrived, one of whom, Arthur Smith, had already withdrawn as his health was not robust enough to cope with the life. The second, David Barnett, served his postulancy in the Prior's absence and entered the noviciate under the name Brother Paul on 5 May 1949. One other postulant, Robert Buttolph, came and went before the end of the year.[15]

A trend was beginning to develop along the lines which Hope Patten had been able to rebut the year before, namely that men were coming and

---

15 Robert Henry Buttolph was ordained priest in Antigua in 1958 and then became rector of St Peter, St Kitts. He returned on holiday to Walsingham in 1960, after Hope Patten's death.

going very quickly, but he was away from the College abroad again in October 1949. This trend continued into 1950, when in January Leo Avery and George Gabriel Koskingen were admitted as postulants. The latter was a novice in a Finnish Orthodox monastery, which had had to re-establish itself after a forced move caused by Russian annexation of part of Karelia. The former left within a month, although some years later he applied to return, and the Finn was recalled to his monastery in May 1950; it had been intended that he work for Anglican-Eastern unity.

On 23 May 1950 Brother Peter (Harbottle) made the unexpected announcement at the chapter meeting that he had concluded that he had no vocation and asked to be released from his vows. This was a substantial blow to Hope Patten, bearing in mind Harbottle's long commitment to Walsingham. He had been to York, where the Dean, Eric Milner-White, had advised him to try for ordination in the West Indies. He stayed in fact until 15 August 1950, when he left for the Caribbean and said he had decided to sever his connections with the College entirely.

The last but one postulant to be taken by the College during this period was John Shepherd, who had been brought up in Walsingham and had been entirely instructed in Hope Patten's view of the Church of England. He was admitted on 2 September 1950. A note was made that his circumstances were unusual because he was then still at Fakenham Grammar School, so for a time he used to come in to the College in his uniform and change into a cassock. On 18 October 1950 Colin Brookman Sparke was admitted; Hope Patten had rather bluntly noted that he was 'a cripple' and would need medically examining before he came. He had malformed legs which made the life very difficult.

There can be no doubt, however, that the College, although far from collapsing, was in a less stable position in late 1950 than it had been in early 1948.

The Sanctuary School began to function under that name from September 1945 in its new location. After the resignation of Alfred Batts, a new headmaster had to be found and it appeared that Hope Patten had located the ideal candidate in Thomas Tapping, who had lived at the vicarage with him when he first came to Walsingham. By this time Tapping was married and his wife also taught at the school. He fulfilled the essential criterion so far as Hope Patten was concerned of being a committed and knowledgeable Anglo-Catholic. In the Jubilee edition of *Our Lady's Mirror* Hope Patten wrote: 'The School is founded to provide a choir for the shrine, and the boys sing at mass and benediction and are taught the faith without any pruning. We hope this will bear fruit in their future lives.'

Apart from Mr and Mrs Tapping, other teachers included Enid Chadwick, who taught art and later also acted as school secretary, Mrs Whittaker, the wife of the parish priest of nearby East Barsham, who taught Geography, Miss D. Vincent (musical adviser) and Anthony Turner (organist and choir master, who joined the staff after leaving the CSA in 1945). Later Moses Harbottle (Brother Peter) acted as choirmaster. Hope Patten himself was not only Chairman of the Governors but also Warden, a somewhat nebulous role which he interpreted as meaning that the spiritual direction of the school was under his personal control. He also provided the religious education to the boys, which, as can be imagined, involved teaching of a most definite type. He had, however, retained the gift of being able to enthuse his listeners, especially the young, and he also had the ability, regrettably rare among the clergy, to communicate his ideas succinctly and in readily comprehensible language.

The school was still very small in 1945. It commenced its new life with 14 boarders, whose fees were £34 per term, three weekly boarders, who paid £30 per term and three day boys, whose fees were £8 8s 0d per term until they were nine and then £10 10s 0d. Since, however, the school bank account was overdrawn by £200 when the new arrangements came into force, the financial position was difficult from the very beginning.

There is no hiding, however, from the fact that the most difficult problem with the school was that Hope Patten himself would not let the staff run it in accordance with their own experience and without interference from him. Although he had many talents, administration was not one of them; in addition his own schooling had been so unsatisfactory that he had no real knowledge of well-run schools. With Quainton Hall itself he was content to allow Father Eyden, who was in any event a strong character, to run the school while he and the other Governors provided guidance and encouragement, turning up at speech days and the like. Fynes-Clinton was particularly assiduous in his attendance at Quainton Hall. With the Sanctuary School, however, Hope Patten was not only on the spot and teaching in the school, he regarded it as being primarily to serve the shrine and thus for the boys to be available whenever required for that purpose.

This interference led to conflict early on. It was clear that Tapping was a very able headmaster with considerable physical presence and a booming voice, and there is no doubt that he did his best to expand and improve the school. However, he and Hope Patten, despite their old friendship, were soon at loggerheads over the amount of time which the boys were to spend in the shrine at the various services, and eventually the two men fell out completely. Another complicating factor was that Tapping and Derrick Lingwood also could not get on.[16] Hope Patten came to the conclusion that Tapping was not the right man to run what he perceived as a 'thoroughly Catholic school'. He was not prepared to compromise on this, and so the headmaster's position became intolerable and in March 1948 he resigned: the resignation was not voluntary and was a means of making more palatable to the outside world what was in fact a unilateral decision by Hope Patten to the effect that he was no longer suitable. It was dressed up as a decision by the Guardians, but that too was something less than the full truth, as was the announcement in *Our Lady's Mirror* for autumn 1948 that 'it was a real sorrow that a change had to be made'.

The departure of Tapping was a severe blow for the Sanctuary School, particularly when he and his wife moved to take over Beeston Hall School, also in Norfolk, which thereafter flourished and to which a number of the parents transferred their children.

Tapping was replaced by Kenneth Hunter, who also brought his wife and her twin brother with him as additional teachers, and a Father Taylor is also recorded as arriving.[17] By his arrival in September 1948 numbers in the school had dropped to a financially unsustainable 16, having been 38 the term before; the overdraft rose commensurately. The new headmaster thought that the school would in any event not survive unless considerable sums were spent to improve the accommodation and to remedy the problems which were caused by the various buildings which were in use being so far apart. Hunter is described in the history of the schools as being 'a charming, easy-going man, who was well liked by both boys and parents'.[18] The main problem with his period in charge was that his brother-in-law became increasingly dependent on alcohol and when he was drunk the housemaids had to barricade themselves in their bedrooms

---

16 Interview with Stanley Smith, 25 March 2006.

17 This was almost certainly Revd Arthur Taylor, who had an Anglo-Catholic background and had also been a school chaplain. His career has a gap between 1947 and 1950 recorded in *Crockford*, which corresponds with this period.

18 See Milner: *Quainton Hall School*, p. 209.

to protect themselves from his advances.[19] Numbers, however, did increase and by the summer of 1949 stood at 46.

At the end of that year work began on a new classroom block at the vicarage, which was to replace the stables attached to it, and at the same time the Friary was converted to be used by senior pupils and also as living accommodation for staff. That work cost about £900, which was about a quarter of the fee income for a year, and could only be financed by the generosity of the Governors, since the overdraft had risen to £3,400, which was £300 above its limit.

In December 1949 Mr Hunter resigned; he too was unable to cope with Hope Patten's well-intended but quite unreasonable interference with the day-to-day running of the school and there was the additional complication of his wife's brother's conduct. The situation was not improved when he circulated parents to tell them of his departure and encouraged them to transfer their sons to his own new school near Northampton.

With this further resignation, the Guardians/Governors became increasingly concerned and, for once, attempted to restrain Hope Patten, telling him that he must allow the headmaster to run the school. It is only fair to the vicar, however, to say that his own interaction with the pupils was remembered by many of them with affection, even many years later. One, who later returned to live in the village and in due course became a Guardian, recalled: 'Fr. Patten was charming, hard working and had time for everyone. He had the most tremendous aura, and one could really feel that he was different from us lesser mortals.'[20] Thus could be seen the two aspects of the man.

The replacement for Mr Hunter was Michael St H. Armistead, who was already a keen member of the Society of Our Lady of Walsingham, and his assistant was an experienced priest and schoolmaster, Revd R. George Darley, who had earlier taught at Woodbridge School. Armistead was to prove the last headmaster, but the final phase of the school belongs to the next chapter.

---

19 See letter from Father Reader, 6 June 1961 (WA).
20 Major Patrick King, in Milner: *Quainton Hall School*, p. 213.

12

WALSINGHAM IN THE FIFTIES, 1951–6

The later years of Hope Patten's life were not a fulfilling time for him. He was increasingly out of sympathy with those changes which were beginning to take place within the wider church as precursors of the revolution which was to occur after the Second Vatican Council. He had a particular distaste for, perhaps amounting to hatred of, the Liturgical Movement, which he regarded as contrary to all the ideas which he had held so dear for so many years, especially its insistence on the laity actively participating in services, although he did compromise to some extent and once a week held what was termed a 'dialogue mass'. His only other concession was sometimes to wear fuller Gothic vestments, although usually over a lace alb; one of Hope Patten's idiosyncrasies was that he disliked lace on cottas, a fashion which was so beloved of many servers, but liked it on albs for the clergy.

One of his acquaintances, who valued his insight and wrote for *Our Lady's Mirror*, was nevertheless rebuked by him on one occasion for saying mass too audibly and also for allowing the congregation to respond.[1] The same source also thought that Hope Patten's ability to dream of what the future might bring was as powerful as ever at this time, while simultaneously being less credible. He wrote: 'I well remember how one Saturday evening, along the sunk road returning from St Mary's, I discussed with Father [Hope Patten] the meaning of the Catholic Church. As he explained it, it was lucid and wonderful, but when related to the existing situation outside Walsingham, and in particular to the protestant-dominated parishes where I laboured [in the Swansea area], it bore no relation to reality.'[2]

---

1 Father Burton, letter of 5 May 1961 (WA).
2 Father Burton, letter of 25 April 1961 (WA).

Although it is not uncommon among priests, as in other fields of life, for a certain rigidity to set in as middle age arrives and then recedes, Hope Patten by contrast did move liturgically, although not in the direction of relaxation of his observances. Rather he moved away almost completely from the Prayer Book and began using the Roman canon. Some attributed this move to the influence of a book entitled *The Great Prayer*, written by Revd Hugh Ross Williamson in 1955 to advocate the use of that form of consecration, which was foreshadowed by articles the author wrote in *Our Lady's Mirror*. Ironically shortly thereafter Ross Williamson left the Church of England over the South India issue and was received into the Roman Catholic Church as a layman; since he was married he could not be reordained, and in any event he soon fell out of sympathy with the new ideas emanating from the Second Vatican Council. It is more likely, however, that this change by Hope Patten was not as a specific result of that book, but rather as a result of influence from his more Papalist friends. So far as the congregation was concerned, it made little difference, since much of the mass as said by him was of course at that time inaudible.

There were a number of changes in the College of Guardians, which reflected the fact that many of those who were either original members dating from 1932, or had arrived in the first influx of new members in 1935, were ageing. Sir Eric Maclagan died in 1951, Canon Claude Powell in 1952, Bishop O'Rorke in 1953 and Father Lester Pinchard in 1956. Father Reginald Kingdon, a Guardian Emeritus, died in 1955.

O'Rorke in particular had contributed greatly to the establishment of the shrine. His ashes were buried in the shrine and an effigy of him in his enormous mitre was set up near the altar of the Annunciation.

The new Guardians were Uvedale Lambert (1952), a substantial landowner in Surrey whose family had been benefactors of the Church of England for many years; Revd A. J. C. B. (Colin) Gill, then a parish priest in Brighton but later to replace Fynes-Clinton at St Magnus (1953); Revd J. Colin Stephenson, then parish priest at St Mary Magdalen, Oxford, who was later to be chosen by Hope Patten to succeed him (also 1953); Patrick Maitland, MP, Master of and later Earl of Lauderdale (1954), who was admitted despite telling Hope Patten that for his constituents' sake he was accustomed to attend morning service at the kirk after low mass in the local episcopal church; and Revd E. H. W. Crusha, parish priest of St Saviour, Saltley, Birmingham (also 1954).

The change in attitude of the Guardians over the years was perhaps shown most clearly by Maitland, who was, as a Member of Parliament, not used to Hope Patten's idiosyncratic way of conducting business in which, as Chairman, he ignored or overruled any expressions of opinion adverse to his own and recorded as carried the resolutions he supported regardless of what anyone else actually said.

In the early 1950s stalls for the Guardians were erected in the shrine church, but a combination of lack of finance and of space meant that room was provided only for 16 to be seated in them at any one time, and thus that some appear to have occupied them for overlapping periods of time.

There was nothing in the constitution of the College of Guardians which expressly prohibited the election of a woman as a Lay Guardian, although the male gender was used throughout. Nevertheless it was tacitly assumed that such a position was inappropriate for a woman. Hope Patten was nevertheless anxious to recognise the very considerable assistance given to the development of the shrine by a number of women, and in 1953 he devised the title of Dames of the Shrine, which was conferred upon six supporters of the work: Miss Chadwick, Miss Doyle-Smithe, Mrs Ferrier and Mother Cicely SSM (all of whom have been mentioned earlier), Mrs Frida Brackley of Blakeney, a longstanding supporter in many ways, and Miss H. Loddiges of Sussex. They were all presented with a gilded medallion with a blue enamel figure of Our Lady of Walsingham on it.

The really important development during the last years of Hope Patten's life, however, was the increasing alienation between himself and Derrick Lingwood.

There is no doubt that Hope Patten got more difficult to work with as he got older. He was depressed by the problems with the CSA and the School and he had increasing problems with his eyesight; by the mid 1950s he was not far off being blind at some times, and these problems were made particularly difficult by the poor lighting in many parts of the shrine church, which he himself had arranged so that an air of mystery could be created. As with other illnesses from which he suffered, his eyesight seemed to come and go according to his mood. He filled his letters with complaints about his vision, but on the other hand was reluctant to accept any medical advice other than to take holidays, which had always been his own cure. He went to see his oculist in either London or Brighton, and this necessitated many visits. However, the local general practitioner, Doctor Sturdie, was adamant that at least there was nothing wrong with Hope

Patten's heart, displaying a confidence which turned out to be misplaced. Rather strangely, despite an intense preoccupation with his health, Hope Patten disliked being asked directly about how he was feeling.

Not only was Hope Patten more difficult and more autocratic, but he was able to do less in the parish because of his other commitments. By the early 1950s he was simultaneously parish priest, administrator of the shrine, Master of the College of Guardians, Prior of the College of St Augustine, Superior of the Fellowship of the Servants of Our Lady and St Augustine, Warden of the children's home, and Warden and Chairman of the Governors of the Sanctuary School, as well as being on the governing body of Quainton Hall. It was inevitable therefore that a great deal of the parish work was left to Derrick Lingwood, who in addition to that had all the responsibility of the financial matters with which to deal. Lingwood was always liable to extend himself too far in a good cause; his relaxation was to serve on the local rural district council, and for a time he was chairman of the housing committee.

The differences between the two men were partly caused by the lack of acknowledgement on the part of Hope Patten that Derrick Lingwood had by the early 1950s been ordained for about 20 years. He was an experienced priest, who had chosen to stay in Walsingham for little monetary reward; he undoubtedly felt a strong sense of obligation to Hope Patten for having secured his ordination and taught him, and in return Hope Patten looked upon him as a surrogate son. However, Derrick Lingwood was unhappy about the increasingly Roman tone to the liturgical observations at Walsingham, and also about the Community of St Augustine. He had never seen his vocation as being a monk, although he had been perfectly content to go along with the early form of the Community involving little more than the saying of prayers together twice a day.

It was a serious personal blow to Hope Patten when, in 1953, Derrick Lingwood indicated that he was not prepared to renew his three-yearly vows to the Community. In fact, as early as 1947 he had written[3] to a third party that he did not want to take even his first three-year vows, but that Our Lady of Walsingham needed him. The taking of the final step of not renewing his vows required a great deal of courage on Lingwood's part, as he must have foreseen the reaction which it would cause. He recorded his reasons by letter dated 16 November 1953, which was sent in advance of

3 In an undated draft of a letter to Sister Benedicta (WA).

the chapter of 21 November 1953, which he did not attend in person. In it he said that he did not believe that the life of the College was his vocation, and that it was impossible for two priests to run three parishes, be responsible for the shrine and pilgrimages and live a collegiate life, as each of these three activities was enough to require full time employment. This may have hurt Father Patten the more because, on analysis, it was true. In *Our Lady's Mirror*, spring 1955 a bald announcement was carried: 'Father Lingwood, feeling he had not a vocation to the Collegiate life, did not renew his promise in November 1953 and therefore should no longer be addressed as "C.S.A." He lives in the College and is still our bursar and pilgrimage secretary.'

The final problem, the straw that broke the camel's back, was in relation to Great Walsingham. In the early days a cottage was made available for the summer months by members of the Gurney family, relations of those in Little Walsingham, to a priest for that period. Hope Patten would then advertise for someone who was prepared, in return for the light duty of holding two services every Sunday in St Peter, to live in the cottage and be paid pocket money. This arrangement went on for many years but then came to an end when the cottage was no longer available, and the church was then effectively closed. The Archdeacon became concerned about this, but Hope Patten thought that he had enough to see to and that any villagers could come the short distance to Little Walsingham to attend St Mary, where of course there was no shortage of religious provision.

In the post-war period a number of new council houses were erected in Great Walsingham and Derrick Lingwood persuaded Hope Patten to allow him to say mass there every Sunday and evensong on alternate Sundays. Lingwood was still unhappy about the Romeward drift in the liturgy and asked to use more of the Prayer Book at Great Walsingham. Hope Patten was quite intransigent; he refused to allow mass to be said in a different form in any of the three churches under his control, although Great Walsingham had never been given the furnishings which had been introduced to Little Walsingham. Lingwood felt that his effectiveness in relation to the cure of the parishioners at Great Walsingham was being curtailed and compromised, and he deliberately made an issue of it. Afterwards he wrote that 'if [Hope Patten] had given me more freedom at Great Walsingham I would have stayed'.[4] It is an interesting contrast to

---

4 Lingwood, 'Rough Notes'.

the control which the vicar sought to demonstrate over him that when Father Augustine Hoey CR came to Walsingham in 1951 to hold a short mission to the parishes he was full of praise because he was permitted to run it in his own way with support from Hope Patten but without any interference.

Although on the face of it the Great Walsingham impasse was a trivial reason for the fracture of the long association between Hope Patten and Lingwood, in fact it was merely a symptom of the distance which had grown up between them. Lingwood later wrote, tellingly, 'I was in danger of becoming the vicar of Walsingham in name, but not in office.'[5]

That distance was also vividly illustrated by a letter written by Lingwood to Hope Patten on 2 January 1956 in which, in his capacity as a Guardian, he officially complained that the Prayer Book had been replaced by the Roman breviary for the offices of the members of the CSA, of which of course he was no longer a member.

Lingwood in due course went privately to see the Bishop of Norwich to discuss his future. The latter suggested that the time had finally come for him to bring his long association with Walsingham to an end. In 1956 Derrick Lingwood was still only 46, but he had lived in the village for the whole of his life, save for the very short period during which he had been in Bradford. He had two offers open to him, one being St Peter Parmentergate in Norwich, the other St Martin, Barton, Torquay, a church which already supported the shrine. He decided that Torquay offered the greater challenge and opted for the move to the West Country.

Lingwood was nothing if not dutiful. He also wrote later that in any event he would not have left Walsingham had there not been a suitable person to take over the duties of bursar, since he knew that Hope Patten had no ability at all with financial matters. His assistant, Stanley Smith, after being a resident at the children's home had then been trained in accountancy when undergoing National Service, during which he lodged in the clergy house of the Holy Redeemer, Clerkenwell. He had returned to Walsingham to learn the ropes from Lingwood and when the question arose, he indicated that he would be prepared to take over.

In addition to arranging the succession to the bursarship, Lingwood arranged, with Hope Patten's approval, for Revd L. P. Franklin, who was already in the College, to assist in the parishes in his place. Father Leonard

---

5 Lingwood, 'Rough Notes'.

Patrick Franklin was a real ecclesiastical rolling stone, who had served for short periods in many places, including long spells in Australia, where he had been born. In Walsingham he lasted a very short time indeed on this occasion, since during the period in which Lingwood took a holiday before moving down to Devon, Franklin was dismissed by Hope Patten.[6] The chapter record indicates that there was an unpleasant scene on 2 June 1956 at which Hope Patten accused him of idleness: he apparently refused to do more than say mass and the office and keep his room clean.

In the summer of 1956 Revd B. P. Elliott Smith[7] came as a replacement assistant priest, initially for three months but with the hope that he would stay longer. However, he had a severe breakdown within a fortnight or so and left, never to return. Hope Patten wrote to a third party that after mass one day Father Elliott Smith had been found unconscious, so the problem was obviously serious.[8]

There is no doubt that Lingwood's departure from Walsingham in June 1956 was taken very hard by Hope Patten, who regarded it as nothing short of desertion, although he commented publicly in *Our Lady's Mirror*, spring 1956, that 'no one could have fulfilled the office of bursar more competently and thoroughly'.

His feelings of rejection were, however, as nothing compared to his reaction later that year when he learned that his protégé was to marry. Hope Patten had always taken clerical celibacy very seriously indeed, and the concept that a priest trained by him and schooled in his ways could even contemplate matrimony was extremely difficult for him to comprehend, still less approve. He wrote to a third party on 20 November 1956, 'Derrick has asked someone or other to marry him', which was a predictably disparaging way of putting things. However, matters went further than that, since he then concluded that the underlying reason why Lingwood had left Walsingham was in order to marry and that therefore he had not been truthful with him. While denying that any understanding

---

6 Father Leo Franklin (as he was known) returned to Walsingham in 1961, after Hope Patten's death, and lived there until 1963 as a member of the Community of Benedictine Oblates of Nashdom which replaced the CSA for some years. He then returned to Australia.

7 Brian Percivall (*sic*) Elliott Smith was ordained priest in 1952 and served as a curate at Rumboldswyke, Chichester, for two years before temporarily disappearing from *Crockford*; Walsingham appears to have been intended as his return to active ministry, but proved a disaster.

8 Letter of 19 November 1956 to R. J. Hill (WA).

had been reached prior to his departure from Walsingham with the lady he married, Lingwood himself later wrote: 'It has been said that I left Walsingham to get married. I cannot deny that this was not in my mind (*sic*) . . .'[9] Certainly the marriage followed very shortly after his departure. It was also the case that he had been worn down by the years at Walsingham and needed to leave for health reasons.

The move by Lingwood to Devon did not affect his position as a Guardian. However, the constitution of the College made it perfectly clear that any Priest Guardian who married thereby automatically ceased from the fellowship. On 8 December 1956 he wrote to the other Guardians announcing his intention to marry and offering to resign, although questioning whether that should be so. By this time relations between the two men who had been so close for so many years were extremely strained, and Hope Patten even accused Lingwood of soliciting money for his new parish from clients of Walsingham. A painful reply dated 5 December 1956 denied the allegation.

Hope Patten would brook no deviation from the prescription in the constitution, and saw it as a matter of supreme importance. In that he was supported by some of the other Guardians, but opinion was divided and Sir William Milner in particular was on Lingwood's side. He and Lingwood were on very friendly terms and had often holidayed together; they were referred to as 'the two Derricks', because of Milner's own use of that name among his friends. Some of the Guardians also took the view that an exception should be made in Lingwood's case because of the unique contribution which he had made to the success of the shrine.

Hope Patten became almost hysterical over this issue. He was simply unable to understand why there should be any support for the proposition that the constitution of the Guardian should be altered to allow Derrick Lingwood to remain as a member of the Fellowship. He began regretting that he had ever established the College of Guardians, and in an undated letter of this period, addressed only to 'Dear Father' (probably Fynes-Clinton) he set out in very forceful terms his views about their position,

---

9 Lingwood, 'Rough Notes'. His fiancée, Cynthia, was a friend of Enid Chadwick, through whom they had met. Some observers, including Stanley Smith, thought that Enid Chadwick herself harboured similar feelings for Derrick Lingwood. There were certainly some at the time, including Miss Williams of St Hilary's, who formed the view that he had decided to marry before leaving (interview with Stanley Smith, 25 March 2006).

thus: 'The College of Guardians was established by *ME* as a body of influential people to back me up in my contention with the B[isho]p etc. and to add lustre to the shrine. I was warned at the time that they would become cuckoos and kick me out.'

Hope Patten's threats became wilder. In a letter similarly addressed but dated 5 December 1956 he said that he would have to resign from the shrine and the parish if the Guardians voted to change the constitution and said he could trust only the addressee, Lord Norton and Father Crusha. In fact Canon Maryon-Wilson was also strongly against the change. He also threatened, that if he did leave, the College of St Augustine would have to move elsewhere with him, which seems odd since its purpose was to serve the shrine.

Hope Patten went so far as to commission a tract on the celibacy of the clergy, which was circulated to all the Guardians. It was written by Revd G. A. C. Whatton, then the chaplain of the Community of St Mary at the Cross at Edgware and a former Master of the Society of the Holy Cross. It was unfortunate that the paper, densely argued and relying on much learning, throughout misspelled its subject as 'celebacy'.[10] The author set out a classic example of Anglican Papalist thinking, of which Hope Patten would much have approved: 'But the question arises whether the Church of England (i.e. a group of provinces of the Western part of the Catholic Church in enforced isolation from the rest) has any more right to "dispense" both Western and Oecumenical Canon Law than e.g. a local County Council to "dispense" from the observance of an Act of Parliament of the Realm?'

The conclusion of the paper was, predictably perhaps, thus: 'it is clear from the Holy Scriptures themselves and still more from Catholic tradition that the celebacy of the clergy is the ideal to which all who value Catholic custom and tradition should be urged . . .'

In the event the meeting of the Guardians reached a classic compromise, mainly because although by this time the members of the College were unwilling to be rubber stamps for Hope Patten, yet they accepted his strength of feeling on this issue. It was eventually decided that the constitution should not be amended, but that the rule, in force since 1929, that priest members of the Society of Our Lady of Walsingham should

---

10 Suspiciously, this was a spelling error also found in an earlier edition of *Our Lady's Mirror*, where there was an advertisement asking for a 'celebate' priest.

automatically lose their membership if they married should be abrogated. The constitution of the Guardians was not in fact to be altered in this regard until 2005.

There were a number of ironic twists to this unfortunate parting of the ways. One was that although Lingwood had been forced to resign as a Guardian, he remained a director of the company holding the shrine's assets and no provision had been included in the articles which required him to resign when he ceased to be a Guardian. Hope Patten was insistent that he should do so, but Sir William Milner was equally adamant in the argument to the contrary and Lingwood did not do so.

The other irony was that, as Lingwood himself graciously accepted later, his departure meant that Hope Patten had of necessity to turn back to the parish and the people and see to their needs again. This he did, which was no mean task for a man of his age and bearing in mind the number of responsibilities which he then held. For the last few years of his life, he again resumed the reins in the village and his parishioners responded to him.

Hope Patten continued to organise anniversary events with aplomb. In October 1952 there was a procession through the village to commemorate the twenty-first anniversary of the translation of the image to the chapel, and Fathers Fynes-Clinton and Gill preached at the festa. The following year the Coronation was marked, perhaps uniquely, by an all-night vigil in the parish church before the exposed Sacrament. After the events of the Second World War, Hope Patten had become more definitely monarchical and patriotic in his notes in the newsletters.

The unfortunate events surrounding Derrick Lingwood's position clouded the Jubilee of the translation, which was celebrated in 1956, very shortly after he had left Walsingham, but before he had announced his intention to marry. On 20 September 1956 there was a solemn mass sung at St Magnus the Martyr by Father Fynes-Clinton, and afterwards a reception at Caxton Hall, where the attendance was recorded as a rather modest 300 to 400. Sir William Milner presented Lingwood with a cheque for £360 and a copy of the Van Eyck triptych of the Adoration of the Lamb. Hope Patten gave a short address dealing with the development of the shrine. Thereafter there was a series of events at Walsingham, and on Saturday 13 October 1956 mass of St Edward the Confessor was sung at his altar followed by solemn vespers and a procession around the precincts of the shrine. The following day there were a number of low masses and at

10.30 a.m. a procession was made from the shrine to the parish church, where it was met by Hope Patten. Father Gill spoke at the parish mass. Later there was sprinkling, benediction and solemn vespers, and at 9 p.m. a torchlight procession down the high street while the rosary was recited, to the parish church and back to the shrine. Both churches were especially lit and the event showed that Hope Patten had not lost his ability to create dramatic events. The procession was followed by midnight mass, and then further masses were said throughout the night while pilgrims kept watch. At 8.30 a.m. there was solemn benediction (an idiosyncratic Hope Patten touch) and then further devotions in the morning. At mid-day on Monday 15 October 1956 Bishop Vernon sang high mass in the shrine church and later the Abbot of Nashdom (Dom Augustine Morris, who had replaced Martin Collett) addressed the Guardians and the other pilgrims on the subject of Christian reunion. The last act of the celebration for that year was yet another procession, again around the precincts, this time presided over by Hope Patten, but the events were continued into 1957 and finished with the Whit Monday pilgrimage.

Although pilgrimages to Walsingham increased in number and size in the 1950s, there was to some extent a sense that matters were not moving forward with the momentum which had characterised the pre-war period and which had been interrupted by the outbreak of hostilities. Hope Patten continued his attempts to publicise the shrine, and in 1954 pub-lished a well-illustrated book on the shrine which was available in either hardback or softback form and entitled *Mary's Shrine of the Holy House, Walsingham*. Although Hope Patten had written many thousands of words for *Our Lady's Mirror*, some of which were of considerable anti-quarian interest, this was his only substantial book.

However, the appeal of the shrine was still to a very small number of parishes, and many who thought of themselves as Anglo-Catholic looked askance at what took place there. In the early 1950s the annual National Pilgrimage was normally attended by between 1,000 and 1,500 people; in other words, it was still a relatively small event.

Hope Patten had always needed company, preferably of those younger than himself. He had relied on Derrick Lingwood in that regard for many years, and also Theodore Williams, Moses Harbottle and others, but in Lingwood's absence he turned initially to his replacement, Stanley Smith, who then lived in the College and was well used to the way in which Hope Patten behaved. On one occasion when Smith was sleeping in the next room to Hope Patten he heard the vicar call out in a semi-conscious state, 'Rudolph, Rudolph, bring me wine.' When he went through to see what the problem was, Hope Patten said: 'Has the drawbridge been let down?' Stanley Smith, who had no wine to hand, took him Lucozade, but after sipping it Hope Patten called it 'dishwater' and again asked for wine.

The extent of Hope Patten's demands on others can perhaps be seen from the fact that at the beginning of this period, when Stanley Smith was only 17 and had just passed his driving test, he was expected to drive him across Europe. This was particularly difficult because although Hope Patten had never learned to drive, he was an enthusiastic passenger seat driver, whirling his arms around as if at semaphore while giving frequent instructions. The young assistant bursar did see at that time and later many sights he would not otherwise have seen, being taken to Belgium, France, Switzerland, and Malta, although of course he had to accept charge of the driving, luggage and money. On one occasion they went to Malta for two or three months. Stanley Smith recalls others telling him how lucky he was, at a time when continental travel was relatively uncommon, to be given the opportunity of seeing so many, mainly ecclesiastical, of the buildings described in Baedeker. However, he missed playing for the village football team, and later, understandably, had no wish to leave his fiancée, Monica Frary, daughter of William Frary, for any prolonged time.[11]

There were in addition occasions upon which Hope Patten stayed in a relatively expensive hotel in Brighton with one of the novices of the CSA, which raised many eyebrows because he was supposed to be living on 10s per week; it also made the other novices jealous, but he could not do without a companion. Those visits at least were not entirely for pleasure, as he wanted to see his oculist on the South coast, but the records show that Hope Patten went abroad nearly every year at least once, sometimes more, from 1951 onwards. He went to various parts of Europe, but after 1955 most often to Spain. In that year he took John Shepherd on a six-week trip around the cities of Spain, travelling by train. The CSA had no vow of poverty, unlike true monastic institutions, but only of chastity and obedience. This was not always appreciated by those who looked at the College from the outside.

The Bishop of Norwich continued during the 1950s to be far more

---

11 Interview with Stanley Smith, 25 March 2006.

accommodating to Walsingham than had been his predecessor. There was a mild falling out in 1950 when it was proposed that regulations be introduced to deal with benediction, and Hope Patten took advice from Raymond Raynes and Bishop Vibert Jackson, a veteran and well-respected Anglo-Catholic who had retired from his episcopate in the Caribbean to Ascot, but in the event the proposed restrictions came to nothing.

The 1950s were also notable for the easing of relationships between Anglicans and Romans in the village, which had been so difficult before the war and had culminated at that time in an absurd dispute about how the local authority was to signpost the two shrines. The new friendliness was largely due to the new Roman Catholic parish priest, Father Gerard Hulme, who was emollient where his predecessors had been provocative.

It is, however, a salutary reminder of how little common ground there was between the churches at this time that an appearance by both priests together on the radio on 6 January 1954, as part of a visit to the village by the well-known personality Wilfred Pickles and his 'Have a Go' programme, should be heralded as a significant ecumenical gesture. Each priest said on air that relations between the two were co-operative, which in those days of an ecclesiastical Berlin Wall around Roman Catholics in this country was perhaps of some little importance.

The ancillary enterprises had different fortunes at this time. The St Hilary home continued to take in and look after children who had been abandoned or whose parents could not look after them, and was in a period of stability. It functioned as well as could any institution in those circumstances, and most of those taken in appeared grateful for the affection and order which were brought into their lives and the extended family which it provided. In 1953 the hostel for working boys, which has already been mentioned, opened under the supervision of John Shepherd's parents; it used the house now known as 'Shields', which had at one time been intended as the Hospice of SS Michael and George and had been acquired again, this time by the Yorkshire subsidiary company. It did not, however, survive to become a long-term feature. Frederick Shepherd continued to work throughout this period as the manager of a local department store.

The CSA had a very unsteady start to the decade. On 1 February 1951 Colin Sparke was clothed as Brother Joseph, but he left before the end of the year, unable to cope with the silence and loneliness of the life. On 14

April 1951 two new postulants arrived, Thomas Bassingthwaite and Malcolm Stubbs, but the latter, who came from Norwich and had visited the shrine frequently before joining the Community, lasted only a few weeks before being told he had no vocation.[12] In July 1951 Brother Paul (Barnett) announced that he no longer felt he had a vocation, and left.[13]

However, Bassingthwaite was clothed as a novice on 1 August 1951, taking the name Brother Thomas, and a week later John Shepherd was clothed as Brother John Augustine. He was, however, forced to leave temporarily in March 1952, as he was called up for National Service with the RAF, despite Hope Patten's best endeavours to prevent this occurring on the basis that he was a member of a religious community. His conduct during his postulancy was described as 'exemplary' and he was clearly Hope Patten's blue-eyed boy at that time. He agreed to keep the rule so far as he could while away and to come back to the College whenever he was free. It was a most unusual situation for a serviceman, but he persevered with his chosen course. This was made easier as he was engaged in air traffic control and was thus on regular shifts. He was stationed near to the church of SS Peter and Paul, Carbrooke, Norfolk, where the parish priest, Revd George Chambers, had been trained by Father Noel at Thaxted. Although John Shepherd found the religion there reasonably familiar, he was somewhat disconcerted by the presence of a figure of Christ with a hammer in one hand and a sickle in the other.

Up to this time, the CSA had effectively been free from outside influences. There was a suggestion some years before that Bishop O'Rorke act as episcopal visitor, but nothing had ever been effected. Hope Patten, however, had applied for recognition to the Advisory Council for Religious Communities, not in order to bring the College under external control, but rather to try to receive official certification so that Shepherd would be exempt from the military call-up.

On 11 November 1952 the Council decided definitively that the CSA was not a monastic institution within their purview, as it lacked certain essential characteristics, and was rather a college properly so called. This decision was conveyed to Hope Patten by the experienced Father O'Brien SSJE, who had assisted with the sisters, by letter dated 13 November 1952,

---

12 He wrote in 1961 with reminiscences of his time in the College, despite being there for such a short time.

13 David Barnett was of Jewish origin. He later became a Roman Catholic.

in which he suggested that the Bishop of Norwich should license the head of the College to use the shrine church under the Private Chapels Act 1871. This statute governed such establishments as school and hospital chapels and provided that the parish priest could not interfere with the worship in such buildings; they were also not required to use the Book of Common Prayer.

Initially, Hope Patten baulked at this sensible proposal, because he was still contending, on the strength of the legal opinion he had been given before the war, that the shrine was a peculiar and therefore extra-diocesan. O'Brien advised him strongly to go down the Private Chapels Act path and Hope Patten eventually agreed with this pragmatic solution. In the meantime, the Bishop of Oxford, Kenneth Kirk, who was on the Council, had communicated their view to the Bishop of Norwich. He immediately wrote to Hope Patten saying that on any change of incumbency (a tactful method of saying when the vicar died) the Bishop would be prepared to treat the shrine and College as coming within the provisions of the Act of 1871, so that he would license a priest nominated by the trustees (i.e. the Guardians) and approved by himself. The following year he said that he would be prepared at that time to license the Provost of the CSA (as Hope Patten had by then become) under that Act, but that it was not a necessary step while Hope Patten was also vicar of the parish.

In that way, many of Hope Patten's constant fears about the future were allayed but never disappeared completely.

The trickle of recruits into the College dried up after Shepherd went away. The situation became even more difficult at the end of 1952 when Brother John (Perry), who was by then the longest serving member apart from Hope Patten and Lingwood, decided to leave in order to try his vocation at Nashdom. Brother Thomas (Bassingthwaite) decided to join him. John Perry did not stay long at Nashdom, and soon went over to Rome, but Thomas Bassingthwaite stayed as a laybrother with the Anglican Benedictines.[14] Since John Shepherd was away, the College had been reduced to two members only and was effectively back to its pre-war state.

For the next year, the College was to all intents and purposes dormant, although Hope Patten and Lingwood continued as many observances as they could. One attractive feature of Hope Patten's personality was his willingness to persevere when others would have abandoned a venture,

---

14 John Perry became a Roman Catholic priest, but later left the priesthood.

and although the state of the College depressed him greatly, he did not give up.

On 17 October 1953 what was in effect a further relaunch of the CSA took place. In order to regularise matters, a new constitution was adopted at the chapter meeting on the recommendation of O'Brien, the main feature of which was to alter the terminology. Thus Hope Patten was to become Provost rather than Prior, and the novices were to be known as Junior Members, the Professed as Senior Members. The Rule and Constitution were typed out and bound for the members in 1955. It was a typical Hope Patten touch that it was specifically provided that: 'The Faith and Practice of the College shall conform strictly with that of the Catholic Church.'

Brother John Augustine (Shepherd) had indicated that he was willing to renew his vows after his national service and thus the Community increased to three at that time. Then on 22 October 1953 David Girling and Peter Wakeling were admitted for an initial three months, but Girling left after a week.[15] On 21 November 1953 came the bombshell that Derrick Lingwood was unwilling to renew his vows. Hope Patten responded by immediately renewing his own for a further three years, but a huge blow had been dealt to the College just when he was hoping to put it back on course.

It was still necessary to ensure that further men came, particularly as it had always been accepted that in due course John Shepherd would go to theological college to prepare for ordination, and this was arranged to commence in October 1954; he was to follow in his patron's footsteps and go to Lichfield. From this time onwards, however, perhaps because the steadying influence of Derrick Lingwood was not present any longer, Hope Patten's judgement became more erratic and a number of those who came were unsuitable. One or two were, in the perception of most observers, obviously homosexual, which led to difficulties in the College and in the public perception of the brothers.

On 6 March 1954 Wakeling became a junior member and took the name of Brother Gregory, but in August he was dismissed by Hope Patten 'owing to grave irregularity and disobedience'. No more detail is recorded in the minutes, but, as often with Hope Patten, more lay beneath the

15 Some years later David F. C. Girling was ordained (deacon 1961, priest 1962) and served most of his career thereafter in the Diocese of Chelmsford. He retired in 1998.

surface. He had in fact known Wakeling for some time prior to him joining the Community, and after he left he continued corresponding with him until his own death. Copies of his letters to Wakeling are in the Archives, but not the replies, and it is clear that Hope Patten was adamant that the younger man had to leave, because he had displayed 'heretical opinions' and developed a violent aversion to John Shepherd, but also because he had formed a surreptitious admiration for a female member of staff at the Sanctuary School, whom in due course he married. Hope Patten was clearly fond of Wakeling, although his letters show how touchy he had become about any perceived slight. The fact that he continued to take an interest in his former novice's career as a teacher and in his marriage does, however, indicate that he was nowhere near as unfeeling to those who had failed to last the course at the CSA as might be thought from the bare minutes.

In May 1954 Matthew Wagstaff arrived and on 27 August 1954 he was admitted as a junior member, retaining his own Christian name in religion. At the end of the year Owen Webber-Jones came to the College, and on 11 February 1955 he was admitted as the second Brother Joseph. He was the son of a priest and had already lived for some time with the Society of St John the Evangelist in Oxford. He was described by one observer as 'a very willowy old queen',[16] or perhaps more kindly by another as rather a harmless old woman,[17] and was said by all to be a great gossip, although Hope Patten was adamant that members of the College should so far as possible stay within the precincts of the shrine and not converse even with the sisters.

Father Franklin, who has already been mentioned, came in July 1955 and was admitted as a junior member on 21 November 1955 as Father Leo, thus providing another priest, which was particularly helpful when Hope Patten was away, as happened in September 1955.

In late 1955 there was an important move in the worship of the College, namely the abandonment of matins and evensong and the adoption of the Roman breviary, which provoked the letter of protest from Father Lingwood to which reference has already been made. This move was

---

16 Letter of 22 April 1961 from a correspondent identifiable only as 'Colin', who had been at the College in the summer of 1955 and was clearly a friend of Revd F. T. W. Smith, who was asking for contributions to his proposed biography of Hope Patten.

17 By John Shepherd, interview 11 March 2006.

championed by Hope Patten and John Shepherd; as already suggested, Hope Patten was further under the influence of the Papalist party by this time, especially because Derrick Lingwood's conservative instincts were no longer a force to be considered whereas John Shepherd was pulling hard in a Roman direction.

There was another crisis in mid 1956. First in June Father Leo was dismissed, as already set out; then in July Brother Matthew (Wagstaff) left, ostensibly because his health was not good and he felt he had no vocation, although Hope Patten wrote in a contemporary letter that he had had a nervous breakdown.[18] He was also one of those whom most observers appreciated had an orientation towards members of his own sex; Hope Patten was intolerant of behaviour of that nature but also naive in seeing it. They were followed out in August by two new postulants, (Herbert) Alfred Stenner and Mervin Douglas Harvard-Brown (Brother Martin), both of whom had joined earlier in the year. Brother Martin left to go over to Rome, but did not in the event secede and went instead to Nashdom.

The College was therefore reduced to Hope Patten, Brother John Augustine (Shepherd) and Brother Joseph (Webber-Jones). Still Hope Patten would not give up, and formal meetings continued to be held.

The Sanctuary School too staggered on from crisis to crisis, which was particularly hard on Derrick Lingwood, who frequently had to burn the midnight oil trying to think of ways of staving off the bank manager. It was particularly hard also on those Guardians who had contributed to the funds required to keep the school running.

Initially Mr Armistead had raised numbers, by creating a pre-preparatory department for both boys and girls in what had once been Walsingham Grammar School. By 1954 there was a record number of pupils, a total of 75 of whom 25 were boarders. That rise was the result of the new department and 22 on the roll were girls. In that year the school was inspected by the Ministry of Education and given guarded praise for its spirit, while the facilities were the subject of criticism. By 1955, however, parents were becoming discontented and a substantial proportion of pupils were withdrawn and not replaced, so that by April of the following year there were only 50 in all. Michael Farrer, who had been a pupil at the

---

18 Letter of 4 September 1956 to R. J. Hill, whom he had been attempting to persuade to join the College since 1952 (WA). In the same letter Hope Patten says that John Shepherd was home from Lichfield after suffering a breakdown in health.

school, returned there to teach in 1955 but saw the way in which the wind was blowing and soon left for a post with Tapping at Beeston Hall.[19] It does not seem in any event that the headmaster inspired much confidence in the parents, but at least he stayed in post. He was also personally acceptable to Hope Patten, not least because he was deeply committed to the religious teaching in the village. He and his wife had a very large family of their own, which led the warden on one occasion to write somewhat sarcastically that 'it isn't possible to run a school and be a nursemaid half the time'.[20]

At that point the almost inevitable decision was made that the boarding house had to close but, optimistically, it was decided to attempt to continue on one site, at the vicarage, at which there were to be both boys and girls. Mr Armistead resigned in July 1956[21] and the school started the new term with only 11 pupils, under a Miss MacMurray.

Hope Patten saw the potential demise of the school upon which he had pinned so many hopes as a personal affront, and never acknowledged that his own conduct might in any way have contributed to its problems. He wrote reams to potential parents and to those who might assist with financial backing, but it was all to no avail and in 1958 the school finally shut its doors. Hope Patten's naivety in matters of education is shown by the fact that, when he was advised that old boys were a good source of financial backing for a school, he wrote round to all the former pupils, failing to appreciate that they were mostly still on National Service and certainly not flush with cash.

The vicar's response to the final collapse was predictable. He had written in *Our Lady's Mirror*, summer 1956: 'The Sanctuary School has closed, much to the great regret of all, but Catholics evidently do not want a Church School of definite teaching and practice, and so it is they who have virtually shut it down.' That sentence did not reflect the better side of him, which was so apparent to other people in other ways. The closure also meant a loss of capital on the part of some of the Guardians who had provided support, and Derrick Lingwood found the prospect of dealing with that aspect particularly embarrassing. In the event, he had left by the

---

19 Another former teacher at the School, Anthony Prescott, was ordained in 1961.
20 On 3 February 1956 (WA).
21 He and his family were received into the Roman Catholic Church shortly afterwards.

time the guarantees were called in and Stanley Smith had to cope with the situation.[22]

What was also galling for Hope Patten was that, while the Sanctuary School was foundering, Quainton Hall under Father Eyden's guidance was surging forward in every respect. Hope Patten attended for meetings and also for important events such as the opening of the new chapel in 1955, but he and the other Governors left the detail of its running to the staff. In many ways, Father Eyden had established what Father Patten foresaw occurring in Walsingham. There was regular worship in an Anglo-Catholic idiom, and a Confraternity of St Francis was established for those confirmed, which in 1954 was given a charter under the seal of the Diocese of London. Benediction was the regular devotion of the Quainton Hall Confraternity, which was the only such organisation apart from that which had been established at St Dunstan, Cranford, by the well-known priest Revd Maurice Child. He had died in 1950 but prior to his death Father Eyden had assisted as an honorary assistant curate at his church.

There is a recurrent theme in Hope Patten's time at Walsingham, of ideas which raised themselves many years before being resurrected and put into effect after a long interval. Another such was the proposal for a home for retired priests as an ancillary to the shrine, which had been in his mind since the original acquisition of property in 1924, but to which effect was not given until the 1950s. At that time, he had what became known as the North Wing reconstructed as the Home of St Thomas of Canterbury. Craze was involved with this, as the conversion was both extensive and expensive. Five new bed-sitting rooms were constructed within the cottages, and in addition a refectory was made which closely resembled a mediaeval hall at first glance. Hope Patten clearly had the potential to have been an architect, provided perhaps that any clients of his were not too worried about finance; the refectory was ingeniously thought through and a very successful adaptation.

The home for retired priests turned out to be another venture which did not succeed. Hope Patten had not really considered the implications of having a number of increasingly aging priests under his control; his simplistic vision of their presence was that they would be able to say mass every day at one of the many altars at the shrine. In practice, priests who had retired were reluctant to move to Norfolk, even with the draw of the

---

22 Stanley Smith, interview 25 March 2006.

shrine. There was in the event only one long-term resident, Revd Sidney Panton, who had been a curate at St Alban, Holborn from 1920 to 1930 and served in various other parishes, lastly as vicar of St Nicholas Cole Abbey in the City. He arrived in about 1954 and stayed until 1962, when increasing infirmity meant that he had to move to a nursing home. As with Hope Patten, he claimed to see ghosts on a regular basis about the College. He died in 1964.

There were at least two other residents for short times. One, from 1955, was Revd Bede Frost,[23] formerly chaplain to the SSM at East Grinstead. The other was Revd G. H. Tugwell, who had been at Caldey but had not gone over to Rome and was subsequently ordained in the Scottish Episcopal Church. He became a secular priest, in London and East Anglia, and lastly, from 1947 onwards, at Hindringham, Norfolk. He was markedly eccentric in his habits and not an easy man with whom to live. He died in 1960.

The empty rooms which did not attract the retired had to be used for other purposes, usually for priests who were visiting the shrine for short periods or attending with their parishioners. A library for the CSA was also constructed in St Augustine's. Hope Patten had asked for advice prior to the venture getting under way from Father Thomas OSB, a frequent visitor to Walsingham, who was intent on setting up a similar scheme at the Benedictine convent at West Malling, Kent, to be known as St Simeon's Home, with himself as Warden. It too was not successful.

It was a sign of the increasing frostiness between Hope Patten and Lingwood that on 20 July 1955 the latter wrote to the former a very formal letter. He reminded him that he had agreed to pay 5 per cent interest on such part of the costs incurred in the conversion work to the North Wing as was not covered by donations. The work had cost £6,000 but only £1,000 had been given, so he was asked to pay £250 per annum, or more precisely £125 per six months, by way of interest. The letter is revealing, as it shows not only how cold had become the relations between the two of them, but also how much money had been expended without real thought about how it could be recouped; £6,000 was a very considerable sum at that time.

---

23 His real name was Albert Ernest Frost; he was ordained in 1901 and after a long career in the Empire he was at East Grinstead from 1940 onwards. He was said to be the only Australian Anglican to use Latin in the liturgy.

The Sisters of St Margaret continued to serve the shrine and look after the pilgrims. The stability which came partly from being part of a well-established order and partly from the fact that Hope Patten had no control over the day-to-day running of the sisters was a welcome change from the conflict which had marked the 1941 to 1947 period. It had been clearly understood from the beginning that he was not to act as confessor to the sisters nor to direct their life other than in the parish and around the shrine.

In 1954–5 a new convent was erected for the sisters, designed by Milner & Craze, in an austere style which would not have been Hope Patten's preference. He would no doubt have preferred a building in the continental idiom which complemented the shrine church and could then be filled with baroque ornaments imported from abroad. It was the only substantial building related to the shrine in the design of which he had no say, a fact which emphasised the independence of the sisters. At the same time, the Walsingham branch became a self-governing Priory with Sister Margaret Mary as the first Mother, a change which was by then appropriate since its foundations had by then been properly established. Originally a wooden chapel was erected for the convent with a permanent altar in it, and then the new chapel was erected around the altar. The Bishop of Norwich came to install Mother Margaret Mary on 10 May 1955 and returned on 9 February 1957 to bless the new chapel.

In this way of course, although not quite as he had envisaged, Hope Patten achieved the establishment within the village of a settled priory, independent of the main order. The twist was that it was outside his control, which is what had in fact enabled it to survive and flourish.

Although Romilly Craze had designed the shrine church, Hope Patten was always interested in the work of Ninian Comper, whose exquisite recreations of the Middle Ages in his early days were in many ways very attractive to the administrator's temperament. The shrine church would no doubt have looked very different had Comper designed it, but the cost would have been prohibitive as his work was always very expensive. Comper had, however, been asked to design a set of six stained-glass windows for the shrine at the time it was constructed, of which three were completed, showing Our Lady herself, Richeldis and St Thomas respectively. Comper also designed at about the time that the shrine chapel was opened a red chasuble decorated with signs of the English saints, which was carried out by the Sisters of Bethany at their famed school of embroidery in Clerkenwell.

In 1954 it was decided to instruct the then very elderly Sir Ninian Comper, as he had become, to design new furnishings for the Holy House itself. The work was not finally completed until 1960, after the death of both Hope Patten and Comper himself, who was almost 90 even when the commission was accepted; a great deal of the work was executed by his last partner and great-nephew, John Bucknall. As was characteristic of Comper's mature years, the design incorporated both Gothic and classical motifs on a gold background, and in addition the finished design drew from earlier work by Comper. The shell design was taken from his altar screen at nearby Wymondham, the crucifix and candlesticks from the chapel of the All Saints sisters at London Colney, and the canopy from that erected over the Stanton chantry in St Alban, Holborn, which formed part of the furnishings of that church lost as a result of bombing in the war.[24]

In 1955–6 further work was done on the site adjoining the Hospice of Our Lady Star of the Sea, and a new building with substantial gatehouse was built leading into the gardens from Holt Road, affording additional rooms for pilgrims. This was made possible by a very generous anony-mous donation of some £10,000, and it gave Hope Patten great pleasure to see a building of such undeniably mediaeval type erected in the 1950s. Few would now appreciate immediately how recently it was constructed.

There is no doubt that the future of the shrine preoccupied Hope Patten as he grew older. By 1955 he was 70 and his health had never been robust. Unlike many people, however, he voiced in public his fears for the future. An unfortunate article appeared in *Our Lady's Mirror*, winter 1955, entitled 'What will happen when Fr. Patten dies?' The author, who was claimed not to be the subject of the article, was correct, but tactless, to say that 'it will never be quite the same of course, because a new man could not possibly maintain a tradition which he had not helped to create'. It was in fact another attempt to encourage vocations to the CSA.

One of the major problems surrounding the position of the shrine was that there was no long-term financial plan or endowment fund in place. Hope Patten himself was always anxious to spend any legacies which were received as soon as possible, preferably on extensions or renovations, because he was strongly of the frame of mind that the more that was erected, the more likely it was to remain in the long term. In 1957 the

---

24 See the note on *Victorian Architects and their Successors at Walsingham* by Anthony Symondson in *Walsingham Review*, 63, 1977.

Guardians persuaded him that an attempt should be made to raise £50,000 so that a substantial endowment fund could be laid down to provide for the stipends of priests who could serve the shrine. The main force behind this was Patrick Maitland, who arranged a launch with a press conference at the House of Commons at which Hope Patten attended. The Appeal for Walsingham, as it was termed, was supported by a number of prominent laymen, comprising John Betjeman, Lord David Cecil, T. S. Eliot, Lady Cynthia Colville, Dame Sybil Thorndike (who had of course sponsored an appeal for the original Hospice in 1926), and the Hon. Richard Wood, MP, the grandson of the co-sponsor of that 1926 appeal, Lord Halifax.

The appeal was supported particularly by a new society which had been formed, the Friends of Walsingham, which, unlike the Society of Our Lady of Walsingham, imposed no devotional duties on its members and was designed as a fundraising organisation. A separate series of newsletters, known as *Occasional Papers*, was circulated for the Friends commencing in July 1955. They sprung from an idea of Derrick Lingwood, who acknowledged later that all the other bodies which were set up had been Hope Patten's own creation, but that this was his.[25]

---

25 Letter of 20 May 1961 (WA).

13

THE LAST YEARS AT WALSINGHAM AND THEIR AFTERMATH, 1956–8

There is no doubt that Hope Patten's ailments were becoming even more frequent as he grew older, but he had been ill so many times that they were accepted by all as part of his life. His eyes by this time were giving him so much trouble that John Shepherd took over the writing of the minutes for the CSA, setting out what was discussed much more fully than had been the case before.

One consequence of these visual problems was that the missal stands in the shrine were constantly heightened by adding portions at the foot, so that it was easier for the administrator to see the book. In April 1957 Hope Patten reported that the sight in one eye had practically gone but that the other eye was capable of being saved with rest. The other members of the College told him to get away as soon as possible, and he later said that he would go away with John Shepherd, who had also been told to relax for a time.

In the last years, there were a few changes to the body of the Guardians. Father Raymond Raynes CR died in early 1958 and was replaced by Revd Philip Husbands, parish priest of St James, Wednesbury, in the West Midlands, who was the last Guardian instituted by Hope Patten in his life-time. The boy whose ear problems had been cured at Walsingham, Cyril Dawes, was a parishioner of his and he had led many pilgrimages.

The most serious problem which Hope Patten faced after Derrick Lingwood's departure in 1956 was that he needed assistance from another resident priest. In the event such aid came from a source which was well known to him, Moses Harbottle, who after leaving the CSA had been ordained in 1950, as he had hoped, by Bishop R. H. Stapley of the Windward Islands,[1] and had thereafter worked for a period of years in the

---

1 Hope Patten may well have smoothed his path because not only did he know

West Indies. Hope Patten had been sympathetic to Harbottle's problem in passing examinations, which echoed his own travails in that regard, and had encouraged him to follow that path to the priesthood although he had not wanted to lose him from the College. In 1956, however, Harbottle returned to England as curate of St Paul, Chiswick, where he remained until the following year. He then returned to Walsingham as assistant curate and was able to help as Hope Patten's health continued to decline. He, like his vicar, was an able preacher with a forceful, simple style.

In fact, Hope Patten received from 1957 onwards more assistance than he had ever had before, as John Shepherd, his new surrogate son and a replacement in his mind for Derrick Lingwood, was ordained deacon on 22 September in that year and was allowed to come to Walsingham to serve his title, while remaining a member of the CSA. He had not yet been priested when Hope Patten died.

The CSA itself was at another low ebb. However, on 1 April 1957 a new young postulant, Arthur Thomas Dance, was received and was immediately reminded that he should bow to the Provost when meeting him. On 16 July 1957 he was joined by Edward Cyril Jillings; in due course they became respectively Brothers Ambrose and Philip. It is not clear what happened to these last two recruits, but it appears that neither was still at Walsingham when Hope Patten died; Philip seems to have left first.

Even at this stage, a new constitution had been prepared and Hope Patten was worried about the situation if the Provost of the College was not also the administrator of the shrine. He raised the question of an episcopal visitor again, and eventually it was decided to ask Abbot Augustine Morris of Nashdom, who eventually declined as he was too busy. It was also decided, on 25 June 1957, to revert to the term 'novice' instead of 'junior member'.

Hope Patten never gave up his efforts to establish the Community, and on 21 December 1957 he was re-installed as Provost for a further five years, which of course he was not to see out. The history of the College was one of heroic struggle coupled with some considerable lack of insight by Hope Patten into what was happening.

Stapley's predecessor, Bishop H. N. V. Tonks, whose episcopate ended in 1949, but Stapley himself had lived in the clergy house at Holy Cross, Cromer Street, as a layman when Hope Patten was a curate there.

However, as 1957 came to an end and 1958 arrived, Hope Patten was indeed beginning to show his years. He presided at the marriage of Stanley and Monica Smith, on 8 February 1958, which was a happy event for all concerned, but the strain of his ministry was telling on him. He was 72 and it was clear to him when he thought objectively on the subject that his cherished ambition to set up a College whose members would serve the shrine was failing, as had done his earlier foundation of sisters and of the school, the final manifestation of which was about to be closed. He was deeply pessimistic about the future of the shrine itself and his eyesight and general health were continuing to cause him trouble.

In June of that year he failed for the first time since he had arrived in Walsingham 37 years previously to have daily devotions to the Sacred Heart of Jesus in June: he was a man of routine and to abandon a cherished 'custom' was quite out of character. On 22 July 1958 he wrote to a younger friend[2] that he was terribly in need of a holiday. He was in fact more ill than he can have known.

During the whole of Hope Patten's ministry Walsingham had largely been shunned by the episcopate. However, it was decided that, since there would be a large number of overseas bishops in England in the summer of 1958 for the Lambeth Conference, an episcopal pilgrimage might be successful, since those from certain dioceses abroad were far more attracted by Walsingham than were those in England. Such a visit was therefore arranged for 11 August 1958.

On the evening before this event was to take place, Hope Patten met John Shepherd in the quadrangle in the College. Entirely out of the blue, but in a serious and considered tone, he said to him words to this effect: 'The time has come for you and I to become Roman Catholics, but we will have to discuss it later.'[3] This was clearly a very important, indeed revolutionary, statement in the light of Hope Patten's career to that date: John Shepherd kept this to himself for very many years thereafter, not least because of what happened the next day.

It may be that Hope Patten was simply exasperated by the failure of the ancillary enterprises, by the tiredness which he was beginning to feel, and by the lack of response to some of his appeals. The recipient of this important confidence, however, had no doubt that it was not a spur of the

---

2 Revd John Foster.
3 Interview with John Shepherd, 11 March 2006.

moment disclosure and that it was a settled decision which would in due course have been taken forward. Circumstances, however, provided that he was unable to ask any further questions about what had prompted this change of mind; the time for the promised further discussion never arose.

The next day Hope Patten and a number of Guardians welcomed the party of bishops on the College lawn. The Bishops of Barbados, British Honduras, Kalgoorie, South West Tanganyika and Zanzibar comprised the group. After rosary and shrine prayers, there was a dinner at the Knight's Gate Café, at which Hope Patten appeared well. It was an unaccustomed experience for him to be sitting at a meal with a sympathetic UMCA[4] bishop on either side of him. It was an extraordinarily hot and humid evening, and after the torchlight procession the shrine was heavy as a result both of the atmospheric pressure and of the heat produced by the multitude of candles. Benediction of the Blessed Sacrament followed without many of those present appreciating that there was anything untoward, and then Hope Patten climbed with the host up the stairs to the chapel in the gallery, accompanied by his servers. He closed the tabernacle door after depositing the Sacrament within, rearranged the veil in a gesture which was characteristic of him in its haste and impatience with untidiness, turned and collapsed. He was caught by the servers and assisted to the College.

The doctor attended and prescribed rest, which the patient resisted on the grounds that the bishops' pilgrimage required his presence. Shortly after the doctor left, Hope Patten collapsed again and died, in his own four-poster bed, with many members of the College of Guardians around him. One or two people had noticed his face displaying pain during benediction, and Father Husbands said he had perceived a glowing light around his head and felt a sense of impending catastrophe.

Hope Patten's death could almost have been stage managed, so dramatic were the circumstances of it. His heart had given way under the continued strain, and cardiac problems may well account for some of his rather difficult behaviour over the preceding few years. Death was certified as being due to myocardial degeneration, and the informant named on the death certificate was Father Crusha, who had been present at the death with the various other Guardians.

---

4 Universities' Mission to Central Africa, then a prominent Anglo-Catholic foundation.

The death was registered the day after it occurred, and the haste may explain why a significant error was made on the certificate in that the deceased was said in it to have been 76, whereas he was in fact only 72, thus leaving another apparent mystery for those looking at his life.

The reason for the very speedy registration of the death was that it had been decided, sensibly, that since so many of the Guardians were already in Walsingham the obsequies should be held as soon as possible.

On the evening of 12 August 1958 the coffin was carried into the shrine and left open for the villagers to pay their last respects to a priest who had changed the lives of all of them in varying degrees, and vespers of the dead were sung. Tom Purdy arranged the funeral in his capacity as village undertaker. Priests said masses every half-hour throughout the night in the Holy House and the next day there was a cortège, with the body on a hand bier, through the streets to St Mary, where, appropriately, Father Lingwood sang the requiem. Despite the serious problems between them in 1956, some part of their old intimacy had begun to return before Hope Patten's death.

Father Gill preached and Hope Patten's body was buried by the west door of the village church. It lies near that of William Frary, whose own premature death at the age of 49 in 1953 had much affected Hope Patten, and who perhaps represented many in the village and outside who had been touched by his charisma, and also near that of Father Francis Baverstock, under whom he had served his title and who had been elected an Honorary Guardian in his later years. The adjacent grave is that of Father Rumball, through whose anonymous munificence the extension had been built in 1938; he had died on 3 October 1953.

The Bishop of Carpentaria, who was also in England for the Lambeth Conference, attended the funeral but neither the Bishop of Norwich nor of Thetford could be there. The Bishop of Central Ceylon came to the shrine a few weeks later.

Hope Patten had left very detailed instructions for his funeral, which he had drawn up as early as 21 February 1937, illustrating again his pre-occupation with his own health. They were, however, not available to the Guardians as they were not found until 4 February 1959, and they were thus not able to follow them to the letter as he would have wished. However, in the codicil to his will, which was of course available, he had asked to be buried either in front of the Hatcham crucifix in the shrine grounds or in St Mary's churchyard in the position which was in fact chosen.

Hope Patten left a will dated 4 July 1957; no doubt that replaced earlier wills in which Derrick Lingwood had been an executor. However, this will named as his executors Stanley Smith, and Peter Hayes, a Fakenham solicitor; the practice was then Mills Reeve & Hayes and is now called Hayes & Storr. The testator left specific gifts of some land at Mundesley, Norfolk, to Stanley Smith, together with personal items of silver and furniture and his books on travel, history and novels, his four-poster bed to Theodore Williams, and keepsakes to members of the Patten, Sadler and Bowling families, including one to his cousin John Patten. He left his theological and hagiographic books together with some vestments to John Shepherd. He left a number of vestments and books which had been used in Walsingham to the College or to the parish church as appropriate; his major asset, a house in Common Place which was then used as the shrine office, was left in one-third shares to Stanley Smith, George Long, and the Walsingham College Trust Association Ltd with a right of pre-emption in favour of the latter. Those premises are still in use as offices. By the codicil dated 14 December 1957, which set out his wishes as to burial, he left any books on art to Enid Chadwick, and, rather plaintively, asked that twenty pounds be applied to the shrine chantry roll for requiems for himself. The will was proved on 5 January 1959 in the sum of £3,616 4s 5d gross, £3,003 14s 8d net.

The College of St Augustine, which after the death of its founder had only two members remaining, namely John Shepherd and Owen Webber-Jones, met the day after the death and elected the former as acting superior. It was never, however, intended by them to continue the College after Hope Patten's death and on 2 October 1958 the two met again and formally resolved to dissolve the Community. Hope Patten's dream of being succeeded by a group of priests and laymen who were already trained to serve the shrine came to an end, as he must have known would happen as he moved into the latter part of his life. Webber-Jones returned to Oxford to work for the Society of St John the Evangelist, although he later retired to Walsingham.

There can be no doubt that the running of the CSA had blighted Hope Patten's later years. He never really thought the project through, and he never managed to attract and retain sufficient members to ensure stability and then slow growth. The readiness to take laybrothers was also a weakness; a group of priests living and working together and running the parishes and shrine may have been more successful. That failure was

exacerbated by his inability to see deficiencies in others which were manifest to most, and the disruptive effect of having unsuitable recruits was
very considerable. It is doubtful, however, whether Hope Patten would
have been temperamentally able to conform with the life of any of the
established communities, because to do so would have involved submit-
ting himself to external discipline administered by others. As it was, he cut
himself off from many of his parishioners while at the same time being
unable properly to establish the College of which he dreamed.

Whether or not Hope Patten would have proceeded to give effect to that
which he had voiced the night before his death must clearly be speculation. Certainly it was a sea change in his thinking from everything which
had gone before. Equally, he was obstinate once set on a path. It may
be that he felt a weariness and lack of fulfilment which was greater than
perceived by anyone at the time. If he had seceded it would have caused
great shock waves among his fellow Anglo-Catholics and reinforced the
feelings of antagonism among those who looked askance at the whole
Walsingham development. On the other hand, the number of those who
had been associated with Walsingham and particularly had been members
of the CSA and who later went over to Rome was considerable, although
they were rather overlooked by those who remained.

In the short-term crisis immediately after Hope Patten's death it was
fortunate that there were two clergy in residence at Walsingham, who
were able to look after the parish and the shrine in the interim. Both in fact
left the following year, 1959. Father Harbottle went early in the year to be
rector of Kedington, Suffolk, a living which was held by the Guardians. In
1963 he moved to St Michael, Edmonton, where he stayed for a number of
years before serving in other parishes. His last appointment was as curate
at All Hallows, Gospel Oak, from 1969 onwards and he died young while
he was there.

Father Shepherd was ordained priest in Norwich Cathedral on 21
September 1958. He sung his first mass in the shrine church two days later,
with Father Smith of South Creake as deacon and Father John Foster, then
curate of St Michael, Ladbroke Grove, as subdeacon. He left Walsingham
in May 1959 partly because he appreciated he would not be able to work
with Colin Stephenson but also to widen his experience by serving as
curate at St John the Divine, Balham. About three months later, and thus
within about a year of Hope Patten's death, he submitted to Rome, a step
which, in the light of the position as it was generally thought by the outside

world to have been, would not have been welcomed by his late mentor. However, it becomes a far easier step to understand after giving due consideration to the conversation which Hope Patten had had with Shepherd the night before the former died. The latter's decision was in some ways a reflection of the views which had then been expressed and a fulfilment of the wishes of the deceased.[5]

John Shepherd then lived as a Roman layman for a number of years, working as a temporary probation officer, then a banker, and finally as personal assistant to Lord Furness of the shipping line. However, by 1967 he had begun to miss the liturgical life in which he had been brought up and thus he returned to the Anglican Communion, first as curate of St Agnes, Kennington. He then held a number of parish appointments, mainly in North London, before becoming chaplain to the then Bishop of London, Graham Leonard. After a spell of about three years in the Diocese of Fort Worth, Texas, he again reverted to Rome after the decision of the Church of England to ordain women, as of course did his new mentor, Bishop Leonard. Father Shepherd was not reordained and is now retired and living in London.

Although it was tacitly understood that Colin Stephenson was to be Hope Patten's successor, and he was fairly rapidly elected as Master of the College of Guardians, he required considerable persuasion to take on the position of administrator. He had been very happy in his parish of St Mary Magdalen, Oxford, and life there suited his gregarious and urban nature. Initially he attempted to persuade one of the male communities to take over the running of the shrine, but none was prepared to do so. The most likely would have been the Community of the Resurrection, but Father Raynes, who would almost certainly have welcomed such a move and driven it from the Mirfield side, had of course died shortly before Hope Patten. Father Stephenson did in due course agree to move and arrived at Walsingham just after Easter 1959. It had been decided that the shrine and the parish should be separated, and at about the same time Revd Alan Roe came to take over as parish priest. It was said then that Hope Patten himself had been considering giving up the parish in favour of the shrine shortly before his death.

At the time, it was thought that the two positions should be divided because the strain of running both had contributed to Hope Patten's ill-

---

5 Interview with John Shepherd, 11 March 2006.

health. Father Stephenson later wrote that he regretted that decision and that he would have found a way of managing, but it is in fact difficult to see how any other course could have been followed, particularly if the work of the shrine was to be extended. It seems, however, that the patron was not in favour of the division.

Although in very many ways Stephenson was a complete contrast in personality to Hope Patten, initially he followed through an idea particularly associated with his predecessor. After instituting the order of Dames of the Shrine in 1953, Hope Patten had considered expanding that concept and had drawn up plans for an order to encompass both the Dames and other men and women, lay and secular, which would provide a recognition of their work for the shrine. Stephenson set up the Order of the Living Rosary of Our Lady of Walsingham in 1960, and each member was allocated to one of the mysteries of the rosary. In that way a number of those who had provided support to Hope Patten were honoured, albeit as it were retrospectively. The clerical members of the new Order were Fathers de Lara Wilson, Eyden, Oldland, and Michael Smith, vicar of South Creake, all of whom have already been mentioned, together with Canon L. G. Harding, parish priest of St Alban, Bordesley, Birmingham, and Revd L. A. Pearson, of St Luke, Hornsey, who had been much concerned with the priests' pilgrimages. The new lay members were Miss Bartholomew and Miss Williams, who had by then run the St Hilary home together for many years, Mother Margaret SSM, Leonard Whitmore, who had replaced William Frary as the shrine beadle, Laurence King, the distinguished architect, F. Bernard Bourdillon, who was instrumental in organising the Friends of Walsingham, Stanley Smith, and Major E. A. Northen.

When Colin Stephenson took over as administrator he resolved not to continue along similar lines to the now-dissolved CSA, but he still felt that it was worth an attempt to establish a community to assist at the shrine. He was himself an external oblate of Nashdom Abbey and he gathered a small group around him to live under the same rule, which was organised formally in late 1960. Those who came for periods included the Australian Father Franklin, whose previous stay had been so short, an American, Revd James Halfhill, and a priest from the West Indies, Revd Y. G. Allan.

However, Stephenson was able in addition to attract three young priests to the shrine community at the same time, which was something Hope Patten had not been able to do. They were Revd (later Prebendary) Derek

Hooper, who served his title there and was officially licensed as curate of Walsingham from 1959 to 1962 before leaving for the West Country, Revd (later Canon) Michael McLean, who was also priested in 1960, and Revd Michael C. G. Johnstone, who was ordained priest in 1959 and came from Holy Trinity, Hoxton. After Father Franklin returned to Australia in 1963, the College was joined by Father Ivan Whittaker, previously of St Michael, Shoreditch, who was an experienced priest, by then widowed, but he left in 1965 to be chaplain at the well-known Anglo-Catholic preparatory school St Michael's School, Otford, which had been founded by Father Tooth. There were also two laybrothers, Anthony Howell and Anthony Burge. This appeared to give a reasonable basis for progress, but in June 1965 Stephenson announced in the *Walsingham Review*, the successor to *Our Lady's Mirror*, that he had decided that 'the attempt to have any sort of Community life in the College here is doomed to failure . . . It therefore seems to me much better to run the College as a clergy house and to have those who are prepared to come for a year or two, as to a parish'. This announcement, made shortly after returning from a trip to the United States and without much notice, came as a surprise to those who still wished to try their vocation in that way, but no similar experiment has been attempted since. Oddly enough, Colin Stephenson continued to refer to the priests of the shrine as being The College, and in 1966 was even considering adopting blue scapulars for those concerned.[6]

Hope Patten's most trusted lieutenant, at least until his 'desertion', remained in Devon after leaving Walsingham. In 1966 Derrick Lingwood moved from Torquay to become vicar of Withycombe Raleigh with All Saints, Exmouth, but as early as 1972 he died, shortly after his 62nd birthday. The years at Walsingham had taken their toll on his health. His widow survived him and is still alive at the time of writing.

Two of Hope Patten's other principal allies in the restoration of the shrine, Fynes-Clinton and Milner, did not long survive him. Father Fynes-Clinton, who was considerably older than Hope Patten, died the year after his long-time collaborator, on 4 December 1959.[7] He had adapted rather better than some of his ilk to the relaxation on fasting before communion which was the first straw in the wind of change about to emanate from

---

6 *Walsingham Review*, 20.
7 Appropriately enough, his requiem was on the feast of the Immaculate Conception of Our Lady.

Rome: he had arranged lunchtime masses for those working in the City before such services became at all common elsewhere, although he himself still did not eat until after the late celebrations.

Sir William Milner died in early 1960 at the age of only 66. His property at Parcevall Hall, while still owned by a Walsingham Trust Company, has since been used as the retreat centre for the Diocese of Bradford and no large sums were released by his death for the work of the shrine. Derrick Lingwood was one of his executors.

Another important figure in the story, Father Eyden, ceased direct involvement in Quainton Hall School in 1969 but then he too moved to St Michael's School at Otford in Kent. He abandoned the liturgical uses of his earlier years and became a strong advocate of the new rites which emerged from Rome. He did not die until late 1988.

Father Roger Wodehouse, another with long involvement in Walsingham, died in 1959. George Long, a faithful helper, died in 1960 and Tom Purdy, the builder, one of those most touched by Hope Patten's ability to communicate the faith simply and clearly, died in 1965.

The Community of St Peter, Westminster, no longer exists, and with some degree of irony the last professed sister of that order is now a member of the Society of St Margaret at Walsingham, which is still serving the shrine, although in 1994 the community there reverted to being an autonomous house of the Society rather than a separate Priory. In 2002 the two remaining members of the Aberdeen convent of the SSM moved to Norfolk to join them.

The Horbury sisters have sold their substantial convent buildings and are now aging in modern accommodation near to their former premises.

It is not part of the purpose of this work to set out the history of the shrine since 1958, but it is evident with hindsight that Colin Stephenson was able to open up the devotion to other sections of the Church of England who had previously stood back. His personality was outgoing and he deliberately involved himself in diocesan affairs, which Hope Patten had shunned. He travelled thousands of miles publicising the work of Walsingham, and in his turn wore himself into a premature grave: he resigned as administrator in 1968 but remained as Master until 1973, when he was succeeded by Father Gill, who had also succeeded Father Fynes-Clinton at St Magnus. Subsequent masters and administrators have been drawn from those who joined the College after the time of Hope Patten's death.

Colin Stephenson had a far greater experience of the outside world than had Hope Patten: he had served for a time as a naval chaplain, during which he had lost a leg in an accident. He was criticised by some for being too open to the new ideas which were emerging in the Church from 1960 onwards, but it is difficult to see how Walsingham could have continued to appeal to the outside world if it had remained in the ecclesiastical time warp in which it had been at least since 1950.

14

A RETROSPECTIVE

There are two aphorisms which apply with considerable force to the life of Alfred Hope Patten.

The first, ironically in the light of his own feelings about the language, is best known in Latin: *Si monumentum requiris, circumspice (if you seek a monument, gaze around)*. While so many changes have taken place in the wider Church since Hope Patten's death, the shrine of Our Lady of Walsingham has flourished, expanded, and, most significantly, reached out to many outside the very narrow constituency to which it appealed at the time of his demise. Although the shrine church has been much extended since 1958, partly by the construction of a cloister in memory of the founder, the basic conception and execution were his alone.

Successive administrators have not altered the Holy House, which remains largely as Comper and his associates designed it. Ironically, the parish church now has much less of Hope Patten's influence visible, since in 1961 it was burned out in a disastrous fire. Laurence King's rebuilding was faithful to the original, but could not attempt to recreate the atmosphere which Hope Patten had established in many small ways over the years. The surrounding infrastructure of the shrine has of course been very greatly altered since 1958, with many new buildings built and more planned. However, the quadrangle, living accommodation for the administrator and College remain much as before. Hope Patten's constant fears that the shrine would not survive his death have proved completely unfounded.

The second aphorism which may be thought to apply to Hope Patten is *A prophet is not without honour, save in his own country and in his own house* (Matthew 13.57). Hope Patten was never more than tolerated by the hierarchy of the Church of England, and usually shunned. No advancement was offered him, not even an honorary canonry of the Cathedral. While time servers and bureaucrats rose effortlessly to the higher echelons of the Church of England, men of real talent and insight were marginalised.

On the other hand, his temperament was such that the administration which inevitably accompanies such promotion would have been anathema to him. He had the characteristic ambivalence towards the episcopate shared by many of his outlook and age.

Hope Patten was a man who excited strong emotions during his lifetime. There were those who were attracted by his personal charisma, by his ability to enthuse others into carrying into effect his own visions, and by his concern for others. The latter, one of his more appealing characteristics, was much more evident during the pre-war years at Walsingham. There can be no doubt that his first few years in the village electrified the religious atmosphere and excited great enthusiasm from many ordinary members of the parish. Although he undoubtedly had snobbish tendencies, which came to the fore on occasion, there is no doubt that he was able to empathise with the personal problems of his Norfolk flock and was prepared to devote a great deal of time to them. They in turn responded, and the 1931 celebrations for the translation of the image to the shrine involved very many people in Walsingham; they were not, as it were, imposed upon an unwilling village.

Not only did he look after the parish, but there is ample evidence that in the pre-war years he was accessible to the pilgrims who came, and would move among them on the vicarage lawn or, later, in the shrine garden, talking and making them feel welcome without any of the somewhat off-putting reserve which repelled some people.

There is equally no doubt that the situation changed in the post-war period, and that that change was mainly attributable to the long-running attempt by Hope Patten to establish the College of St Augustine. That took him away from his parishioners and indeed exiled him internally from the pilgrims who continued to come to Walsingham. Many who visited in the 1950s found that they either did not see Hope Patten at all, or merely caught a glimpse of him around the shrine.

One of his most severe critics, who had been a member of the CSA for a time, wrote later that he was 'for the most part acting a part'.[1] That may well contain more than an element of truth: Hope Patten's early enthusiasm for amateur theatricals may have had more effect on his life than at

---

1 Letter from Revd Frank Reader, 6 June 1961 (WA).

first sight appears. He undoubtedly had an ideal of how a priest should behave, which included an absolute dedication to his vocation, which sometimes struck others as too perfectionist. However, throughout his life there are examples of how, particularly when out of the public gaze, Hope Patten was able to relax and thus to allow a somewhat childish sense of fun to break through.

It may be that another comment of the same critic, namely that he continued throughout his life behaving like a spoiled child, also has some force.[2] Certainly his lack of much formal education meant that he lacked the common experience of nearly all his contemporaries and he lost out on the social and frivolous side of growing up. The over-indulgence which his parents seemed to have applied to him, especially during the period 1901–11 when he made no attempt to earn his living and simply took it for granted that they would continue to support him, would appear also to have had long-term effects on his emotional development.

There is a difference of course between being selfish and being self-centred. Hope Patten was not selfish in the commonly understood use of the word, but he was extremely self-centred, in that he saw the whole of the outside world through his own prism, and he could never understand why others did not appreciate, as he did, that his latest project, whatever it might be, was the most important governing factor in that world. This aspect of his personality undoubtedly fascinated some, who appreciated the drive behind his desire to establish the shrine, but it also grated on others. He could not understand that other churches might want to rebuild, repair leaking roofs, or even erect rood screens, and that their parishioners might then prefer to subscribe for those objects rather than to give money towards the provision of yet more *objets de piété* for the shrine. His many gifts did not include the ability to criticise himself: he never appeared to accept that he was in any way to blame for the failure of the Sanctuary School or for the destabilisation of the sisters at Walsingham in 1941–2, although the letter of apology that he later wrote to Laleham is some counterweight to that criticism. While it could be said that that self-centredness was a character defect, it also enabled him to focus his monocular energy on that which he wanted to do. He was also able to shut out unpleasant realities which did not accord with his own thought.

---

2 Letter from Revd Frank Reader, 6 June 1961 (WA).

There again, the earlier part of his ministry, and particularly the pro-
ductive years from 1930 to 1938, when the shrine chapel was built and
then extended, shows the fruits of that single-mindedness. He was
undoubtedly much assisted in that period of progress by the fact that so
many of the mundane realities which afflict most people were either of no
interest to him, or if they were unavoidable, such as paying bills, were
taken off his shoulders by Derrick Lingwood.

There is no doubt that Hope Patten completely failed to achieve what is
nowadays known as the work/life balance. He became so engrossed in any
project which had taken his fancy that he worked himself into a state
of collapse and had to take a long holiday, which itself usually led to
problems at home which arose when he was away. He was indubitably
very highly strung, and there seems no doubt that his frequent collapses in
health were realities, even if sometimes the physical problems resulted
from mental pressure. More is of course now known about the interrela-
tion of the two than was the case during his lifetime.

This almost neurotic temperament also showed itself in Hope Patten's
fascination with the supernatural, which showed itself throughout his life
and has perhaps excited disproportionate interest. He frequently asserted
that when he came to Walsingham the parish church was haunted by
ghosts, but that he began their rout with holy water and completed it when
the Blessed Sacrament was reserved in the church.[3] He always refused to
walk down the sunk road at Walsingham by night, and inevitably took the
longer way round, because he claimed it was haunted. Some even thought
that he could bilocate – that is, be seen in two places simultaneously. Hope
Patten treated these matters seriously but without any sense that they were
out of the ordinary, and his interest in the paranormal was shared by a
number of others of his acquaintance, including particularly Father
Fynes-Clinton.

It may well be that of more value in gauging this aspect of his life is the
well-known story, retold by Leslie Oldroyd in his reminiscences, of a
mysterious knocking being heard in the shrine church. Hope Patten's
immediate reaction was to pick up a bucket of holy water and to announce
that there were ghosts who should be dispelled. In fact, it was one of the
sisters hammering on the walls of their own nearby chapel as she put up
the stations of the cross. On another occasion, Father Patten was with

---

3 Letter of 10 April 1961 from 'Colin'.

Stanley Smith in the administrator's cottage when they heard a curious intermittent rattle from upstairs. He immediately sprang to the conclusion that the noise had a supernatural explanation, but the more sceptical Stanley Smith ran upstairs to find that a large rosary was being blown by the wind against a metal oil stand from which it was hanging.[4] In other words, as with many facets of Hope Patten's life, there are often simple and straightforward explanations for what appear at first sight to be mysterious events.

Hope Patten's problem as the years went on was that he was so buoyed up by the real accomplishment of establishing the shrine and supervising the buildings which were erected that he began to think that he could not fail in his attempts to extend the spheres of influence of Walsingham. His vivid imagination soared ahead of reality, and foresaw the village and shrine as one of the centres of an alternative Anglicanism, owing its allegiance to the tradition of the Western Church, which would in due course so influence the wider Church of England that it would realign itself to Rome.

There is no doubt that Hope Patten was a Papalist, in the sense that he saw no future for the Church of England unless it returned to communion with Rome under the leadership of the Pope. Equally, until the very end, there was no sign that he was not a loyal Anglican, in that he had never expressed any doubt about the validity of his orders and certainly would have no truck with *episcopi vagantes* and their like. He had always affirmed that the Church of England was the real Ecclesia Anglicana and the Church of Rome was an intruder in this country.

In *Our Lady's Mirror*, spring 1945, Hope Patten set out what he conceived as Our Lady's part in the reunion with Rome which he regarded as the inevitable consequence of the Oxford Movement and what followed it. He wrote thus:

> If England is ever to be reconverted: if these Provinces are ever to be reunited to their parent stock, devotion to Mary must become widely accepted among us, for it is impossible to hold the true Faith apart from Our Lady. She is the instrument all through the divine plan of redemption; leaving out the Mother of God it is impossible to begin to get a right understanding of God Himself or the meaning of salvation. It is because Mary is so patently left out in the scheme of English religious

---

4 Interview with Stanley Smith, 25 March 2006.

teaching that thousands, nay millions, of our countrymen have no grasp of the first principles of Christianity. Walsingham, therefore, has a real place in the scheme not only of restoring the fundamental principles of the faith, but in preparing for the outward reunion of Christendom.

The powerhouse which Hope Patten conceived as centring on Walsingham would in his imagination have encompassed a choir school, a number of other schools across the country, all teaching a most undiluted Anglo-Catholicism, and communities for both men and women serving the shrine. When priests retired from their parishes, they could live in the shrine grounds and participate in all the functions appertaining to it. Against this model, his later years can be judged as a failure. Apart from Quainton Hall, which was a well-established school with a strong tradition when taken into the Walsingham orbit, and the Sisters of St Margaret, who were similarly well established before they were taken into the work of the shrine, his other attempts to set up new institutions were ill thought out, hastily executed, inadequately capitalised and subject to too much interference from him.

The conversation which Hope Patten had with John Shepherd the night before he died is clearly very significant. No one can tell what may have happened had he lived, but there is no argument but that a defection would have shaken many on his wing of the Church of England. There is little doubt that had he indeed gone over to Rome, he would not at his age have been reordained, and in any event that the arrangements which he had himself put into place as insurance against a successor taking that step would have safeguarded the shrine. There was nothing at all in Hope Patten's life to suggest that he had ever at any stage been disloyal in the sense that some Anglo-Catholics were, in that they actively encouraged their adherents to move to Rome.[5]

---

5 For example, Revd T. Victor Roberts, Warden of the Community of the Holy Cross at Hayward's Heath, advised Colin Stephenson not to take Anglican orders, which the former thought was the greatest mistake of his life. Hope Patten's former vicar Father Corbould, when faced with a wholesale defection from his church of the choir and servers in 1944, is said to have remarked with resignation that one of his tasks was to prepare people for Rome. At an earlier date, Revd C. F. Hrauda, an eccentric priest of Austrian origin, often referred to Anglo-Catholics as 'Amateur Catholics' and Roman Catholics as 'Real Catholics', and on one occasion advised the Nashdom Benedictines to go over to Rome.

It is, however, very easy to be over-critical of Hope Patten because he is now being viewed from the standpoint of the early twenty-first century. In many ways he exhibited all the strengths and the weaknesses of an Anglo-Catholic priest of his generation, and it is not difficult to focus on the weaknesses without paying sufficient attention to the real strengths. It is difficult now to recall how different was the teaching which was expounded at the time of his death, less than 50 years ago. Hope Patten and his contemporaries were brought up in a system in which, for example, fasting communion was absolutely de rigueur. Thus, not only were there no evening celebrations but even at the main mass of Sunday there were generally no communicants. Benediction of the Blessed Sacrament was the evening service not only because of the importance placed on eucharistic adoration but also because mass could not be celebrated at that time.

It could perhaps justly be said that that state of affairs arose because Anglo-Catholics tended to follow Roman use without the liturgical discipline imposed by Rome. It was that contradiction which led to grave problems once Rome, suddenly and with very little advance notice, changed radically not only the content of its liturgy but also the tone and ethos. Fellowship among the congregation took the place of non-participation. The veneration of relics almost disappeared. The saints were relegated to the periphery of the liturgy whereas in some cases previously they had seemed to overshadow it. The autocratic priest could no longer rule his flock without involving them in any way. Anglo-Catholics had steered by a compass pointing to the Seven Hills; once the electrical storms started in Rome their sense of direction was lost, in some cases for good. Some followed the new ways slavishly, others clung obstinately to uses which no longer had the imprimatur of the Holy See.

It is an interesting, but ultimately fruitless, line of speculation to consider how Hope Patten, if he had not seceded, would have coped with the radical changes which affected liturgical and devotional practices and which came forward so soon after his death, still less how he would have reacted to the idea of ordaining women. Many others had to face the dilemma of whether to adopt the new ideas or to hang on so far as they could to what they had always known. Hope Patten's undoubted loyalty to Rome would have conflicted with his inflexible attachments to the way in which he had always said mass, to fasting communion, and to the collection and veneration of relics. While it is quite impossible to conclude definitively how Hope Patten would have coped with those revolutionary changes, there are substantial grounds for thinking that he would have found it very difficult to abandon his mindset, which was established early on and did not change much as he grew older.

The autocracy, rigidity and fussiness, which are all words which can justly be applied to the religion at Walsingham during Hope Patten's day, went hand in hand with a very strong devotion to duty and an ingrained routine, coupled with an elevated and serious commitment to the priestly state; these are all virtues much less often found today.

There were many Anglo-Catholic priests of Hope Patten's era who combined those virtues with the weaknesses inherent in such a system of belief. They laboured in parishes with varying degrees of success, but they are now largely forgotten. Hope Patten's name, on the other hand, is still honoured and his life remains a subject of some controversy. That was not only because, against many odds and in the midst of many failures, he managed to restore the shrine of Our Lady, but also because he had a human side to him which was not always obvious at first sight.

His early work in the village was remarkable and also enduring. A large number of perfectly ordinary Norfolk villagers were so attached to him and his teaching that they not only adopted his religious ideas but also were prepared to assist him in many different ways with their time and talents. His very great gift of not only seeing the potential in a man or woman but also then letting them develop that potential, which unfortunately did not extend to potential members of the College of St Augustine, did lead to the ordination of Derrick Lingwood, John Shepherd and others, the artistic work of Enid Chadwick, and the encouragement of many more people. Undoubtedly also he contributed to the lives of many in the confessional and with personal advice, which is obviously not recorded, but which affected a large number.

The shrine is, however, his memorial. His own vision of a realigned Church of England moving steadily towards Rome and encouraged by devotion at Walsingham has long since faded. In its place, however, there has been a much more subtle effect, which began when Colin Stephenson moved the shrine back towards the mainstream of the Church of England. When Hope Patten went to Walsingham in 1921, it was extremely unusual to see any image of Our Lady in an Anglican church. By the time he died, it was commonplace. The aftermath of the Reformation discouraged Anglicans from even thinking of the unique part played by the Mother of

Jesus in Our Lord's appearance on earth, or in the divine scheme of things. Walsingham was one of the important factors which have contributed to the recognition by Anglicans as well as Nonconformists that Our Lady cannot be ignored in Christian thought.

Coupled with that has been the increasing acceptance that places such as Walsingham do have a place in an increasingly secular age and that atmosphere can be important in concentrating the modern mind on spiritual matters.

The unique atmosphere of Walsingham is the product of Hope Patten's flawed, but undoubted, genius. Although there are easy explanations for many of the mysteries surrounding his life, the message conveyed by the shrine and its surroundings remains incapable of such simple analysis.

Appendix

Leaflets, Appeals and Plans of the Extension to the Shrine

The Twelfth Annual May and the Eleventh Annual August

PILGRIMAGE TO OUR LADY OF WALSINGHAM, 1934.

May Pilgrimage under the auspices of the Society of Mary and the Catholic League.
August Pilgrimage conducted by the Society of Mary.

Preacher in MAY :
The Rev. Fr. Biggart, C.R.
(of the Hostel of the Resurrection, Leeds)

Preacher in AUGUST :
The Rev. Fr. Monahan,
(Rector of S. Martin's, Worcester)

PROGRAMME.

First day—Tuesday (May 22nd and Aug. 21st):

12-15 p m.   Mass and Blessing of the Pilgrims at the Church of S. Magnus by London Bridge.

3 p.m.   Leave King's Cross Station for Walsingham.

7 p.m.   Arrive at Walsingham and first visit to the Sanctuary and Holy House.

7-30 p.m.   Supper.

8-30 p.m.   Vespers, Address and Benediction.   Confessions.   Evening visit to the Holy House. *Shrine closed at* 10-30. *Confession and Holy Communion are essential to the making of a good Pilgrimage.*

9-30 p.m.   Tea and Biscuits in the Refectory.

Second day—Wednesday (May 23rd & Aug. 22nd):

7 a.m.   High Mass with Holy Communion.   Private Masses of Pilgrim Priests as arranged. *All Priests are asked to bring their own Missal, amice, alb, girdle, and Cotta.*

7-45 a.m. (onwards)   Breakfast.

10-15 a.m.   Stations of the Cross, followed by visit to S. Giles and the Slipper Chapel, at Houghton. *(Invalids and elderly people desiring cars should notify the Secretary when booking rooms).*

12-30 p.m.   Lunch.

2-30 p.m.   Admissions to the Society of O.L.W. in the Holy House.

3 p m.   Intercessions and "bathing" of the sick. *After this Pilgrims are free to visit the Priory ruins and the mediaeval Picenas or the extensive remains of the Franscian Friary. Entrance in each case 6d.*

4-30 p.m.   Social at the Vicarage.   Tea, &c.

6 p.m.   Rosary and Salve (this is not necessarily part of the Pilgrimage, but the daily Devotion said all the year in the Holy House at 6).

6-30 p.m.   Supper.

7-30 p.m.   Pontifical Vespers, Sermon, Procession and Benediction.   Evening visit to Holy House *(where Credo, Salve and Te Deum will be sung).* Shrine closed at 10-30 p.m.

8-30 p.m.   Tea and Biscuits in the Refectory.

Third day—Thursday (May 24th and Aug. 23rd):

8 a.m.   Mass with Holy Communion. *Private Masses of Pilgrim Priests as above.*

7-45 a.m. (onwards).   Breakfast.

10-15 a.m.   Mass with music and last Address.

11 a.m.   Veneration of S. Vincent and last visit to the Holy House and Blessing of the Pilgrims.

11-15 a.m.   Tea and Biscuits in the Refectory.

12 noon.   Leave Walsingham.

Pilgrimage programme for 1934.

THE PROPOSED EXTENSION
OF
The Shrine of Our Lady of Walsingham.

TWO years ago, a devoted and generous client of Our Lady of Walsingham gave a sum of money for these plans for the extension of the Shrine to be prepared, with, we understand, every intention of aiding very substantially in their construction, but she did not live to see the actual drawings completed.

As we are constantly being asked by pilgrims and visitors if we propose enlarging the outer Church of the Sanctuary, as the present accommodation is so very limited, we have prepared this leaflet in the hope that those who are interested may help forward the scheme.

Ever since pilgrimages began to visit the reconstructed Shrine in 1931 it was realised how inadequate the new buildings were for the accommodation of large numbers of people.

The dimensions of the Holy House and the Outer Church were regulated by two factors: first the wish to rebuild these Chapels according to the exact dimensions of the original Church as described in the 15th century by William of Worcester and in the 16th century by Erasmus; and secondly by the amount of money at our disposal.

From historic and sentimental reasons we propose keeping the present buildings as they are, but to add as large an extension to the " East " end as the space allows, to accommodate the fast increasing number of pilgrims and others who come each year to Walsingham. By removing the existing " East " wall and inserting a great arch at this point, the Shrine will be connected with the extension and provision made for all purposes. It is our aim also to erect some domestic buildings to accommodate a small College of Priests and Laymen who will be in charge of the Sanctuary.

No public appeal is being made at present, as it is hoped that donations will come in without this. The various parts of the new work can be erected separately, if necessary, and by consulting the list of costs, some may be moved to build a chapel, or a bay of the nave, or part of a cloister, either as a thankoffering or in memory of some friend. Of course it is rather more expensive to build in sections than all at one time, but something ought to be done as soon as possible.

We cannot and do not expect those friends of Walsingham, who have done so much already, to help in this, beyond interesting their friends and those who are able to assist in raising this Votive Church in honour of Our Lady and as a witness of the devotion of English Catholics to the Mother of God.

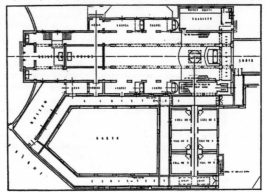

COST.

For Nave £2,000.

For Chapels £1,200 (£300 each).

Sanctuary and Sacristy £3,000.

Cells and W. Cloisters £2,000.

Remaining Cloisters £700.

Parts in proportion.

Leaflet describing the proposed extension to the shrine, 1935.

THE EXTENSION
OF
The Shrine of Our Lady of Walsingham.

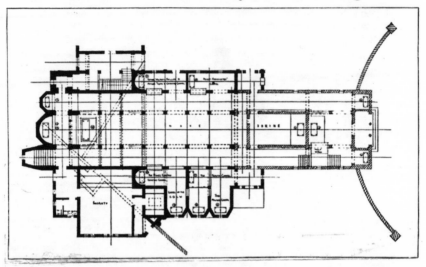

EVERYONE who visits the Shrine, or who is interested, will be thrilled by the building operations which are going on, and all will wish to have **a share in the honour** of enlarging the historic and ancient National Sanctuary of the Blessed Virgin.

WHEN the existing buildings were put up it was realised, at once, how inadequate they were at the time of large pilgrimages, but we had felt compelled to reconstruct the Shrine exactly as recorded in the fifteenth and sixteenth centuries, hence its confined space.

IN those bygone days the pilgrims had the advantage of the great Priory Church within a stone's throw.

THREE years ago, a devoted friend of Walsingham gave a sum of money for the preparation of plans for the work now in hand, with, we understand, every intention of aiding very substantially towards their construction, but she did not live to see the drawings completed.

IN 1936, an anonymous donor made it possible for us to make a start with the necessary extensions, but the generous **support of all who visit** or are interested in the work of the Shrine is **necessary**, in order that the building may go on and the work completed.

THE smaller of the two plans is that of the Chapel upon which we are at present engaged, while the larger shows the layout of the Chapel in block and by its side the domestic buildings and cloisters which are to be built to accommodate a small College of Priests, retreatants, and men visiting the Sanctuary.

THE different sections of the scheme **can** be put up separately, but it is always more expensive to build in that way. So will you be generous and put what you can in the boxes provided; or send a cheque when you get home.

Amended plans for extension, 1937.

242

IF you **can** help we are confident you will do so.

IF you cannot help yourself do not forget the work, but try to interest your friends and get them to assist.

PERHAPS you who are reading this can give a larger sum than others; would you like to give—

£1,000 to complete the Chapel.	£2,000 for the Library Wing & East Cloister.
£1,350 for the Museum and West Cloister.	£700 for the adaption of S. Augustine's.
£300 for the North Cloister (abutting on Chapel).	£390 for the South Cloister.

or any part as a thank-offering or in memory of some departed friend or relative?

*Postal Orders and Cheques made payable to—***The Bursar, The Sanctuary of Our Lady, Walsingham, Norfolk.**
*Cheques crossed—***" Building Fund."**

Treasurers of the Fund—THE RT. REV. BISHOP O'RORKE and THE REV. A. HOPE PATTEN.

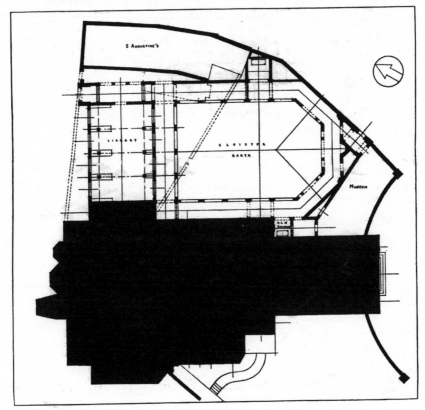

Reverse of the last leaflet.

PLAN
Showing the Complete Scheme for the Buildings already erected or to be erected at the
Shrine of Our Lady of Walsingham

THE burden of providing the necessary Buildings for the working of a place of Pilgrimage such as this, is a heavy undertaking, and may be compared to the erection of a College or small Monastic Establishment.

THE SHELL

of the Shrine Church has been built by the generous donations of the faithful, but there still remains a sum of **£3,000**

before it is free of debt. To raise this amount therefore is our **immediate aim,** and one that will be the concern of all Pilgrims to the

HOLY HOUSE OF OUR LADY.

THEN the Shrine must have priests to minister to the pilgrims and a staff to tend and guard the Sanctuary. With the rapidly increasing number of those who visit the Shrine it is essential to form a College. There are those who are willing to undertake this work, when and if adequate accommodation is provided. Section A, marked on the plan "College of Priests," shows the position and arrangement of these buildings. For this a sum of **£7,000 IS REQUIRED.**

ON the plan, B indicates the position of the New Refectory with bedrooms for pilgrims above, service room, kitchen and scullery, &c.

AT C is the site of the North Gate House, giving access to the precincts, and the old house adjoining is to be converted into the Offices of the Secretariat with pilgrims rest rooms, &c. on the first floor. All these Domestic Buildings are to be linked to the Church by cloisters.

THE total cost of all these necessary extensions, including the Cloisters and the Priests' College, will amount to **£20,000**

THIS is not a very large sum when we remember that it is less than some people spend on a private house, a church hall, or a club.

ANY sum, small or large, will be welcome, and remember, it is for the Restoration of

ENGLAND'S ANCIENT NATIONAL
SANCTUARY OF OUR LADY.

Donations or promises should be put in one of the boxes provided or sent to—
The Pilgrimage Secretary, Sanctuary of Our Lady,
Walsingham, Norfolk.

I enclose...(or) I promise to send by (date)...................................

the sum of...to help pay off the debt on the Shrine of Our Lady of Walsingham (or for the Building of the College and Precincts).

Signed..

Address..

Cheques and Postal Orders should be crossed "Building Fund" and sent to the Secretary as above.
Treasurer: THE RT. REV. BISHOP O'RORKE, D.D.   *Bursar:* THE REV. D. A. LINGWOOD.

Further appeal for money, 1938.

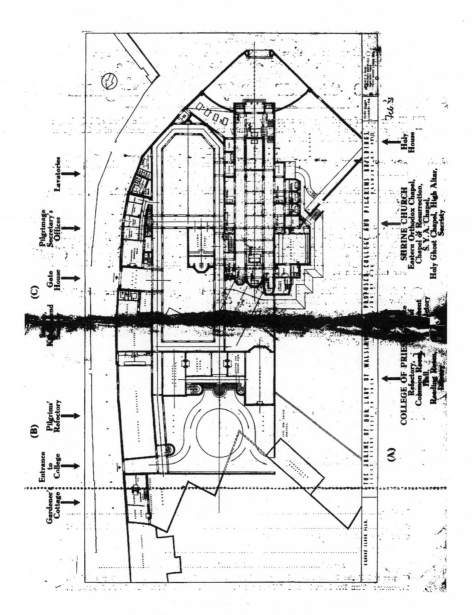

Amended plans showing further proposed work, 1938.

ALFRED HOPE PATTEN

URGENT APPEAL - WILL YOU HELP?

———•••———

At the request of those responsible for the Walsingham Clergy Fund we print this message:—" We lay the following before you in great **urgency** as we know you will be profoundly concerned about the future of the Shrine and its work: Either money must be found for the Clergy Fund or **the two priests at Walsingham must resign,** which would be a most serious problem, at this stage, for the future of the Shrine and its work.

The position is that we have an overdraft at bank of £58; bank loan owing, £43; owing to Miss Doyle Smithe and another, £70—total £171.
We have to find £280 for stipends per annum. (The parish contribution of £40 to make up the inadequate stipend of £150 for the Assistant Priest is often not reached.)

The annual donations from subscribers have greatly diminished owing to deaths, cessation of pilgrimage and the war stringency, and it has not been possible to hold the usual sales on which we have much depended.

Can Collapse be Averted ?

Many of those who receive this appeal no doubt send personal donations to the Clergy Fund through Miss Doyle Smithe, for which we warmly thank them, but we **urgently ask you to respond to this SPECIAL APPEAL in this critical time**

CAN YOU ASK FRIENDS TO HELP ? For the honour of Our Lady and her Shrine, surely this will be possible.

Contributions may be sent to any one of us.

Signed on behalf of the Committee: M. C. O'Rorke, Bishop, Blakeney Holt, Norfolk; C. R. Deakin, St. Augustine's, Queen's Gate, S.W.1; J. H. C. Twisaday, All Saints', Clydesdale Road, W.11; E. H. Whitby, St. Mary's, Graham Street, S.W.; the Rev. H. J. Fynes-Clinton, 145 St. Ermin's, S.W.1 (Chairman of the Council); Miss Doyle Smithe, Walsingham (Hon. Secretary); Mr. S. W. Hodgkinson, 7 Crichton Road, Carshalton (Hon. Treasurer).

The desperate war time appeal. Note that Bishop O'Rorke's address is still given as Blakeney although he had left Norfolk long before then.

246

INDEX